Soul Cycles

Dear Twyla,
A Leo with a
Compassionate heart!

by *With Blessings*

Elaine Kuzmeskus

Elaine Kuzmeskus, M.S., P.M.A.F.A.

First published by Author House 07/13/04

ISBN: 1-4184-2591-5 (e-book)
ISBN: 1-4184-2592-3 (Paperback)

Printed in the United States of America
Bloomington, IN

This book is printed on acid free paper.

Elaine Kuzmeskus, M.S. is a professional member of the American Federation of Astrologers and Director of the New England School of Metaphysics. She combines her background in counseling and metaphysics with a humanistic approach to astrology. Edited by Susan Roberts

SOUL CYCLES is lovingly dedicated to my teacher and friend, Dorothy Lynde, past president of the New England Astrological Association. Dorothy taught her students to see our squares as "stepping stones, not stumbling blocks", and to be a blessing to others. She truly lived the words of her favorite poem by Emily Dickenson:

Make me a blessing, Lord help me
To help those needing help, to be
A blessing to my fellow man.
Instruct me when to speak,
When to hold my speech, when to be bold
In giving and when to withhold,
And if I am not strong enough,
Then give me strength, make me tough
With my own self, but tender toward
All others, Let there be outpoured
On me the gentleness to bless
All who have need of gentleness.
Give me a word, a touch to fill
The lonely life, faith for the ill
And courage that keeps hearts up though

My own is feeling just as low.

When men have bitter things to meet

And quail and would accept defeat

Then let me lift their eyes to see

The vision of Thy victory.

Help me to help, help me to give

Thy wisdom and the will to live.

Dorothea Lynde, Boston astrologer

TABLE OF CONTENTS

CHAPTER ONE

"AN UNEXAMINED LIFE IS NOT WORTH LIVING"

Socrates

Why are we here? What meaning will our lives have a hundred years from today? My twenty-five year career in astrology began with these questions. In the midst of studying English literature at University of Massachusetts in Boston, I read Jess Stearn's, <u>The Sleeping Prophet</u>--a biography of Edgar Cayce. For the first time I connected with someone who had answers to these questions. Edgar Cayce's remarkable channeling validated the intuitive experiences I had since the age of three. If according to Cayce, "the psychic was of the soul", so apparently was astrology: "The signs of the zodiac are Karmic Patterns; the Planets are the Looms; the Will is the Weaver." His guides cautioned that "the mind was the builder" and no outside force even astrology could surpass the will of man--if he chose to apply it.

Paramahansa Yogananda echoed this sentiment in Autobiography of a Yogi:

A child is born on that day and that hour when the celestial rays are in mathematical harmony with his individual karma. His horoscope is a challenging portrait, revealing his unalterable past and its probable future results. But the natal chart can be rightly interpreted by a few man of intuitive wisdom; these are few.

One such astrologer was Yogananda's guru. When he saw an early death for his pupil, the wise guru made an amulet to protect the young Yogananda during the upcoming disastrous cycle. Impressed by this story, I began to believe there was something to this pseudo science after all.

Up until this time, I felt astrology was nonsense and those people practicing it were charlatans manipulating a gullible public. In fact as a child I had come upon an astrology reading my mother hid in her drawer. I was truly embarrassed by her lack of intelligence. However, being a wise college junior, I decided to investigate. So I sent my birth data, March 25, 1947, 2:00 A.M., Boston, MA; checked the block marked female; and mailed the form to Time Pattern Research in Long Island. I was amazed at the twenty-page computer report. On page three it stated, "You will have an interest in occult matters and a very balanced attitude toward them.". On page five, "You will have much to do with male relatives other than your father." Both statements were true. I certainly had been intuitive all my life. And while very close to my grandfather, I had not been close to my father since the age of eight when my parents divorced. I returned to Boston to live with my mother's family, while my father remained in Los Angeles. Maybe this was just a coincidence; however, being "progressive in outlook and both original and prolific in ideals" (page 4), I had to find out more about astrology.

After receiving a B.A. in English, I started classes at the New England School of Astrology in September of 1969. Classes were conducted by Frances Sakoian and Louis Acker, who later coauthored The Astrologer's Hand Book. Both were astrological wizards. I took most of my classes with Frances,

3

an attractive red-headed grandmother who gave great encouragement to all of her students. Since I was taking a journalism class at Boston University at the same time, I decided to do a piece on the school for BOSTON AFTER DARK. Frances loved the article and felt that I would make an excellent writer. However, my focus was on astrology and the esoteric sciences and I continued to study under the direction of two professional mediums--Rev. Gladys and Rev. Kenneth Custance. I completed my mediumship certificate in May of 1972 and I was now free to prepare for the American Federation of Astrologer's Professional Exam.

Frances Sakoian who had a flair for teaching taught me the basics of astrology--planets, signs, houses, aspects, progressions, and transits. However, after three years of study I had taken almost all the classes the school had to offer. I needed a private tutor to prepare for the upcoming eight hour exam. Through another astrologer, Mary Letourney, I met my mentor, Dorothea Lynde. Unfortunately, Dorothea never wrote any books. She always said, "My students are my books."

4

In 1975 after five years of study, I received my teacher's certificate from the American Federation of Astrologers. Over the years, I have been grateful for the many fine books written by Frances Sakoian and Louis Acker. Even though Frances has passed on, I still feel connected to her through her writing. Dorothea Lynde and I remained close until her death in 1995. In fact I can still feel her over my shoulder, when I need some advice. About this time, I realized I wanted to leave a more permanent record for my students. This book is the result of my twenty years as a professional astrologer.

During these twenty five years, I have added to my skills. I obtained a Masters in Counseling from the University of Hartford in 1978. I have also been an adjunct instructor in psychology since 1979 for the Connecticut community college system. I use cognitive psychology and, Jungian dream analysis when indicated, and with my astrology clients favor humanistic psychology with its emphasis on human potential. However, I always go back to the client's chart because used correctly astrology is a valid predictor of human behavior. It truly was the psychology of the Ancients. The Egyptians and Greeks of past centuries knew something our modern psychologists have forgotten. We are not just the body and mind, but soul--an individual portion of the Divine.

Why study astrology? The answer is three-fold: One, astrology gives a blueprint of our constitution, character, and personality. Two, it can provide a road map for future reference. Most of us would not think of going on a long distance journey without a well marked map, yet we go blindly through life's journey. However, the final reason is the one for which the book was written. Astrology shows most eloquently a Divine blueprint for each and every one of us. This Divine blueprint is shown in our aura, the palm of our hands, and in the light of our eyes. And it was written in the heavens well before our birth.

Soul Cycles looks at astrology on these three levels. On the first level, the physical health is seen. Here the astrologer can ascertain potential for longevity and areas where future illnesses may occur. In Tibet all physicians study astrology in medical school. Rightly used, astrology can be a valuable took for maintaining health. In the United States, though, the most common use of astrology is for psychological counseling. This second level of astrology shows the character, personality and psychological lessons one will face in this life. In fact, an accurately cast chart, interpreted by a professional astrologer has an advantage over a traditionally trained counselor since it can predict future as well as present inclinations. Dr. Carl Jung, who utilized the clients' horoscope in diagnosing and treating mental illness, knew this occult factor:

The great decisions in human life usually have far more to do with the instincts and other mysterious unconscious factors than with conscious will and well meaning reasonableness. The shoe that fits one person, pinches another; there is not a universal recipe for living. Each of us carries his own life-form within him and irrational form which no other can outbid. (The Practice of Psychotherapy, Volume 16, Collected Works).

Correctly employed, astrology can be a

diagnostic tool for a psychologist. A horoscope can point out maladaptive patterns as well as sources of strength, and help to time treatments for maximum benefit. If more psychologists would take a note from Dr. Jung, they would increase their cure rate and decrease time in therapy.

Rightly employed, astrology not only can be used as a physical and psychological diagnostic tool, but as a spiritual indicator. This third level of astrology can free us from cycles of rebirth, while benefitting humanity as a whole. From the words of the ancient Greek oracles, "Man know thyself" to those of the modern Avatar, Sai Baba, "The proper study of mankind is man" looking inward is the key. After careful review of a horoscope, an astrologer tells the seeker which karma he has chosen to work out in this life and the talents he has brought with him and the timing of events. Without such knowledge, the esoteric student may be doomed to repeat maladaptive patterns, avoid necessary lessons, and pursue many detours before finding his path in life. As Edgar Cayce points out, "The purpose for each soul's entrance is to complete a cycle, to get closer to the infinite, that it may know the purpose with the entity in the earth."

The spiritual practice of astrology is the most demanding level. It is imperative to have compassion and positive regard for the client as well as possessing a greater spiritual awareness. And the astrologer should be of the highest moral quality. In India, the Kuritekey School prescribes this code of conduct for palmists and astrologers: "The practicing palm reader should observe all the niyama prescribed in the Yoga Sutra. He should be an expert on the science of breath.....He should have a knowledge of omens.....He must be a strict follower of truth. He must be kind and considerate to one and all. He must have a contented heart." (Everyone's Guide to Palmistry, page 4)

The professional counselor should try to uplift the spirit of his client. If a negative aspect is seen in a chart, always add the antidote or time sequence. For example, Frances Sakoian saw an accident coming in her son's chart the night of the senior prom. She insisted he take his date to the prom in a taxi, which he reluctantly did. Were her judgments correct as an astrologer and a mother? Well Francis did protect her son, but she couldn't hold back fate. The taxi was in an accident on the way to the prom! Fortunately, no one was hurt except the cab.

An old Hindu tale further illustrates this point. Two swamis were walking along the Ganges River. Suddenly they heard the desperate cries of a boy, "Help, I'm drowning!" The first swami just watched while his fellow guru dove into the water to rescue the lad. When his friend returned after saving the boy's life, pious swami asked, "Why did you interfere with the boy's karma?" His friend answered, "It was not his fate to drown because I was here to save him. If I had tried to save him and failed, it would have been his karma!" Free will has saved many a soul.

Just as negative predictions can be overcome, so often are the good opportunities missed because of depression or mental unrest. Sensitive assessment of the client is necessary before an astrologer can accurately predict events. For example, there are levels of prediction. Transiting Uranus square Venus may indicate a divorce for unhappily mated clients. However in a devoted couple, it may indicate some time of separation--perhaps a business trip abroad for the husband.

Effective counselors, astrological or psychological utilize perceptive analysis as well as faith in human nature. Dr. Carl Rogers terms this essential faith "unconditional positive regard". No teacher can impart this, although many counseling schools do their best to encourage respect and empathy. However these qualities come from within. Without respect, empathetic listening and faith in the client, counseling can only be marginally effective.

Finally, if we are to grow as a profession, we need to adhere to the highest standards of professional conduct. In the United States, the American Federation of Astrologers, the organization responsible for certification of astrologers, has their own code of ethics. Members agree to give only information based on the date, time, and place of birth and to maintain confidentiality.

In closing, remember, "The stars impel, they

do not compel". Regardless of how well aspected or afflicted a chart is, free will is the deciding factor. Never underestimate it. It is our greatest gift on the Earth plane. Often when few opportunities are present in the outer world, much is taking place to refine the character from within. Professional astrologers know this and will encourage their clients to use their "slow cycles" as planning periods, knowing when the time is ripe, new plans can be set in motion. As the esoteric astrologer, Alan Leo points out:

Will is the driving power of soul

One ship drives East, another West

With the self same wind that blows

Tis the set of the sails

And not the gales

Which tell the way to go

Like the winds of the sea are the ways of fate

As we voyage through life

It is the set of the soul that decides the goal

And not the calm or strife.

CHAPTER TWO

HISTORY OF ASTROLOGY

The story of astrology is as old as man, for man has always had a fascination with the stars. Cave men carved phases of the moon on reindeer bones 10,000 B.C. The ancient Egyptian's knowledge of the occult sciences goes back some 6,000 years ago. Historian Sir Ernest Wallis Budge describes Egypt as a civilization "with lofty spiritual character" in which prophecy using trained clairvoyants played a central the Chaldeans learned astrology from the Egyptians.role. The first horoscope was found in Egypt, and it is believed

The Great Pyramid of Gizeh, dating back to 10,000 B.C. the time of Ra, was a hall of initiation. We still do not know much about its construction, but clairvoyant Edgar Cayce's "forces" stated that the Great Pyramid is a record in stone from the time of Ra to 1998. Scientists have been fascinated by this structure which covers over 13 acres and measures 1,000 yards around its base. These

13

gigantic limestone blocks, weighing as much as 54 tons apiece, are set with a half a millimeter of precision. While scientists cannot explain their construction, Edgar Cayce in <u>Stranger in the Earth</u> explains: "It (the pyramid of Giza) was erected by those universal force of nature which cause iron to float". His words suggest the Egyptians knew how to reverse gravity.

The mathematics of the pyramids are also interesting as they are based on the teleios, a series of numbers and proportions found in the musical scales, designs in snow flakes, and in distances of the planets from the Sun. The shape of the pyramid with the King's Chamber has been shown to have the ability to keep razor blades shapE and preserve organic matter. Channeler, J.Z. Knight first saw her guide Ramtha, when she placed a pyramid on her head. Sheila Ostrander and Lynn Schroeder in their classic, <u>Handbook of Psychic Discoveries</u>, pages 195 to 196 explain the dynamics of pyramid power:

"Most experimentors agree for the model pyramid to work well and for material to be dehydrated or blades sharpened, the material must be placed one-third of the way up at the king's chamber level and the pyramid must be aligned north-south."

In (Eric) McLuhan's view this means several energies could be involved:

*The king's chamber, the major energy center in the pyramid, is also the center of gravity. This can't be a coincidence he believes.

*The pyramid is aligned north-south parallel to the earth's magnetic axis. This is no coincidence either and would indicate that the energy waves involved are somewhat polarized. This coincides with the complementary theory of magnetism being somewhat polarized, he feels.

*The Egyptian pyramids are solid masses of rock with specifically shaped cavities (chambers) hollowed out and interrelated in a specific way. These cavities are "resonant cavities", according to McLuhan, that is, enclosed spaces in which electromagnetic energy may be store or excited, something like a hi-fi speaker.

More recent research shows the pyramids were positioned astrologically. Robert Bauval in his book, <u>The Orion Mystery</u> correlates the position of the three pyramids of Giza, two of which are in alignment, and one off center, with the stars of Orion's "belt". These pyramids line up perfectly with the night skies of 10,000 B.C., not only in terms of the fixed star, Orion; but with the fixed star, Sirius. It was discovered in 1986 that a shaft from the King's Chamber in the Great Pyramid of Giza aligns with Orion; and the shaft from the Queen's Chamber aligns with Sirius. The Egyptians obviously knew of these distant stars and considered their influence paramount.

In any event, the perfect alignment of the two shafts indicates a tremendous knowledge of astronomy. They knew how to cast horoscopes as early as 4,200 B.C. as well as determine the position of planets. They also used this knowledge to predict famine, the weather, and the destiny of their leaders. Records dating back 3,000 B.C. show they had ten signs of the zodiac and they were the first to use astrology to foretell a person's destiny. They assigned each planet a God. Osiris, for example, was the god of the dead who ruled all things pertaining to death, rebirth, and burial.

Not only does the structure of the Great Pyramid of Cheops at Giza reveal occult expertise, but its function was occult in nature. Originally, the pyramids were thought to be tombs. However, for tombs, there is little evidence of burials and mummies. The Great Pyramid was a tremendous undertaking in its day, just as our space program. Many occultists such as Edgar Cayce, Rudolph Steiner, Elisabeth Haith, and writer Joan Grant, describe the Great Pyramid as a place of imitation. Edgar Cayce also states the structure contains records of man dating from the time to Ra to 1998. Writers Elisabeth Haith in Initiation and Joan Grant in Winged Pharoh describe the process of initiation. The priest involved in the rite wore the symbol of the ank, a circle with a cross underneath. The circle, the soul, is on top of the cross of matter, signifying an initiate. The actual process involved being placed in a stone sarcophagus, in an induced trance state. There, according to Elisabeth Haith, they met the forces of the astral world and shining face of the Master.

Not only do the pyramids show knowledge of astrology, but the Sphinx is a monument to astrology. This massive stone structure has the body of a bull (Taurus), the paws of a lion (Leo), the wings of an eagle (Scorpio) and the face of man (Aquarius). These four signs represent the fixed sign of the zodiac. The lesson of Taurus, with its key phrase I HAVE, is that of maintaining material existence. The lesson of Leo, with its key phrase I WILL, is that of the personal will and ego. The ancient astrologers sometimes portrayed Scorpio as an eagle, so the wings on Sphinx stand for Scorpio. The lesson of Scorpio, with its key phrase, I DESIRE, is overcoming the material world with knowledge of secrets of death, afterlife and reincarnation. The lesson of Aquarius, with its key phrase I KNOW, is spiritual wisdom poured on a thirsty humanity by the Aquarian water boy. Is the Sphinx deliberately set up with the face of man to direct humanity to the Aquarian Age? Why does Edgar Cayce's guide state the records in the Great Pyramid go from the time of Ra to 1998? It may well be a time when the occult knowledge of the ancient

Egyptians, which included a deep understanding of death, rebirth, and science and astrology, will be available for humanity. In 1998 both occult planets Uranus and Neptune will be in the sign of Aquarius, signifying vast change in both technology (Uranus) and spirituality (Neptune).

The ancient Egyptians, as well as the Druids, Hindus and Incas, were all Sun worshippers. In Egypt, the Sun god is called Ra. His influence became prominent in the reign of Akhunaton and his consort Nefertiti as they tried to establish the Law of One God--the sun God. In India, Vishu, the embodiment of life, is the Sun God. The Druids designed Stonehedge to predict eclipses. Both the Mayans and the Egyptians erected pyramids to be closer to their gods. In the United States American Indians aligned their structures to the four points of the compass. For example, Casa Grande in Arizona, built in 1300 B.C. was set up to predict equinoxes and solstices.

Historians place the beginning of astrology in China around 2800 P.C. with the reign of Emperor Fu Hsi. In the Bamboo Annals the twelve signs of the zodiac and the twenty-eight mansions of the Moon are recorded. The Chinese assigned a sign to each year in a twelve year cycle.

Besides the ancient Egyptians and Chinese, the ancient Hindus studied astrology. The Veda, the Hindu Bible, written in 1500 to 1000 B.C. speaks of the importance of the Sun, Moon and seasons. Even today modern Hindus use astrology to choose careers, marriage partners, and promote healing with gemstones. BV Raman, a well-known modern astrologer explains the Hindu view:

According to the ancient text when one dies, his soul which is enveloped in a subtle body and invested with the sum total of good and bad Karma passes after some time into another body, leaving off his gross body as a man, casts off his worn-out clothes and puts on new ones. His reincarnation takes place in a physical body corresponding with the deeds done by him in a previous life. The process of death and birth goes on until the person has obtained emancipation. The cardinal doctrine of Karma is the law of cause and effect in accordance with the maxim "as a man sows, he reaps".*

*B.V. Raman PLANETARY INFLUENCES ON HUMAN AFFAIRS (Bangalore 1BH Prakashana 1982) pages 29-30)

Both Hindu and Western astrology have been heavily influenced by the Babylonians and Greeks. Historians place the beginning of modern astrology in Babylonia, from 4,000 to 125 B.C. The Three Wise Men in the Bible who followed the star to Bethlehem were Babylonian astrologers. The Babylonians also knew the seven planets and the basics of astrology still used today. Their priests were able to divine the time of floods, earthquakes and weather patterns vital to their agricultural society. The earliest horoscopes were those of kings and queens. Even after being conquered by the Persians in 539 B.C., the Babylonians made great strides in planetary charting and predictions. It was the Babylonians who taught astrology to the Greeks who, in turn, refined the science.

The Greeks had great respect for prophecy. The oracle at Delphi was described by Justine Glass in her book, They Forsaw the Future P 41.

The clients of the Pythia included the greats

of her time. Oepidus came to learn his tragic fate and the historian Herotus who believed, "It is my business to record what people may say I am no means bound to believe." Furthermore, Alexander the Great was told., "My son thou art invincible", he went on to conquer the world.

The Oracle told Nero bluntly, "Your presence outrages the gods...The number seventy-eight marks the hour of your downfall." Nero known for his cruel persecution of the Christians died at seventy-eight. Two truths written on the walls of the Temple of Delphi apply to man today: "Know Thyself" and "Nothing in excess". Both the Greeks and later the Romans held prophecy and astrology in high esteem.

CHAPTER THREE

HOW ASTROLOGY WORKS

The planets transmit their influence through geomagnetic vibrations. Just as the Earth's tides are affected by the pull of the Moon, so our bodies are influenced by the magnetic pull of the planets. Our physical bodies are made up of 30 percent solid and 70 percent liquid--just as the Earth itself! The ancient Egyptians understood this principle well. In fact, they constructed the King's Chamber in the Great Pyramid of Cheops to insulate the initiate from outside influences such as planetary vibrations. Gregg Braden describes this ancient knowledge in Awakening to Point Zero:

Human experience is, and always has been, intimately tied to the strength or density of the magnetic fields, surrounding the Earth. The decrease in planetary magnetic seen today has a profound effect on all life. Many remains of the ancient technologies, when viewed today, indicate a preoccupation with the building of specialized chambers; tuned resonant cavities of experience. Frequently these structures of precise geometry provide an environment lessening the effects of planetary magnetic within the chamber during use.

Perhaps the best example of this technology may be seen in the Great Pyramid of Giza where the upper chambers have significantly lower readings of Earth magnetic than the lower chambers.

(Gregg Braden, <u>Awakening to Zero Point: The Collective Initiation</u>, 1997, New Age Press, page 32)

The Egyptians excelled in astrology. They named the major planets and many of the brightest stars. Research done by engineer Robert Bauval in 1989 showed a tie to the shaft found in the King's Chamber with Osiris and a shaft found in the Queen's Chamber to Sirius, when placed against the night sky of 2750 B.C.

While our scientists are just beginning to explore outer space, the ancient Egyptians made their own contact through the astral world. According to metaphysician Rudolf Steiner, the initiate would be placed in a stone sarcophagus. Once the lid was in place, the initiate had to leave his physical body in a hibernation state and journey to the Moon in his astral body. On his second initiation, he would journey in his astral body to the Sun. In his final initiation, he would merge with the energy of

Sun and achieve unusual psychic powers.

While the initiation process described was unique to Egypt, many societies acknowledge the astral body. In India, it is called "prana" in China it is called "chi" In Japan "ki". It is through this astral body with its seven energy centers that the magnetic energy of the planet is registered. In fact, we are constantly creating our own bodies through our thought patterns of the present as well as astrological influences. As Carolyn Myss states: "Biography becomes biology."

A horoscope simply gives us a starting point in this life in terms of past biography which we are doomed to repeat unless we are brought into conscious awareness. For example, a woman with Venus square Jupiter may crave sweets because she feels unloved. This astrological inclination if unchecked can lead to obesity and problems associated with sugar. If she is informed of this destructive tendency and directs her energy to activities that enrich self-esteem--perhaps using positive affirmations, the negative health problems need not manifest. Often people with cancer have severe Neptune affliction-

-sapping their energy and keeping them in denial. Some reality testing and immune system rebuilding could avert an early demise.

Perhaps the best explanation of karmic influence is given by Theosophist C.W. Leadbeter. Leadbeter likens our karmic condition to a pitcher out of which we take a cup to work in one lifetime. We remain in our bodies until we finish the lessons for this life. Some who finish their "cup of karma" early may exit suddenly such as by a heart attack; others may elect to remain and work out karma from the larger pitcher. Thus, there is a Divine plan in the chart, but sometimes more advanced souls transcend their horoscope with judicious use of free will.

Edgar Cayce's guides further this explanation by stating in between lives we dwell on different planets to gain knowledge while in our astral state: "Astrological urges are not existent just because of the position of the Sun, Moon, or any of the planets at the time of birth, but rather of the universal consciousness AND HAS DWELT IN THOSE ENVIRONMENTS. (Reading 2132-L 1)

For the student of astrology, suffice it to state that the child becomes imprinted with astrological forces when he takes his first breath. Later planetary transits will trigger those lessons he has chosen to work out in this lifetime. Transmission of astrological influences affect the mind and physical body through the astral body with its seven chakras which interface with the glandular system of the body. Studies of the ancient Egyptians and modern metaphysicians--Gregg Braden, Carolyn Myss, Edgar Cayce, Rudolf Steiner, and C. W. Leadbeater--point to a Divine intelligence at work in the universe to perfect the soul. Since the process of evolution takes much energy and attention, it is likely the soul will take many births in order to evolve. "A wise man guides his destiny; astrology points the way!"

CHAPTER FOUR

THE BASICS OF ASTROLOGY

Astrology has its own language based on the planets, signs, and house of the horoscope. What is a horoscope? A horoscope is a planetary picture of the heavens at the exact time of birth--when the infant takes his first breath. It is a unique moment. When you include the positions of the fixed stars that exact planetary pattern will not be repeated for 26,000 years!

The planets tell us WHAT is happening. The signs HOW this is expressed. And the houses WHERE this will be utilized. On a basic level, the horoscope can be read according to key-word analysis. For example if a woman had her Sun in Aries in the third house, an astrologer would read it this way: Your ego (Sun) is assertive and dynamic (Aries) and could be utilized in teaching, writing or communications (third house).

Astrologers also use a short hand for the planets and signs called glyphs. This is a universal language. Early in you studies, it is important to memorize glyphs and key words for planets and signs and key words for houses. Just as a student of mathematics cannot progress to higher math without memorizing the multiplication tables, so the student of astrology cannot progress without memorizing the basics given below:

Planetary Chart

Glyph	Planet	Ruler	Detriment	Exaltation	Fall
☉	Sun	Leo	Aquarius	Aries	Libra
☽	Moon	Cancer	Capricorn	Taurus	Scorpio
☿	Mercury	Gemini Virgo	Sagittarius Pisces	Aquarius	Leo
♀	Venus	Taurus Libra	Scorpio Aries	Pisces	Virgo
♂	Mars	Aries	Libra	Capricorn	Cancer
♃	Jupiter	Sagittarius	Gemini	Cancer	Capricorn
♄	Saturn	Capricorn	Cancer	Libra	Aries
♅	Uranus	Aquarius	Leo	Scorpio	Taurus
♆	Neptune	Pisces	Virgo	Sagittarius	Gemini
♇	Pluto	Scorpio	Taurus	Aquarius	Leo

Note: Astrologers do not have all the data on

Neptune and Pluto, so there is still speculation on their exaltation and fall.

The following are key words for retrograde planets in a horoscope:

Mercury retrograde   Difficulty in concentrating. May learn more by experience. Can slow thinking and speech. May be more introspective.

Venus retrograde   May complicate conditions in love life. In a male chart may be attracted to women who are inferior.

Mars retrograde   Slows physical energy and motivation. In a female chart may be attract to men who are dependent on her.

Jupiter retrograde   May indicate one who does not follow the conventional road.

Saturn retrograde   Fatalistic attitude, needs to be more positive

Uranus retrograde   May slow, but deepen higher mind.

Neptune retrograde	Needs to be recognized for spiritual deeds.
Pluto retrograde	Compulsive qualities intensified. May bring out suspicious or mysterious circumstances.

Planets are at home in the sign that they rule and considered to be in detriment or weaker position in the sign opposite the ruler. This would lessen their qualities. For example, the Sun rules Leo and gives individual power a boost in that sign. When it is in its opposite sign Aquarius, executive ability is less strong, and technical or scientific work as part of a group is more favored.

Planets are considered exalted in one sign-- meaning best placement. When in the sign opposite the exalted sign, they are their fall or worst position. For example, the Sun is exalted in Aries where individual initiative is at its zenith, but at its fall in Libra where the Sun is more dependent on others.

In order to understand the signs of the zodiac

we need to be aware of the basic qualities in their makeup. Signs may be either masculine which means active or positive energy or may be feminine which means receptive or a negative charge of energy. They are in term made up of one of the four element: fire, warmth and enthusiasm, earth, practical firm, air, communicative and social, or water, emotional and sensitive. In addition to the four elements, they may be found in any of three states: cardinal which gives initiative, fixed which gives staying power, or mutable which give flexibility.

SIGNS OF THE ZODIAC

Glyph	Sign	Qualities	Ruler	Key words
♈	ARIES	m,cardinal, fire	Mars	Assertive, dynamic, impulsive
♉	TAURUS	f,fixed, earth	Venus	Conservative, loyal, stubborn
♊	GEMINI	m,mutable, air	Mercury	Versatile, social, restless
♋	CANCER	f,cardinal, water	Moon	ensitive, protective, moody
♌	LEO	m,fixed, fire	Sun	Proud, romantic, demanding

♍ VIRGO   f,mutable, Mercury Analytical,
          earth   perfectionist,
                             worrisome

♎ LIBRA   m,cardinal, Venus   Diplomatic,
          air   artistic,
                              vacillating

♏ SCORPIO f,fixed,   Pluto   Resourceful,
          water   passionate,
                              jealous

♐ SAGITTARIUS m,mutable, Jupiter Aspiring,
          fire   philosophical,
                               scattered

♑ CAPRICORN f,cardinal, Saturn Ambitious,
          earth   organized,
                              depressed

♒ AQUARIUS m,fixed,   Uranus   Friendly,
          air   tolerant, non-
                              conformist

♓ PISCES f,mutable, Neptune Sensitive,
          water   compassionate,
                              shy

NOTE ABBREVIATIONS: masculine-m and feminine-f.

A horoscope is divided into twelve parts. Each division represents a different department of life. For example the Sun (basic self) will have different opportunities if placed in the tenth house of career as opposed to the fourth house of home and family. House positions are fundamental to reading a horoscope.

HOUSES

1. Physical   body,   early   childhood, personality

2.   Finances, values, portable wealth

3.   Communication, short journeys, relatives

4.   Home, mother, inner self, end of life

5.   Children, romances, speculation

6.   Work, health, service

7.   Marriage, partnerships, legal matters

8.   Higher mind, long journeys, philosophy, publishing

10. Career, status, authority, public image

11. Friends, hopes, wishes, groups

12. Unconscious mind, limitations, solitude, psychic

The angles of the chart are formed by the 1st (ascendant), 4th (nadir), 7th (descendant), and 10th (midheaven). These houses are considered to be more powerful than the other houses of the zodiac.

CHAPTER FIVE

SUN SIGNS: SOLAR POTENTIALS

"To everything there is a season under the Sun" ECCLESIASTES

The Sun is the center of our universe, governing not only the seasons of the year, but the seasons of life. In astrology the placement of the Earth in its orbit around the Sun determines our basic nature or Sun sign. The Sun with its radiance rules the ego, the conscious mind, and the male principle. In a man's chart, it is his father and his own leadership qualities, and the type of husband and father he will become. In a woman's chart, it will also show the type of husband that she attracts, as well as her relationship with her own father.

The Sun also governs the vitality of the person and has rulership over the heart. A well aspected Sun will strengthen the heart and the immune system. Afflictions will weaken both.

The Sun also shows our status and ability to

shine in the community. For, example if your Sun trines or sextiles Jupiter, the native will prosper and be well respected because he is honorable by nature. If on the other hand, the Sun is square Uranus, he may be too demanding and impatient with others which would create many misunderstandings and breaks in relationships. The Sun trines Saturn, on the other hand, will give patience and staying power. Most people will have some good and some adverse aspects, which brings our free will into play. Using the above examples, of a male with the Sun in good aspect to Jupiter and Saturn, but in adverse aspect to Uranus, he would be advised that his patience and leadership skills would bring success, as long as he kept his impatience and ego in check. Often with this position one would fare well in life, but suffer some setbacks because of breaks in relationships or abrupt changes in attitude. To be more specific, the astrologer would chart the Uranus transits, so the client could be ready for any adversity.

With this in mind, let us begin with the basics for each sign. Since the Sun enters each sign of the zodiac around the same date each year, the dates given are approximate.

SUN IN ARIES

March 21 to April 20

NOTED ARIES MALES: Alec Baldwin, Thomas Jefferson, Marlon Brando, Harry Houdini, Warren Beatty, Eugene McCarthy, Joseph Campbell, Tennessee Williams, Vincent VanGogh, Willhelm Reich, and Gregory Peck.

FAMOUS ARIES LADIES: Gloria Steinem, Billie Holiday, Diana Ross, Betty Ford, Gloria Swanson, and Bette Davis.

The sun is exalted in the sign of Aries. Its key phrase is I AM. Instinctively, Aries knows he possesses all creative power within his soul. He can create his own reality. Known for their courage and generosity, Aries can be a true friend in need.

Much like their symbol, the ram, Aries are capable of climbing steep mountains with their head thrust forward, tolerating no obstacles. Aries can be a man (or woman) in a hurry! Ambition, leadership, and ego make this a dynamic sign.

In order for lasting success, they need to learn patience and curb their tempers. If not, they may find themself alone more than they would wish. As a sign Aries can be quite sensitive to loneliness.

Ruled by Mars, Aries is born to lead. Much courage is given to the sign by the red planet Mars! Mars also makes Aries restless and fond of debate--sometimes they forget to rest. If well aspected there is a great passion to this sign--pugnacious if afflicted. Aries always has bright eyes and a spring in his step. In matters of romance, Aries puts the beloved on a pedestal.

Aries is a fire sign and as such is full of warmth, physical passion and genius--but also the flame of temper. A cardinal sign, Arians love to start new projects, but do not enjoy putting the finishing touches on them. Aries, ever the pioneer, enjoys blazing trails and is not afraid to go it alone if necessary! President Jefferson showed the intelligence of the sign, Harry Houdini, the daring, and feminist Gloria Steinem, independence!

THE ARIES CHILD

The Aries child is full of energy and enjoys travel and new projects, but loath details. Often fond of sports and physical activity. He is bright and may not enjoy sitting still long in school. Learn best with an individual approach allowing some choice in subject matter. If crossed, can be headstrong, but will respond well to praise. Since Aries is ruled by Mars, watch out for minor accidents as Aries may have more than their share of scrapped knees!

THE ARIES MALE

He can be delightfully original or downright domineering. He likes to be in charge. Often his bark is worse than his bite. He is not too domestic, unless other planets such as the Moon in Taurus or Cancer are found. As a mate, he prefers some time to peruse his own interest, but is willing to be an equal partner. Prefers gentle, feminine women who he can idealize. Can be quite generous. As a Dad, the type who likes to take his kids camping and would encourage achievement.

THE ARIES FEMALE

She is usually attractive and likes to be well presented--loves bright colors; ruby is a favorite stone, The Aries lady enjoys her outside interests and may be very career oriented, unless her Moon is in a more home-loving sign such as Taurus or Cancer. As a wife she is willing to be an equal partner. She is a doer and often a cheerful family organizer. She can withstand any obstacle except being ignored! While Leo makes the most expensive wife in the zodiac with extravagant tastes, Aries makes a close second with a love of diamonds and the latest fashions. As a mother, she is very proud of her children, both ambitious and generous, but may need to spend more time at home.

SUN IN TAURUS

April 21 to May 20

FAMOUS TAURUS LADIES: Cher, Jessica Lange, Queen Elizabeth, Florence Nightingale, Shirley

Temple, Traci Lords, Candice Bergen, and Barbra Streisand.

NOTED TAURUS MALES: George Clooney, Harry Truman, Valentino, Mike Wallace, Ulysses S. Grant, and Perry Como.

The Sun is more restrained in Taurus, releasing its rays slowly. This gives longevity to the sign. Its key phrase is I HAVE. Possessive by nature, they are the stewards of the zodiac. Taurus is known for his loyalty and staying power. He wants peaceful environment, and can be a stubborn foe to one who threatens home.

Much like their symbol, the bull, they are capable of great strength, just like a bull great anger if you wave a red flag in front of them. Many a Taurus is known for their thrift and financial success. They have an innate sense for business and the patience to stay with projects. In order to have lasting success, they need to be more flexible, willing to seek new methods when the old order is not working.

Ruled by Venus, Taurus can have an eye for beauty. Artistic abilities are given by the planet of love--Venus. They enjoy their creature comforts, are fond of music and art, and often enjoy gardening. Not one to sacrifice comfort to style. Taurus prefers a worn sofa to the most elegant French Provincial settee. If well aspected, there is material abundance and lasting partnerships. If afflicted, they tend to hold a grudge and need to go past hurts. In romance, Taurus may be shy at first, but as a lover has staying power.

Taurus is an earth sign, practical, sensual--but at times stubborn. A fixed sign, Taurus is loath to change. They make excellent managers and organizers. Since Taurus rules the throat, many Taurean have beautiful speaking or singing voices. President Truman showed loyalty to country and family, Barbra Streisand the sensuous voice, and Jessica Lange the classical beauty of Taurus.

THE TAURUS CHILD

The Taurus child is quiet, kindly, and has a sweet tooth! He may need to be encouraged to be outdoors, but once outside, he enjoys nature. He makes a loyal playmate and usually prefers one or two close friends. Don't attempt to change his mind. Give him alternatives. Since Taurus rules the throat, or throats and colds may be a problem if afflicted.

THE TAURUS MALE

He can be very thoughtful or deep in thought. Either way, he knows what he wants in a relationship and may have strong likes and dislikes. He prefers a traditional marriage and love his creature comforts--good food, a warm hearth, and a loyal mate. Practical by nature, he'll build his family a real house with solid wood. As a Dad, he enjoys cooking breakfasts, watching the children's games, coaching from the sidelines. He is a firm, but fair disciplinarian and expects his children to play by the rules.

THE TAURUS FEMALE

She is a Venus beauty--prefers pink and blues and loves diamonds. She has solid values and prefers a traditional marriage. As a wife she can be quite supportive. She prefers a mate who can give her the good life she craves. As a mother she is at her best. The Taurus mother is loyal, organized, and very nurturant. Not as interested in the latest fashions as Aries, she chooses comfort over style. An excellent cook, she knows "the way to a man's heart is through his stomach". However, she may have to watch a tendency to become an "enabler" for less responsible people in her life.

SUN IN GEMINI

May 21 to June 20

NOTED GEMINI MALES: Michael J Fox, John F. Kennedy, Bob Dylan, Walt Whitman, Henry Kissinger, Ralph Waldo Emerson, and John Wayne

FAMOUS GEMINI LADIES: Marilyn Monroe, Judy Garland, Wynonna Judd, Alice Bailey, Queen Victoria, Ally Sheedy, and Isabella Rossellini

The Sun brightens in Gemini. Its key phrase is, I THINK. Geminis are natural communicators and can make excellent teachers, researchers, and sales personnel. They have a love of short distant travel. Known for their quick smiles and wit, they make good travel companions and always enjoy a change of place. Occasionally, their quick wit may make them tricky and their need for change superficial. However, they are never boring.

Sometimes like their symbol, the twins, they can be two people in one body. However, they do have trouble sitting still and may get bored easily. In order to be successful, they need to stay with projects longer. They also need to watch their lungs, as Gemini rules the lungs and if afflicted may cause lung problems.

Ruled by Mercury, they are naturally intelligent. since Gemini rules the hands, they may also excel in mechanics or crafts. In matters of romance, Gemini likes to be friends first. They like a partner they can talk to, who has a sense of humor and doesn't mind surprises.

Gemini is an air sign which makes them logical sequential thinkers--perfect for the computer age. They make friends easily and may enjoy friends of both sexes. A mutable sign, they enjoy work with varied activities or some travel. Geminis prefer the light touch and are known for their sense of humor. John F. Kennedy, with his elegant speeches, showed the Gemini power of communication, Bob Hope, the sense of humor, and both Judy Garland and Marilyn Monroe, the duality of the sign.

THE GEMINI CHILD

The Gemini child has great curiosity and loves to ask questions. He responds well to reason and travels well. Take time to answer his questions, be sure to give him the reason behind decisions, and allow time for frequent outings. Otherwise he can bore easily and be a "Dennis the Menace" type.

THE GEMINI MALE

The Gemini male likes to be busy. He may be handy around the house with his tools or full of advice on everything from toys to taxes. He loves to talk. Often enjoys female friends and is willing to travel. What this philosophical male does not like is irrational temper tantrums or frowns. Too much unpleasantness and he may get lost. As a mate, he is willing to do his share, but prefers a wife who is an equal. As a Dad, he's a great teacher, loves field trips and is never at a loss for words. However, when responsibilities pile up, he needs to hang in there a little longer.

THE GEMINI FEMALE

The Gemini female can be quite independent. She enjoys travel, likes to change her hairstyle and clothes often, and doesn't mind surprises. She has a sense of humor. She enjoys dating and the fun times in a relationship, but is not too domestic. As a wife, she will want to work at least part time. Like the Gemini dad, the Gemini places great stress on the child's education. In her desire to optimize her child's education, she may over schedule activities. She needs to allow some "down" time in both her and her child's schedule. Like the Aries mother, she may need to spend more time in the home, to give her child a stable base.

SUN IN CANCER

June 21 to July 22

FAMOUS CANCER LADIES: Princess Diana, Meryl Streep, Linda Ronstadt, Natalie Wood, Rose Kennedy and Mary Baker Eddy.

NOTED CANCER MALES: Tom Cruise, John Quincy Adams, Bill Cosby, Neil Simon, Marc Chagall, Yul Brenner, and Art Linkletter.

The Sun in its midnight position in Cancer--giving the sign a penchant for seclusion. Its key phrase if I feel like the proverbial Jewish mother, Cancers like to nurture and nudge. Just like our nation which is a Cancer country born on the fourth of July, Cancers love Mom, home, and apple pie. Cancers collect everything from string to Tupperwear. And of course, they love a bargain!

Much like their symbol, the crab, they retreat under attack. Sensitive to criticism, they may miss much helpful feedback. They need to get out of their shell in order to be more successful in the world. Isolation can lead to psychological problems.

Ruled by the Moon, Cancers can be moody. Their intuition is strong. If well aspected, they are ahead of the trends. They often like to work in retail or real estate and are good business people. Since Cancer rules the stomach, they are often good cooks--even the men like to barbecue. If afflicted, they may be prone to ulcers and digestive problems. In matters of romance, they tend to be shy--at least at first.

Cancer is a water sign and is most relaxed on the beach or in the pool. A cardinal sign, they may have to make time to relax. They tend to bring the office home at nights and may treat co-workers as family. John Quincy Adams showed Cancer patriotism, Princess Diana and Rose Kennedy, dedication to family, and Bill Cosby, Cancer's sense of humor.

THE CANCER CHILD

The Cancer child loves his mother--and father too or course. He is a homebody and may enjoy building forts or playing house. They often are shy outside the home and seek the comfort of food when under stress. Outwardly compliant, this child tends to stuff his feelings and may hold a grudge.

Try involving him more in decision-making process-
-"What do you think is a fair punishment?" Most of
all your little Moon child needs the security of a
night light and a good night hug. Take time to give
him the emotional security he needs as a youngster,
and he will care for you well in your later years.

THE CANCER MALE

The Cancer male needs reassurance. He likes
to lead, but he's not sure you will follow. When
he commits, it is for life. Cancers really do make
the best husbands--as they are natural homebodies.
They will build you your own love nest. As Dads,
they are "hands on" fathers. They like to provide
both food and fun for their youngsters. And are not
shy about giving advice. They know the value of old
fashioned discipline and hard work. Occasionally
they will try to parent their mate to the detriment
of the marriage.

THE CANCER FEMALE

The Cancer female is a domestic goddess. She

loves her home and family. Sometimes she has a hard time separating from her parents. She is intuitive, compassionate, and always there for those she loves. She knows "the way to a man's heart is through his stomach" and is an excellent cook. Home always comes first. She may even prefer to work from a home office. She can excel in fields of real estate or interior decorating. As a mother, she will sacrifice much for her child. If afflicted, she can be a "smother mother".

SUN IN LEO

July 23 to August 22

FAMOUS LEO LADIES: Jacqueline Kennedy Onassis, Martha Stewart, Tipper Gore, Cathy Lee Gifford, Madame DuBarry, and Lucille Ball.

NOTED LEO MALES: Dr. Carl Jung, Robert Redford, Robert DeNiro, Dustin Hoffman, Alan Leo, Benito Mussolini, George Bernard Shaw and Napoleon.

Leos are born to shine. Their key phrase is, I WILL. They may excell in management, the arts or in sports. They love the limelight. Leos love to party and make better hosts than guests. They are generous to a fault, but have a quick temper when not appreciated.

Like their symbol, the lion, they have a loud roar and refuse to be ignored. They also love their lair and are known to lounge. Like the king of the jungle, they are born to rule, taking great pride in their accomplishments.

Ruled by the Sun, they are born to rise in life. Status is important. They prefer center stage. Leos also like to bask in the Sun. Since Leo rules the back and heart, these may present problems if afflicted.

Leo is a fire sign and as such can be artistic and creative. The fire energy is stabilized, giving them great warmth and loyalty. When crossed or their authority is challenged their fixed nature becomes apparent. Napoleon shows the determination of the sign, Martha Stewart, its innate good taste, and Jacqueline Kennedy Onassis, Leo's love of luxury.

THE LEO CHILD

The Leo child is the pride of the family--with

his zest for life and sunny disposition. Love of sports, music, and of course arcade games is strong. Their fun loving and generous nature attracts many friends. They can be demanding and a bit bossy--if afflicted a strong willed child, whose temper needs curbing. Leo children like to be seen in only the "hottest" fashions.

THE LEO MALE

The Leo male likes to be in charge. Appreciation is key to his character. As a husband, he is generous and loyal. His need for attention is apparent from the moment he enters the house with a loud, "Honey, I'm home!" As a father, he shines. Nothing is too good for Junior. He will be glad to coach and organize his children. However, after a workout, he is known to retire to his den.

THE LEO FEMALE

The Leo female loves gold and finery. She dresses well and may have a long golden mane. She is a gracious hostess and makes a loyal mate. With her elegant taste, she is the most expensive wife in the zodiac. As a mother, she is in her glory. She will lavish both time and money on her child. She takes great pride in their accomplishments-- always there in the front row applauding.

SUN IN VIRGO

August 23 to September 22

FAMOUS VIRGO LADIES: Leann Rimes, Mother Theresa, Marcia Clark, Joan Kennedy, Patsy Cline, Lauren Bacall, Maria Montessori, and Sophia Loren

NOTED VIRGO MALES: Scott Hamiliton, Lyndon Johnson, Peter Falk, Roal Dahl, Hank Williams, B.B. King, Peter Sellers, and Leonard Bernstein.

The Sun is in the house of service in Virgo, making it a perfectionist. Their key phrase is, "I ANALYZE". Quiet Virgo can surprise you the day the boss is out by their vast knowledge and capable nature. With their analytical mind, they are drawn to science, medicine and computers--all run by logic. Known for their patience, they make hardworking nurses--but may lack warmth. Perhaps Virgos wouldn't be so "picky", if they didn't do so much picking up after others.

Their symbol is the virgin lying on her side with a sheath of grain in her hand. The virgin stands for purity and the sheath of wheat is wisdom gleaned from experience. Virgos are very discriminating in romance and may marry later. True to their symbol, they value hard work and may have a tendency to overwork.

Ruled by mercury, they enjoy pursuits of the mind. They often worry needlessly. If afflicted, they can be high-strung and may be prone to ulcers as they hold emotions in. Since Virgo rules the intestines can be a problem area if afflicted.

Being an earth sign, they value material good and are given to small thrift. Even though Virgos love a bargain, they are drawn to good quality and will take time to carefully examine purchases. Since they are a mutable sign, they enjoy mental diversions and a change of scenery--with a well planned itinerary. Marcia Clark showed the intelligent analytical side of Virgo, Roal Dahl, writing ability, and Mother Theresa exemplified Virgo's desire to serve.

THE VIRGO CHILD

The Virgo child is considerate by nature, but a bit frail. He is often timid and may have to be drawn into conversations. He prefers a best friend to a gathering. Since he is ruled by Mercury, he loves to read and makes a good student. If afflicted, his insecurities come to a head. Since he had a good mind, he can sense there are more things to be concerned about in the world. Shy, by nature, he may need encouragement to display his talents--which are considerable. He can also have more than his share of stomachaches. However, nothing that a bland diet and a dose of empathy won't cure.

THE VIRGO MALE

The Virgo male may sometimes be so involved in his work, he neglects his social life. Hence he remains a bachelor longer than other signs. When he does marry, it is after careful consideration. He has discriminating tastes, and looks for refinement in a mate. When he does marry, he is a good provider. He is a loyal if not expressive mate. As a father, he takes his duties seriously and will teach his child the value of hard work and discipline. He may need to show more affection especially with younger children. He does take time to watch their diet, help with homework, and support the team.

THE VIRGO FEMALE

The Virgo female is often well presented. She enjoys well-made clothes that are in fashion. She is very much a lady and has high standards. Interested in health, diet and exercise, she may even appear younger as she ages. At first, she may seem shy or not interested in romance, but she is just waiting for the right partner. Once married, she is an excellent homemaker and a loyal mate. If afflicted, she can be a nag. It may be her way of trying to improve her man, but it usually backfires. A concerned mother, she will attend to the child's diet and wardrobe. Hard work, however needs to be balanced with play, or both the mother and child will suffer.

SUN IN LIBRA

September 23 to October 21

FAMOUS LIBRA LADIES: Alicia Silverstone, Susan Sarandon, Helen Hayes, Tiffany Trump, Sarah Ferguson, Eleanor Roosevelt, Margaret Thatcher, Savannah, Heather Locklear, and Catherine Deneuve.

NOTED LIBRA MALES: Dwight Eisenhauer, John Lennon, E.E. Cummings, Mahatma Ghandi, Ed Sullivan, Paul Simon, and Jimmy Carter.

The Sun is descending in the sign of Libra, bringing both an interest in partnerships. Libras are marriage oriented and enjoy an active social life. They have respect for the law and a desire to please others, sometimes too much. However, they need to be more decisive.

Like their symbol, the scale, they have a need to weigh and balance carefully before making a decision. Their key phrase is, I FEEL. Their fine intelligence helps them to succeed in life. They have long memories and may stuff their feelings.

When angry, they are apt to bring up a long Landry list from the past.

Ruled by Venus, they are attractive and well spoken. They abhor coarse language. They can be attracted to artistic professions from cosmetology to fine arts. Their sense of color, proportion, and taste are excellent. Hence, they may be attracted to architecture and interior design. While Libras love beauty, they dislike all the scrubbing of cleaning and can be indulgent at times. Their "sweet tooth" may cause them to gain weight in middle age if left unchecked. However, Libra women are the most beautiful women in the zodiac with classic beauties such as Rita Hayworth and Catherine Deneuve.

Libra is an air sign, who love company, gossip, and fashion. They communicate well. Since they are a cardinal sign, they can overcome a tendency to be laid back and show intelligent leadership. Presidents Eisenhower and Carter showed intelligent leadership, John Lennon, Libra creativity and Catherine Deneuve the exquisite beauty of the sign.

THE LIBRA CHILD

The Libra child is often quick, intelligent and enjoys popularity. He may be fair of face and full of fun. He shows concern for others and has good manners. Naturally intelligent, he looks forward to school and excels in his studies. Cleaning his room is another matter. Often content to sweep under the bed and pile his tangle of toys in the clothes basket. His charm make him hard to discipline, but he does need help with practical matters. Ruled by Venus he may prefer dessert to the main course.

THE LIBRA MALE

The Libra male has classic good looks and nice manners. He very much is attracted to beautiful women, and prefers a lady for a mate. He wants a soul mate--someone to share the struggles of life with. As a father, he has high standards for his child's education and is well informed. He likes to pal around with his child and may leave the discipline to Mom.

THE LIBRA FEMALE

The Libra female is a princess and wants a fairy tale marriage. She is willing to work hard on a relationship and makes an attractive wife. She dislikes the drudgery of housework, but loves to decorate. As a wife, she is an excellent companion- -as long as she receives the attention she knows she deserves. She can be loyal and loving. As a mother she takes pride in her children, cheerfully, decorating their bedrooms, creating spectacular parties, and carefully grooming them. At times her high standards may seem tedious, but her care and concern make her a mother you want to please.

SUN IN SCORPIO

FAMOUS SCORPIO LADIES: Hilary Clinton, Princess Grace of Monacco, Marla Maples, Madame Marie Curie, Sylvia Plath, Indira Ghandi, Jodie Foster, Whoopie Goldberg, and Linda Evans.

NOTED SCORPIO MALES: Bill Gates, Theodore Roosevelt, Billie Graham, Johnnie Carson, Will

Rogers, Pablo Picasso and Kurt Vonnegut.

The Sun is ambitious in the sign of Scorpio. Its key phrase is, I DESIRE. It has great determination and staying power. Power is important. Known for their hard work and loyalty Scorpios make excellent organizers. Known for their courage and desire to excel, they are keen competitors since they tend to go to extremes. They can be either saints or sinners--sometimes both in the same lifetime. There are two traits that hold them back--jealousy and control. Scorpios need to "let go, and let God" to be successful in both their professional and personal lives.

Like their symbol the Scorpion, they can sting and be a bitter enemy. However, the wise Scorpio will hold back his sarcasm and concentrate on the details at hand. They often are called on to manage other people's resources and can be successful in banking, insurance and corporate life. Their hunches usually pay off. They make shrewd investors and seldom die poor.

Ruled by Pluto, they can be ruthless when crossed. They have a good ability to create a second chance for themselves and others. They are reformers at heart and have a penchant for recycling or buying at discount. Pluto gives them a determined, serious appearance. If afflicted, they can be lone wolves, trusting only a few.

Scorpio is a water sign in touch with intuition and willing to play a hunch. Fixed by nature, they can also be stubborn and are known for their strong likes and dislikes. They can be a most loyal friend or bitter foe. Theodore Roosevelt showed the determination of the sign; Grace Kelley, the loyalty, and Pablo Picasso, the Scorpio genius.

THE SCORPIO CHILD

The Scorpio child may prefer to play alone. He has good concentration and likes puzzles, mysteries, and the unusual. He may appear shy, but will extend himself when he is ready. He is a loyal friend. Sometimes his temper will get him into trouble. His strong drive to compete may also cost him a few friends. Encourage him to be all that he can be-- but to be fair.

THE SCORPIO MALE

The Scorpio male may seem too engrossed in thought to notice you but he does. He likes to lead and will let you know he's interested when he has a plan in place. He is an ardent lover and a determined suitor. But he likes to have some money in the bank before proposing! As a husband he has strong likes and dislikes. He makes a loyal mate believing marriage is "till death do ye part". As a father, he believes in discipline and will provide well for his child. He is quick to spot a lie, but just as quick to lend a helping hand to his offspring. You may have to read between the lines, as he is apt to be brief in communications.

THE SCORPIO FEMALE

The Scorpio female may be a top executive or a "femme fatale". Either way, she likes to have her way. She can be quite proper at times, and yet very sensual underneath. Once she decides to marry, she will work hard to help her mate rise to the top. Hillary Clinton is a good example. She is also a most dedicated mother--disciplining, grooming, and educating her child with exacting standards. By nature, she is a hard worker and expects others to work just as hard. However, nagging and knitpicking bear watching!

SUN IN SAGITTARIUS

November 22 to December 21

FAMOUS SAGITTARIAN LADIES: Margaret Meade, Tina Turner, Leslie Stahl, Emily Dickinson, Amy Grant, Caroline Kennedy and Patty Duke.

NOTED SAGITTARIAN MALES: Brad Pitt, Mark Twain, Frank Sinatra, Kahlil Gibran, William Blake, Sai Baba, Kirk Douglas, Walt Disney and Dick Clark.

Sagittarians are born seekers. Their key phrase is, I PERCEIVE. They love travel, sports and adventure. Like their sign, the body of the centaur and head of the archer, they are half party animal, half square shooter. The lower side of Sagittarius can stretch the truth a bit. The higher side is a seeker of higher truths. Sagittarians have a sense of humor and usually enjoy the outdoors. They may have a temper, but are quick to forgive. They need to concentrate more on matters at hand and less on future sights to be truly successful.

Like their symbol the body of the beast and the head of an archer, they can be half square shooter. While the lower side, may enjoy sensual pleasures, the higher side aims at the stars. Sagittarius rules the thighs of the body. If afflicted this area and also the liver (ruled by Jupiter) may be a trouble spot--usually from excesses whether it be exercise or food.

Ruled by Jupiter, they have a jovial nature. They can inspire others with their faith. Fond of debate and a passion for the truth, they can make excellent professors, lawyers, or writers. They are also drawn to fields connected with travel. Their positive nature and strong faith can be an inspiration to many in the fields of counseling and ministry as well.

Sagittarius is a fire sign, full of swagger. They enjoy creative work, but dislike the drudgery of detailed analysis. A mutable sign, they prefer a variety of tasks, rather than repetitive work. Like all fire signs, when crossed, they display a temper! Mark Twain with his love of a good story and travel down the river is a perfect example of Sagittarius. Margaret Meade, the anthropologist and writer shows the more serious side of the sign. And Tina Turner shows the creative, fun loving side of Sagittarius.

THE SAGITTARIAN CHILD

The Sagittarian child is a spiritual warrior. He loves to explore, so give him plenty of space. He will also enjoy games from Little League to Olympics of the Mind. Once he has found his path life, he can be a born crusader. Never content to keep still, he will wear out many a pair of sneakers. This child may be high in creative intelligence, but low in concentration. He'll tell some great stories, embellishing the truth as he goes along. In school, he'll need to be told to sit still and get his facts straight. Sometimes he takes unnecessary risks. Parental supervision is a must. As much as he dislikes restriction, he needs to learn to finish one task, before starting the next.

THE SAGITTARIAN MALE

The Sagittarian male is part swashbuckler, part "Good Neighbor Sam". Given to travel and lofty goals, he may be hard to catch. Once married, he is a loyal mate. He needs his space, but is willing to give his mate her freedom too. While he loves a large house, he probably will not spend much time in it, as he loves the outdoors. As a father, he is more a pal. He likes to take the kids on trips, but will shy away from discipline. His love of sports and fair play makes him a cheerful coach!

THE SAGITTARIAN FEMALE

The Sagittarian female believes in equal rights. She is willing to work shoulder to shoulder with her man to achieve success. Since her career is important to her, she may choose to marry later after she has gotten it off the ground. As a wife, she is a most pleasant companion. A nature girl, she prefers casual attire to the latest fashions. She is a team Mom encouraging her child and her neighbor's as well. She does prefer being outside the home, and is not too domestic. She will often cheerfully delegate dusting to others!

SUN IN CAPRICORN

December to January

FAMOUS CAPRICORN FEMALES: Mary Tyler Moore, Janis Joplin, Joan Baez, Erin Gray, Loretta Young and Marlene Dietrich.

NOTED CAPRICORN MALES: Woodrow Wilson, Swarmi Vivekananda, J. Edgar Hoover, Pablo Casals, Albert Schweitzer, Martin Luther King, Sr., and Paramanhansa Yogananda.

The Sun is at its zenith in the natural zodiac in the sign of Capricorn. Capricorns seek recognition and status. Career is important to both males and females. Serious, hard working, and thorough, they have natural executive ability. They may even schedule vacations around work. They need to worry less about details and learn to relax between assignments if they want to enjoy their trip to the top.

Like their symbol, the seagoat, they may take three steps forward and two steps back in life.

They will succeed because of their focused energy where many others give up. They usually thrive on hard work and will stay with challenges. Their key phrase is, I USE. As they age, they may learn to lighten up. Born with old heads on young shoulders, they are one sign that may actually grow younger as they age.

Ruled by Saturn, they are determined to overcome life's obstacles. Saturn, the planet of restriction demands this. They tend to be shy and closed mouth, even cold at times. Since Capricorn rules the knees, bone structure and teeth, these can be problem areas, if afflicted.

Capricorn is an earth sign which give makes them thirty. They definitely need material security behind them. Since they often live long lives (Saturn's influence), they instinctively put something aside for a rainy day. Since they are a cardinal sign, they have initiative and leadership ability to become materially successful. The Reverend Martin Luther King showed the determined leadership of the sign. Mary Tyler Moore, with her high cheek bones is a Capricorn beauty and J. Edgar

Hoover exemplified Capricorn's ability to keep a secret.

THE CAPRICORN CHILD

The Capricorn child is your "little professor"--serious, hardworking, and reasonable. He may have more than his share of colds and flu during his first seven years. Quiet by nature, he tends not to complain. He may be shy and should be encouraged in friendships. He desperately wants attention, but may be too introverted to express his feelings. Take time to read to this young scholar and draw out his concerns.

THE CAPRICORN MALE

The Capricorn male takes his work home and may tend to marry later. He is a traditional husband, likes economy, neatness and a refined wife. He works hard to provide well, but not lavishly for his family. As a father, he may be a disciplinarian. He takes his role as a parent seriously and will surely save for his child's education.

THE CAPRICORN FEMALE

The Capricorn female may appear cold on the surface, with her high cheek bones has an air of refinement. Always a lady, she dislikes coarse language and immature behavior. Serious about her career, she may marry later or choose a more serious mate. She is an excellent housekeeper and a devoted mother who may tend to be worried about her child's progress but is well intentioned. The Capricorn mother stresses breeding, manners, and morality. Affection is more difficult. She will work hard on behalf of her child, but may need to give more hugs.

SUN IN AQUARIUS

FAMOUS AQUARIAN LADIES: Cybil Shepherd, Eartha Kitt, Molly Ringwald, Mia Farrell and Betty Friedan.

NOTED AQUARIAN MALES: Abraham Lincoln, Franklin Delano Roosevelt, Ronald Reagan, Charles Dickens, James Hoffa, Paul Newman and Burt Reynolds.

The Sun is revolutionary in Aquarius. The

United States has had three Aquarian presidents all changing our country--Abraham Lincoln with the Civil War, Franklin Delano Roosevelt with the New Deal, and Ronald Reagan with decentralization of government. Aquarians love to reorganize and thrive on change. Democratic in spirit, they attract friends from all walks of life and many friends of both sexes. Drawn to the unusual, they may explore the occult and astrology. President Lincoln invited medium Netty Colburn Maynard to the White House for seances. Jeanne Dixon in her autobiography tells of smuggling a crystal ball past the White House guard to do a "reading" for President Roosevelt and Nancy Reagan kept President Reagan safe in the Oval Office with regular consultations with San Francisco astrologist, Joan Quigley. Perhaps the only thing idealistic Aquarius will not tolerate is a lie.

Their symbol, the water bearer is most interesting--the lad gazing at the heavens, while all his water is flowing out his pitcher hoisted backwards on his shoulder. However, don't worry it isn't water in the pitcher--it's knowledge. The key phrase for Aquarius is, I KNOW. True to their symbol they are drawn to the stars and can make excellent astrologers and wise counselors.

Ruled by Uranus, a higher octave of Mercury, they can be quite inventive, and may be fascinated by gadgets. They can bore easily and may be highstrung. Since Aquarius rules the legs, they may be prone to problems there if afflicted.

Aquarius is an air sign who needs their freedom. They can be drawn to group associations and can be idealistic. Since they are a fixed sign, they may show a stubborn streak. However, they make loyal and tolerant friends. Abraham Lincoln showed the humanitarian greatness in the sign. Evangeline Adams, the love of astrology, and Paul Newman their classic good looks.

THE AQUARIAN CHILD

The Aquarian child is a natural explorer. An air sign, he needs fresh air and fresh ideas. He delights in tales from fairy tales to science fiction. Since he values liberty, restraint is unnatural to him. Encourage his independence, when applicable and appeal to his sense of reason and fair play before disciplinary actions. Aquarian children have much to share for they are children of the New Age.

THE AQUARIAN MALE

He can be quite independent, but longs for a mate who will be a friend. Since he is not too domestic in nature, he wants a wife who balances home with a career. Appeal to his humanitarian instincts and you will have an equal partner. As a Dad, he wants to be a pal. He loves to travel, camp, and explore with his child.

THE AQUARIAN FEMALE

She may be hard to catch as she values her independence. However, once married, she makes a loyal mate. She can be a great companion and will not tolerate being left home. Not too domestic, but a true friend to her husband. As a mother she is quite sensible, emphasizing education, human rights and playing by the rules.

SUN IN PISCES

February 19 to March 20

FAMOUS PISCES LADIES: Alicia Silverstone, Drew Barrymore, Elizabeth Taylor, Tyne Daley, Glen Close, Pat Nixon, Joanne Woodward, Dinah Shore, and Elizabeth Barrett Browning.

NOTED PISCES MALES: Grover Cleveland, Desi Arnez, Jackie Gleason, Edgar Cayce, Rudolph Steiner and Jack Kerouac.

Pisces are born dreamers. Their key phrase is, I BELIEVE. And they seem to believe in everyone except themselves. Gentle, soft spoken, and shy, they may need to learn to assert themselves, if they desire material success. Their sense of humor, kindness, and faith make for devoted friendship.

Their symbol is that of the two fishes swimming in opposite direction, but tied together. Fish represent Christ-like compassion, which they have in abundance. However, they need to sort out their emotions, which can go in different directions, to be successful in life. It is hard for them to make a decision as they are sensitive to both their own concerns and those of others. However, procrastination in itself is a decision. Better, to go within and stay with that choice which is most correct--as no decision can be one hundred percent.

Ruled by Neptune, they are mystical in nature. They enjoy music, art and poetry. What they lack in assertion, they make up for in devotion to duty.

Pisces is a water sign and loves the beach. They are emotional and intuitive. However, being mutable, they are subject to vast changes in feelings due to their sensitive streak. Elizabeth Taylor with her violet eyes showed the lush beauty of Pisces; Jackie Gleason exempliefied the gentle Pisces humor, and Edgar Cayce showed the psychic sign of the sign.

THE PISCES CHILD

The Pisces child is a blessing. This gentle soul may be content to daydream by a fishing hole or play quietly in the corner. Either way he's no bother. However, there is a great deal going on inside. Intuitive by nature, he misses little emotionally. He will surely appreciate music, love a mystery, and have a sense of humor. Occasionally, forgetful, a well-timed reminder will get him back on track. Quiet by nature, he may lack confidence and need encouragement to express his feelings. When he does people, will be surprised at how insightful he is. While he enjoys the companionship of sports, he doesn't like the competition. He may seek to escape the harsher side of life. If his family is not available to encourage his spirit, he needs a mentor.

THE PISCES MALE

The Pisces male is sensitive and gentle. He loves music and is definitely sentimental. He shines in romance, remembering important occasions with flowers and notes. As a husband, he is most devoted. Creative by nature, he has his own plan for a dream house. He may not be great at hammering a nail, but can outline the details for others to implement. He likes to escape from reality and is sensitive to criticism. While you can't live on love alone, he sure helps. As a father, he is a loving protector. Kind to both animals and children, he truly takes time to listen.

THE PISCES FEMALE

The Pisces female enjoys being a woman. A sensual, but gentle charmer, who longs to have someone stronger to carry the burden. She is most willing to support her mate emotionally. As a girlfriend, she is unforgettable, as a wife, never far from your thoughts. She will create a decorative home, romantic dinners for two, and makes a loving mother. She may forget to pay the phone bill on time, be oblivious to dust, but never deliberately! As for her children--she is always on their side. Reluctant to deal with unpleasant issues, she may have to learn the value of "reality testing", priorities and goal setting, is she decides to peruse a career.

CHAPTER SIX

THE MOON: EMOTIONAL SIDE OF LIFE

"If the Sun and Moon should doubt, They'd immediately go out"--Blake.

In ancient times, the Moon was called Isis after the Egyptian goddess and the Sun was called Ra. While the Sun is our power center ruling worldly stratus, the Moon is our inner source of power, governing the home and women. The Moon rules the unconscious mind of habit; the Sun governs the conscious mind. Each planet has a very vital role to play in the chart.

In traditional astrology, the Moon represents the emotional side of man. It represents women in general, the native's mother; in a man's chart, his wife; and in a woman's chart, the type of mother she would become. Furthermore, the moon represents the public. In electional astrology it is an important tool in planning public functions. In Hindu astrology, the moon would have a past life influence, and the nodes of the moon indicate our most recent life and the direction needed for soul growth. Psychologically, the moon shows the influence of the parents and the seeds planted in childhood. It also shows how we are programmed to receive energy and those habits deeply ingrained in our subconscious mind.

The Moon has a greater influence in childhood as it represents what we have garnered emotionally from past lives. It is instinctual by nature. Since it rules the unconscious mind, it plays a strong role in our psychological makeup. If afflicted, there may be psychological blocks to expressing the personality. For example, if the Moon is squared by Saturn there may be a lack of nurturance in the child's life. This could be the forerunner to adult depression if not addressed by a therapist or a caring adult. Sometimes influences may be mixed. A child may have Moon square Saturn, but the beneficial aspect of the Moon trine Neptune. Here the child's mother may give him up (lack of nurturance), but a grandmother or adopted mother (Moon trine Neptune) may take over his care. To fully understand the Moon, we need to look at the sign it is in, the house position, and the aspects it makes to other planets.

MOON IN ARIES

The Moon in Aries likes to dramatize his feelings, may have a temper, and may become easily distracted. While quite enthusiastic in nature, there is a need for patience at times. If well aspected, he is decisive in nature and a strong leader. If afflicted, he may puff up the ego to create a petty dictator. Often this moon signifies a strong, but domineering mother influence. In a woman's chart, all or nothing attitude toward children-either loves being a mother or definitely prefers a career. In a man's chart, it attracts a passionate, creative, headstrong wife, whose ambitions will match his own.

MOON IN TAURUS

While the Moon may be restless in Aries, it is full of patience in Taurus because it is exalted. The Moon in Taurus is quite domestic--he may even prefer to work at home. It is kind and deeply feeling--but prefers to keep his feelings private. If well aspected they may excel in home-making skills, gardening, cooking and business. If afflicted they can be too stubborn and may need to be more flexible in thinking. In a woman's chart brings out the maternal nature. She is a good mother--establishing rules and routine, but is kind and considerate to the child. In a man's chart it brings an attracted, traditional wife who will be his strongest ally. For good or ill, people with the Moon in Taurus are tied to their roots. In childhood they may have difficulty separating either physically or psychologically from their home. Later in life they may have difficulty letting their own children go.

MOON IN GEMINI

The Moon in Gemini is quite friendly, enjoys travel and change in general. Restless in nature, it seeks stimulation. Frequently people with their Moon in Gemini are people watchers and may enjoy analyzing emotions. They have a healthy curiosity and a good sense of humor. If well aspected, they can have writing or speaking ability. If afflicted they may be too worrisome, fearful, or highstrung. In a woman's chart it shows a capacity for communication and the type of mother who fosters her child's education, but she is not especially maternal in nature. In a male chart, the Moon in Gemini attracts an intelligent wife, who enjoys being an equal partner.

THE MOON IN CANCER

The Moon is very much at home in Cancer as it is in its own sign. Both men and women with the Moon in Cancer like to nurture. They are sensitive, sometimes shy, and very emotional people. Often they enjoy cooking, homemaking and real estate. Sometimes the natives will have strong resemblance to their mother, either physically or psychologically. Often they see their home as a place of retreat from the harshness of the outer world. Innately intuitive, they have their pulse on the public. This can give them an edge in business. If well aspected it means good parents and a happy home life. If afflicted, many responsibilities in these areas. Men with Moon in Cancer attract home-loving mates who like to nurture. Women with the Moon in Cancer are natural mothers. If they don't have children, the office becomes their family.

MOON IN LEO

The Moon in Leo likes to dramatize feelings and can be theatrical. Often they enjoy working with young people, love games, and sports, and can be kids at heart. If well aspected their romantic nature sparkles. If afflicted, they can be too domineering. In a man's chart, it attracts a very loving but possessive wife. She will be generous with a vibrant personality, but has a temper when crossed. In a woman's chart she is a mother who takes great pride in her children and/or creations.

MOON IN VIRGO

The Moon in Virgo may be slow to express emotions and even shy at times. He likes an orderly environment and likes to analyze. Often there are skills in research, writing, medicine and accounting. If well aspected he is a good worker. If afflicted he may be petty or worrisome in nature. In a man's chart, the Moon attracts a quiet, neat, industrious mate. In a woman's chart, this Moon attracts a mother who works hard for the good of the child, but may need to show more affection. Sometimes it decreases fertility as Virgo is a barren sign.

MOON IN LIBRA

The Moon in Libra is refined and sociable. Drawn to luxury, the Moon in Libra has discriminating taste. He is quite intelligent, fair, and able to see both sides of an issue. If well aspected, artistic abilities are strong. If afflicted, may be too indecisive. The Moon here is partnership oriented and marriage is emphasized. In a man's chart, the Moon attracts a lovely, refined wife with a taste for the "better things of life". In a woman's chart, this Moon makes for the type of mother who encourages her child's education, but may be a social butterfly. If well aspected, she has good methods of child psychology.

MOON IN SCORPIO

The Moon in Scorpio finds it difficult to express his deep feeling nature as the Moon is in its fall in Scorpio. This can make him moody and at times judgmental. Often he is intuitive and shrewd, and will work hard to overcome obstacles. If well aspected, he can overcome much adversity in life. If afflicted too jealous and demanding and may indicate a lone wolf type. In a man's chart, the Moon attracts a magnetic, passionate, but possessive mate. In a woman's chart, this Moon can give problems with female reproductive systems, if afflicted. While she is fiercely protective of her child, she can be a disciplinarian as the child matures. Taking great pride in her child, she may be oblivious to the child's faults. To improve relationships, she should use more intuition and tact when dealing with the public.

MOON IN SAGITTARIUS

The Moon in Sagittarius gives a friendly

disposition, one with an open mind, and helpful nature. He can be a bit shy early in life, but has a flair for the creative and may enjoy music. He may marry later, as he prefers not to be tied down emotionally. Men with the Moon in Sagittarius may attract an independent, idealistic mate who wants to be an equal partner. She will definitely have a twinkle in her eye. Women with this position enjoy children and make excellent teachers. As mothers, they are devoted, encouraging creativity and intelligence, but may feel too tied down by motherhood.

MOON IN CAPRICORN

The Moon in Capricorn is in its detriment. He keeps a tight lid on his emotions and needs to be in control. Often sensitive to criticism and subservient to authority. Known for their stoic nature, they would make a good nurse--organized, systematic, and can give a shot with little empathy for the patient's discomfort. If well aspected, their ambition is strong and their business ability keen. If afflicted, they may appear cold and unloving. In man's chart, he attracts a practical, down to earth, mate. In a woman's chart, she makes for a devoted and hard working mother who can discipline well but may lack warmth at times.

MOON IN AQUARIUS

The Moon in Aquarius is idealistic and upbeat. They are everyone's friend. Since they have a quick wit and enjoy people, they do well in fields which require communication such as writing, sales, and teaching. If well aspected, they can be humanitarian and progressive in thought. If afflicted, they may become impractical daydreamers. In a man's chart, he attracts a charming, but independent mate, who will be a friend for life. In a woman's chart, a mother who makes learning fun. She knows the value of education and has her own views on raising children. Like the Moon in Sagittarius, she may prefer interests outside the home.

MOON IN PISCES

The Moon in Pisces has a gentle personality

They are kind and sympathetic, sometimes shy, with an unhostile sense of humor. If well aspected, drawn to the arts and spiritual pursuits. They can be gentle and indecisive at times, but their hunches turn out to be true. If afflicted they may try to retreat from reality with alcohol or become involved in relationships which are codependent. In a man's chart, attracts a gentle, feminine wife who is very devoted to husband and family. In a woman's chart, makes for a warm and caring mother. Often she will sacrifice much to make her family happy. She has faith in everyone--but herself.

CHAPTER SEVEN

MERCURY: THE MIND

In Greek mythology, Mercury was the messenger of the gods. In Western astrology, Mercury is the planet of communication. It is a neutral planet, requiring aspects to be activated. Therefore, even negative aspects are better than no aspects to Mercury.

Mercury rules our style of communication-- the way we speak, gesture, and form ideas. It also shows native intelligence and writing ability. Psychologically, it indicates our ability to make decisions and use our rational mind. If well aspected, the individual will be intelligent with good communication skills; if afflicted, he may still possess intelligence, but may have difficulty making decisions or communicating with others.

In a fire sign Mercury is passionate, but impatient in speech. If afflicted he can show a temper. In an earth sign Mercury thinks more deliberately. If afflicted, he is too practical or self-serving. In an air sign, Mercury is at its best, using intelligence and communicative skills. If afflicted, he may be argumentative. In a water sign, Mercury is intuitive and gentle. If afflicted he can be worrisome.

MERCURY IN ARIES

Mercury in Aries has a quick mind and likes to be heard. He enjoys trying new things, likes to travel, but may become bored easily. With his energetic mind, he is a good starter, but tires with too many details and may have to push himself to finish. If afflicted, his ego may be out of control. If well aspected, he can have a flair from drama, debate, or leadership. Either way, Mercury in Aries has strong definite opinions.

MERCURY IN TAURUS

Mercury in Taurus has a quiet firm voice and good concentration. She prefers just the facts and likes to concentrate on one issue at a time. She can be stubborn if afflicted--the "I'm from Missouri" type. If well aspected, she has a good head for business and a soft spoken pleasant manner. She is a person of steady habits, loyalty and firm convictions.

MERCURY IN GEMINI

Mercury is well placed in Gemini as it is in its own sign. Here is one who enjoys travel and communications. She may have a friendly, easy-going manner. If afflicted, she can be a chatterbox. If well aspected, she possesses good planning, mechanical ability, and intelligence. It gives a keen wit which can make her critical at times.

MERCURY IN CANCER

Mercury in Cancer is sensitive, soft spoken, and can be intuitive. They may be fond of history. If afflicted, they are worriers and may take things too personally. They may speak with a lisp or lack confidence in themselves. However, if well aspected, they are sentimental and can use their sensitivity in a positive way to help others in fields such as counseling.

MERCURY IN LEO

Mercury in Leo gets his share of attention, with a sense of humor and a flair for drama. He may have a deep melodic voice and a sense of command. If afflicted, he can be boisterous, opinionated, or a ham. If well aspected, he is a good speaker, well organized, and entertaining. Either way, he dislikes being ignored.

MERCURY IN VIRGO

Mercury is well placed in Virgo as it rules the sign. It is precise and polite in speech. She has good abilities for detail analysis in fields from medicine to bookkeeping, and carpentry. If afflicted, she is too analytical and may bore others with trivial details and can be a worrier. If well aspected she is an excellent worker, soft spoken, and modest about success. She can be a perfectionist at heart.

MERCURY IN LIBRA

Mercury is softened by Libra. He is polite,

sociable, and well mannered. If afflicted, he can be affected in speech. If well aspected, he has a pleasant modulated voice and an interest in the arts, theater, or music. He can see both sides of an issue and make a fair judge. Sometimes, he has difficulty making decisions because he wishes to be fair. He needs to watch a tendency to procrastinate.

MERCURY IN SCORPIO

Mercury in Scorpio has strong likes and dislikes. They may have a deep or unusual voice. If afflicted they may be conceited, judgmental, or stubborn. If well aspected, they have a keen sense of intuition and make a good judge of character. They do not like to waste their time or yours. They may have an interest in investments, banking, insurance, and corporations. Usually they have good financial sense.

MERCURY IN SAGITTARIUS

Mercury in Sagittarius is friendly and breezy

in manner. Since Mercury is in its detriment here, they may lack concentration and have a tendency to disregard the facts when telling a good tale. If afflicted, they may be superficial or chatterboxes. If well aspected, they can be humanitarian, interested in travel, and be good story tellers. More serious natives may have an interest in philosophy and the legal profession. Sometimes, their mind can be one place and their body another. To be successful, they need to focus more on matters at hand.

MERCURY IN CAPRICORN

Mercury in Capricorn is a planner and an organizer. He has a serious mind and likes to be thorough in his research. He prefers just the facts and doesn't like any surprises. If afflicted, he may have a tendency toward depression and worry. If well aspected, he is a capable leader with the strong voice of reason. He tends to have a more serious tone and perhaps a deeper voice. He often commands the respect of others.

MERCURY IN AQUARIUS

Mercury is exalted in Aquarius. He is original and rational in thought. His manner is friendly with an upbeat quality. He sees people as friends and is usually well liked. If afflicted, he may not be reliable about details or truthful. If well aspected, he has a good ability to persuade others and an excellent memory, a capable mind, and even a flair for invention. Definitely, he should take time to listen to his inner voice.

MERCURY IN PISCES

Mercury is soft spoken and gentle in Pisces. However it is in its detriment and may lack faith in himself. There is more of an intuition rather than a rational side. This can increase artistic and musical ability. If afflicted, he can be forgetful or "sketchy" in speech. If well aspected, can be a good detective, psychologist, or nurse because of his intuitive insight into human nature. Either way he needs to do some reality checking and watch his tendency to be too trusting or to be a martyr.

CHAPTER EIGHT

VENUS: THE SWEET THINGS OF LIFE

Venue rules love, romance, creature comforts, money, art, music, and all "sweet" things. Sometimes a chart may have many afflictions , but if Venus is well aspected, people will still feel happy among life's disappointments because they feel loved. Conversely, a well aspected chart may miss opportunities for happiness in relationships because they do not feel loved. If Venus is sextile or trine the higher octave planets--Uranus, Neptune, or Pluto, individuals have given much service in past lives to others and in this life others will wish to assist them. Conversely afflictions may bring out compulsive relationships, homosexual tendencies, or misplaced affections that may cause rejection or embarrassment. Sometimes the best way to handle these aspects is to remain honest and moral in all relationships and accept some "learning experiences" in love. Love does not always have to be sexual; it can take the form of friendship or creative expression.

In general, Venus in a fire sign, Aries Leo, and Sagittarius, can be quite passionate and enthusiastic in expressing love. Generous if well aspected; demanding if afflicted. Venus in an Earth signs, Taurus, Virgo and Capricorn, are more practical. They work hard to give their loved ones material comforts. They can be wealthy if well aspected, but if afflicted, materialistic. Venus in an air sign of Gemini, Libra, and Aquarius likes to talk about love and is very idealistic. They love to flirt. They can be quite charming if well aspected but too flirtatious if afflicted. If Venus is in a water sign,

Cancer, Scorpio, or Pisces, emotions rule. Here Venus is a sensitive lover and often lucky in love in Pisces where Venus is exalted. Pisces, more than any other sign, believes love is all. Venus is also at home in Taurus and Libra but it is at its fall in critical Virgo, and in its detriment in domineering Scorpio or demanding Aries. Love, after all, can never be taken--only given.

VENUS IN ARIES

Venus in Aries is in love with love. He likes to idealize his beloved, putting her on a pedestal. He enjoys a nice appearance and the show or romance. He is both passionate and idealistic. If afflicted, he may try to dominate his lover or be too demanding. Love goes out the window when coerced. If well aspected, he can be very giving and attentive. He may enjoy the limelight and have leadership qualities.

VENUS IN TAURUS

Venus in Taurus knows the value of love. Their sense of touch is strong. Women with this position love the Venus colors--pink and blue. Known for their loyalty and their love of family, they make stable mates. If afflicted, they can be stubborn and controlling. They may have to learn to be more generous. If well aspected, they enjoy the good life, a beautiful home and harmonious family. Since they are an earth sign, they may enjoy decorating with plants and gardening.

VENUS IN GEMINI

Venus in Gemini is friendly, often with a good sense of humor and repartee. They may be hard to catch as they have many friendships and enjoy travel. If afflicted, they may be flighty and need to take more to cultivate romance. If well aspected, they can be poetic and expressive in love. In either case, they are usually well liked and may excel in sales or teaching.

VENUS IN CANCER

Venus in Cancer loves Mom, home, and apple pie. They have a strong devotion to family and enjoy cooking. If afflicted, they seek a "parent" in their mate and may be too dependent. If well aspected, they reap the benefits of a happy home life and enjoy being a parent to their children. Either way, they are sensitive and may wear their feelings on their sleeve.

VENUS IN LEO

Venus in Leo makes an art of love. They are

romantic idealists with strong charisma. Men with this position can be courtly lovers; the women quite attractive with a flair for dress and love of jewelry. If afflicted, they may overdress or wear too much cologne or perfume. They may also be conceited. If well aspected, their noble ideas bring them much happiness and true love in this life. Either way, they enjoy the chase and love games of chance.

VENUS IN VIRGO

Venus in Virgo may be picky, but they are also winning to work hard for their loved ones. Unfortunately love can go out the window with too much criticism. If afflicted, they may lose friends by too much fault finding. This can be corrected by focusing more on the positive qualities and keeping criticism to a minimum. If well aspected, they make loyal friends and sincere lovers. Since work is important to them, they may meet their significant other through work. Both males and females under this love sign are discriminating when it comes to love. Sometimes they wait too long as they want a "perfect" partner. They need to remember love is not always a rational choice.

VENUS IN LIBRA

Venus in Libra loves romance--roses, candlelight, and soft music. And why not? Venus is in its own sign. These people were born for partnerships and dislike doing things solo. Frequently drawn to the arts, they have a love of beauty, decorating, and design. If afflicted, they may be indecisive in relationships or too dependent on others. If well aspected, they can benefit from marriage and partnerships. Either way, they usually have good manners and dislike coarse language. Women with their Venus in Libra love to dress in the latest fashions and may be drawn to a profession dealing with beauty, culture or fashion.

VENUS IN SCORPIO

Venus in Scorpio can be passionate, loyal, and magnetic. Since Venus is in its detriment here, they have a tendency to be jealous and possessive.

More than any other placement, they need to learn to "let go and let God." Distrust can kill any relationship. If afflicted they may have to watch their temper and their desire nature. If well aspected, they have everything under control and may do well in corporate work or financial institutions. They will work hard for family and can overcome many obstacles with their determined spirit and spark of intuition.

VENUS IN SAGITTARIUS

Venus in Sagittarius is hard to catch. They love their freedom and may enjoy the outdoors. They are well liked with a friendly, helpful nature. Men with Venus in Sagittarius may attract an independent mate. Women with this position may have a feminist perspective on life. If afflicted, females may need to cultivate a more demure manner and males may need to be less brusque. If well aspected, they attract many friends of both sexes and may enjoy many romantic adventures before settling down.

VENUS IN CAPRICORN

Venus in Capricorn takes romance seriously and prefers a traditional marriage. They are often good providers and work hard for their families. They don't like surprises and may have a passionate streak under conservative attire as they are, after all, an earth sign. If afflicted, they may have a tendency to use others or indulge their passions in secret. If well aspected, they are attracted to people with the right connections and may prosper materially. In terms of marriage, they see the value of "the tie that binds."

VENUS IN AQUARIUS

Venus in Aquarius loves everyone and views the world as their family. They are born humanitarians. They are apt to rebel against social conventions. They have a friendly flirtatious nature and a ready smile. If afflicted, they may adopt "a rebel without a cause attitude." If well aspected, they benefit from friends and group associations. Either way, they may be drawn to New Age interests and are always ready to explore new horizons. They are tolerant in nature and make loyal partners once wedded.

VENUS IN PISCES

Venus in Pisces lives for love. Here Venus is exalted. They enjoy romance, flowers, and memories. They truly believe in a "happy ever after ending." If afflicted, they may be martyrs or be attracted to people who are not available. If well aspected, they are apt to have a story-book romance. In general, marriage is favored in the chart because they are willing to make whatever adjustments are necessary for a lasting union. More than any other sign, they know the true nature of love is spiritual.

CHAPTER NINE

MARS: THE MOTOR OF THE CHART

Mars is the motor of the horoscope. It represents the way we get started, our sex drive, and physical stamina. For example, Mars in a fire sign, Aries, Leo, or Sagittarius, starts with great enthusiasm, is passionate, and enjoys physical activities such as sports. It may also indicate male pattern baldness as the ancient astrologer felt it burned the roots of the hair. If afflicted, they have a temper. Mars in earth signs, Taurus, Virgo, Capricorn, is more cautious, but has more staying power. They like to take their time making decisions and prefer to concentrate on the matter at hand. They can be practical, organized, and make good business decisions. If afflicted, Mars can be too materialistic in earth signs. Mars in an air sign can have mechanical ability, a sharp intellect, and may be fond of debate. They like to think things over and plan their strategy before starting a project. If afflicted, may be too critical.

Mars is weaker in water sign and may be slower to take action, but has an intuitive edge. They are very protective of loved ones. If afflicted, they may lack motivation or stamina.

MARS IN ARIES

Mars is at home in the sign of Aries as Mars is the ruler of Aries. People with Mars in Aries are physically strong, fond of sports, enjoy debate, and are very active. They may prefer to work alone or be their own boss as they have good leadership skills. If afflicted, they can be wasteful and may have a temper. If well aspected, they can excel in their own enterprises. They enjoy the pursuit of romance and make ardent lovers.

MARS IN TAURUS

When Mars is in the sign of Taurus the senses are strong. They enjoy their creature comforts and may procrastinate before starting a project. Often they have charm and a gentle touch. If afflicted, may be stubborn or lazy. Sometimes their sensual nature gets them into trouble. If well aspected, they can be a gentle lover--loyal and kind in nature. They are hard workers who succeed through strong will power. In love, they are true.

MARS IN GEMINI

Mars in Gemini may have mechanical skills and enjoys doing a variety of tasks. They are always on the go and enjoy short distance travel. Routine work and desk jobs bore them as they prefer to do a variety of activities. If afflicted, they may have too many irons in the fire and have difficulty finishing projects. If well aspected good reasoning ability-may possess mechanical or speaking ability. They can charm the opposite sex with their polite speech, sense of fun, and grace.

MARS IN CANCER

Fiery Mars is watered down in Cancer. These people like to take their time making decisions and assimilate change slowly. They have a strong attachment to family and are sensitive to family differences. Their hunches are good. If afflicted, they can be procrastinators. If well aspected, their sensitive nature favors work in the "helping professions". They have patience in love relationships and many endearing qualities.

MARS IN LEO

Mars in Leo does things in style as they have a lot of pride. They have confidence, leadership, and enjoy being in charge. If afflicted, they can be overbearing or lazy. If well aspected, they make natural executives and may excel in athletics. They enjoy courtship, lovemaking, and children. Their enthusiasm fuels romance.

MARS IN VIRGO

Mars in Virgo can be a perfectionist. They often make good housekeepers-"with everything in its place and a place for everything". They take their time and work hard at projects. If afflicted, they may be too fault finding. If well aspected, they are skilled workers and may excel in medicine, engineering, or writing fields. They are patient lovers willing to wait for the right time.

MARS IN LIBRA

Mars in Libra is "the iron fist in the velvet glove. They can be very persuasive. Their innate charm conceals a strong will. They have an artistic side and may appreciate fine art and music. They also have a strong sense of fair play and sociability. If afflicted, they may have difficulty making decisions as they want to please everyone. If well aspected, they are diplomatic, popular, and excel at romance.

MARS IN SCORPIO

Mars in Scorpio is the strongest of the water positions as Mars is the old ruler of the sign. Mars has great stamina and passion here. People with this position can keep a secret. While Mars in Aries shows a temper, Mars in Scorpio holds a grudge. If afflicted, they can be jealous and resentful. If this tendency goes unchecked, they may become loners. If well aspected, their resourcefulness makes them good leaders and confident lovers.

MARS IN SAGITTARIUS

Mars in Sagittarius likes to play. Often enjoys games, sports, and travel. They have great enthusiasm starting new projects, but may get distracted easily. If afflicted can be "jack of all trades, master of none". If well aspected, can show a humanitarian nature. When in love, they can come on strong.

MARS IN CAPRICORN

Mars is exalted in Capricorn. Here the fire of Mars is harnessed to the ambition of Capricorn. These people work hard and make excellent executives. They calculate their moves and are able to climb the ladder of success. If afflicted, may have a tendency to use others. If well aspected, they will excel in any enterprise they take on. In romance, they are willing to wait for the right one.

MARS IN AQUARIUS

Mars in Aquarius likes to organize and has good methods of operation. They begin projects by getting set up properly. They seek out information as they have a natural curiosity. They like to appeal to reason and have a belief in democracy. If afflicted, they may waste their time in day dreaming and trivial pursuits. If well aspected a skilled worker and/or fair boss and can have good teaching ability. They make friends easily and may become romantically involved with one.

MARS IN PISCES

Mars is gentle and romantic in Pisces. It doesn't like the harsh reality of the world. These people like to start their day slowly so they can acclimate themselves. They definitely don't like to rush. They are sensitive and may have artistic or musical abilities. They like romance with all the trimming--candles, music, and fine food. If afflicted they are too sensitive to criticism and must guard against using pills or alcohol to solve their problems.   If well aspected, they have a strong spiritual nature and may possess intuitive gifts.   They can excel in "helping professions" as they genuinely care about others.   In romance, they have a "feeling" for chemistry.

CHAPTER TEN

JUPITER: THE GREATER BENEFIC

Jupiter is the largest planet in our solar system. It takes twelve years to orbit the Sun, and it stays about one year in each sign. Jupiter is called the greater benefic because it represents good fortune. It expands and improves whatever planet it contacts. Malefic aspects represent excesses. In addition to good luck, Jupiter stands for courage, optimism, and success. When Jupiter is strong in the chart by placement in the angles--houses one, four, seven, and ten; you are blessed. Jupiter in the first gives popularity and leadership; in the fourth, a happy home life; in the seventh, a happy marriage; and in the tenth, a successful career, often before the public. When Jupiter is well aspected, personal happiness is multiplied. When afflicted, over-confidence, excesses, and pride may get in the way of success. Sometimes affliction will make the person lazy or indulgent. This could also indicate health problems due to excesses such as gout, high cholesterol, or diabetes. While these diseases are not life threatening, they can be precursors to more serious ailments. Often they can be corrected in their early stages with more discipline in diet and exercise.

Think of Jupiter as "money" in the bank earned from past lives. The house position show where success will come easiest. The sign shows how you express your Jupiter energy. Examine Jupiter first by element--fire (Aries, Leo, and Sagittarius)' earth (Taurus, Virgo and Capricorn); air (Gemini, Libra, and Aquarius); water (Cancer, Scorpio, and Pisces). Jupiter in a fire sign enhances enthusiasm and spiritual nature. When Jupiter is in an earth sign, creature comforts and material success are emphasized. When Jupiter is in an air sign, idealism and intelligence are enhanced. And in a water sign, sensitivity and intuition are strong.

JUPITER IN ARIES

Jupiter in Aries confers leadership and courage. They frequently like to be their own boss. They have a good ability to influence others. People look to them for original ideas. They may also have an interest in the arts, particularly theater, and athletics as they thrive on being in the limelight. If afflicted, they may promise more than they can deliver. If well aspected, they are resourceful and respected as leaders in the community. Careers in management, small business, arts, sports, and promotion are favored.

JUPITER IN TAURUS

Jupiter in Taurus loves their creature comforts. These individuals enjoy spending on luxuries and like quality. Since they manage money well, they often obtain financial success. They possess sound business sense and good values. If afflicted, they may be greedy and extravagant with their resources. They need to learn the test of stewardship. If well aspected, they are more than willing to share the wealth, which in turn, will bring true abundance in their lives. Careers in finance, nursing, organizing, and farming are favored.

JUPITER IN GEMINI

Jupiter in Gemini expands the intelligence. They enjoy learning, travel, and people. Their sense of humor and light touch with the public makes them popular. Sometimes there is mechanical or engineering ability. Jupiter is at its detriment in Gemini (opposite its Sagittarius its ruling sign). The benefits of Jupiter can be scattered. If afflicted, they may be the "jack of all trades and the master of none." Good aspects reverse this, giving intelligence and mastery of their trade. Careers in teaching, sales, communications, carpentry, computers, and mechanics are favored.

JUPITER IN CANCER

Jupiter is exalted in Cancer, making this one of the luckiest places for it to be. Jupiter in Cancer promotes family relationships. Love of home and parents is strong. Real estate is favored. Often they are patriotic. Intuition is favored. They often enjoy cooking and domestic activity. They will spend heavily on their home and use it as a place of retreat. When afflicted, they may be too attached to their parents. Conversely, their parents may neglect them or be too indulgent. Family problems require attention. If well aspected, there is harmonious family life and they have honorable family ties and may well inherit. They make excellent parents and enjoy good relationships with their children. Careers in real estate, insurance, home design, child care, and nursing are favored.

JUPITER IN LEO

Jupiter in Leo makes one lucky in love--and children and sports. They want romance with a capital "R" and are often very attractive to the opposite sex. Leadership and executive ability are also strong. They may have a flair for drama, public relations, and advertising due to their optimistic nature. If afflicted, their ego can get in the way and they may over extend themselves. If well aspected, they will reach the top of their profession. As parents they excel, taking great pride in their offspring. Children enjoy their good humor and generosity. Careers in advertising, public relations, the arts, education, and the stock market are favored.

JUPITER IN VIRGO

Jupiter in Virgo likes to work and may be attracted to the medical profession. Often they maintain good health through informed diet and discipline. They can be economical and willing to start. They know instinctively that "oaks come from little seeds". They are ethical in business dealings, a fact which earns them success in the long run. If afflicted, they may pinch pennies and worry too much about work. Health problems occur, due to excessive worry and anxiety. They simply don't know when to stop working. A regular schedule with adequate rest is important. If well aspected, they adopt good work methods and balance work and health. They can prosper financially through business investments. Careers in business, accounting, medicine, nutrition, and cleaning services are favored.

JUPITER IN LIBRA

Jupiter in Libra favors marriage and partnerships. In fact, marriage may bring a step up socially and financially. They are joiners and have many acquaintances. Their sense of justice is strong, and they may have an interest in the law. The arts are also favored. If afflicted, people with Jupiter in Libra may be snobs or social butterflies. If well aspected, they are popular due to their genuine warmth and compassion. They often do well in court. Marriage brings much happiness. Careers in public relations, the arts, cosmetology, the law, marriage counseling, and social work are favored.

JUPITER IN SCORPIO

Jupiter in Scorpio increases magnetism. They exude sensuality and a sense of mystery. Psychic faculties are strong, and they often play their hunches. They are generous in nature, but once they help you they expect you to stand on your own two feet. If afflicted, the sexual side of

Jupiter in Scorpio can dominate. They may be drawn into secret romances or may be too judgmental in nature. If well aspected, they enjoy a passionate marriage and gain through joint finances. Careers in banking corporations, psychology, the occult, and recycling are favored.

JUPITER IN SAGITTARIUS

Jupiter in Sagittarius is everyone's friend. And why not, for Jupiter rules Sagittarius. They enjoy travel--especially to far away places. If unable to travel, they will take travels of the mind through reading and imagination. They love a good story and are not above spinning a few yarns themselves. Their prophetic nature may show up in dreams. Sometimes they choose to settle far from home and may benefit from foreign lands. If afflicted, the opposite can occur with foreign countries becoming a source of frustration. If afflicted, they can be dreamers and schemers. If well aspected, they make excellent writers. Careers in writing, law, higher education, travel and sales are favored.

JUPITER IN CAPRICORN

Here Jupiter is at its fall, opposite Cancer where Jupiter is exalted. Jupiter's strength is expressed in material ambition. People with their Jupiter in Capricorn have great pride and ambition. They like to govern and may choose to work for the government. If afflicted, they may work too hard for material comforts, neglecting their spiritual side. If well aspected, they have good earning potential and gain in status as they progress through life. Careers in corporation, politics, and public service are favored.

JUPITER IN AQUARIUS

Jupiter in Aquarius are seekers of social justice and are true humanitarians. As such, they are rebels without a cause. They enjoy many friends from all stations of life. They frequently have mass appeal. If afflicted, they may be too far out for people to understand. Sometimes their friends can be a downfall. If well aspected, the reverse is true and they benefit from friendships. Careers in television, radio, computers, teaching, and technology are favored.

JUPITER IN PISCES

Jupiter in Pisces appeals to the heart. They are warm and sentimental, known for their concern for others. They will often champion the underdog. Mystical in nature, they "tune in" to man and nature. Love of music, poetry, and art is strong. If afflicted, they may be impractical dreamers-- always chasing rainbows. If well aspected, they can make their dreams come true with their intuition and magnetic personalities. Careers in medicine, music, art and cosmetics are favored.

CHAPTER ELEVEN

SATURN: LESSONS OF LIFE

Saturn shows our lessons of life. Jupiter rules expansion, while Saturn rules contraction. It has a twenty-nine year cycle around the Sun and stays about two and one-half years in each sign. Saturn can influence public fashion. For example, in 1997 and 1998 with Saturn in Aries, nose rings and body piercing are in style. When Saturn goes into Taurus, more conservative fashion and neckwear, collars, and necklaces will be highlighted.

Saturn in the horoscope shows the karma the individual has brought in this life--the sign the type of karma. For example, Saturn in Aries may have to watch their ego. The house shows where it needs to be worked out. For example one with Saturn in Aries in the seventh house would have to watch the ego and the tendency to dominate others in relationships and marriage.

Saturn rules Capricorn, the sign of career, making it also indicator. People with a well aspected Saturn tend to rise in life. Those with weak aspects may experience many setbacks. Saturn indicates our ability to handle responsibility. For example someone with Saturn in Leo would take on much responsibility for children.

Saturn conjunct the benefic planets, Sun, Venus, and Jupiter, may be a stabilizing force on these planets. Saturn conjunct the Sun gives a serious outlook on life. Saturn conjunct Venus deepens responsibility in relationships. Finally Saturn conjunct Jupiter may be a sign of an advanced soul who takes religious or civic duties seriously. Saturn conjunct all other planets has a suppressive effect, depressing energy of the planet. For example, Saturn conjunct the Moon gives a "wet blanket" personality--one who tends to be pessimistic.

Saturn in Fire signs (Aries, Leo, or Sagittarius) is more outgoing in energy, but may have problems expressing affection. Saturn in earth signs (Taurus, Virgo, and Capricorn) is more conservative, but may be materialistic. Saturn in air signs (Gemini, Libra, or Aquarius) is a serious thinker, but may be anxious or depressed. Saturn in water signs

(Cancer, Scorpio, and Pisces) is compassionate and willing to help the underdog, but may lack faith in life at times.

SATURN IN ARIES

Saturn is at its fall in Aries as it is opposite Libra, where it is exalted in placement. Saturn in Aries may be a capable leader, but may have problems initiating activities or persuading others. They tend to be sensitive to criticism or may overstep their bounds, recognizing the rights of others. Sometimes they are defensive or self serving. If afflicted, these people may be demanding and egotistical. If well aspected, especially to Jupiter or the Sun, the ego is in check. Patience, diplomacy, and hard work bring well deserved success.

SATURN IN TAURUS

Saturn in Taurus does not enjoy hard work and may resent it. Since they have a strong desire nature, they may have to endure difficult work.

Sometimes, they make good business men and may be successful in accounting or banking. If poorly aspected, they lack initiative or motivation. When well aspected, they can hang on to their resources and will prosper materially as they go through life.

SATURN IN GEMINI

Saturn in Gemini has a well developed systematic mind, but they may be critical or sarcastic in speech. They often have good ability in math, science, or engineering. If afflicted, can have problems in written or oral communications, which can lead to disputes. For example, they may be unsympathetic or suspicious in nature. If well aspected, they are capable of serious study and make good teachers or researchers.

SATURN IN CANCER

Saturn in Cancer places a high value on home and family. However, since Saturn is at it detriment in Cancer, there may be many family obligations.

If afflicted there can be estrangements from or heavy obligations to parents. Sometimes the early home life is strained by poverty or a difficult parent. There may be a tendency to stomach or digestive problems. If well aspected, parents may be conservative but fair. There would be strong family ties, and a tendency to inherit from parents. These natives are very protective of children. There may also be benefit through real estate investments.

SATURN IN LEO

Saturn in Leo has great pride and needs to feel appreciated. They can be generous and are fond of children. If afflicted, they can be dogmatic and may have difficulty expressing affection. Sometimes there are heavy responsibilities around children or they take on too many obligations. Ancient astrologers considered Saturn at its detriment in Leo as it is opposite Aquarius, which was ruled by Saturn before Uranus was discovered. Afflictions may also indicate problems with the heart or circulatory stem. Watch the health transits carefully to see when these may occur. The opposite is true when

Saturn is well aspected for longevity and health are indicated. Those with Saturn in Leo can be good organizers or have leadership potential, and may have an interest in working with youth.

SATURN IN VIRGO

Saturn in Virgo indicates a hard worker, concerned with accuracy and detail. If afflicted they can be too much of a "nit picker" and worry excessively about their health. Often this can cause digestive problems. If well aspect, the opposite is true and they make excellent doctors, diagnosticians, and nurses. Work is very important to them.

SATURN IN LIBRA

Saturn is exalted in Libra. Justice and fair play are important. These people really believe in the golden rule, "Do unto others as ye would have them do unto you." They know the value of cooperation in achieving anything of lasting value. Since they had an innate sense of responsibility, they may be drawn to law or government work. If afflicted, legal disputes are best settled out of court if possible. Partnerships can be problematic under affliction. For example, their marriage may lack warmth and stimulus. Sometimes these individuals lack empathy, or interpret the law too literally or strictly. If well aspected, legal matters and partnerships are favored. Saturn in Libra often signifies a long-lasting marriage, and partnerships tend to work in their favor.

SATURN IN SCORPIO

Saturn in Scorpio indicates financial responsibilities. They may be drawn to corporation and banks. Often they are perfectionists. They take matters of sexuality and relationships seriously. If afflicted, these areas are sensitive. It may indicate a tendency to miscarriages, hysterectomies, or problems with the urinary tract or bladder. Sometimes sexual liaisons and/or resentment are the source of their undoing. If well aspected, they have confidence and good organization skills which can bring success in business.

SATURN IN SAGITTARIUS

Saturn in Sagittarius takes education, philosophy and legal matters seriously. They may travel for business. If afflicted, there may be a loss through a fatalistic philosophy or religious fanaticism. They may be prone to leg injuries or liver problems under certain afflictions. If well aspected, they may benefit from foreign lands or products. They can make good salesmen or teachers.

SATURN IN CAPRICORN

Saturn is at home in the sign of Capricorn because Saturn rules Capricorn. They have an innate sense of business and make good managers. They may work for government and often are good organizers. They enjoy work and prefer being in charge. They like to progress materially as they go through life. If afflicted, they may be too materialistic or have a tendency to be ruthless in their ambitions which can cause a fall from power if unchecked. If well aspected, power is earned legitimately and the person will rise in life.

SATURN IN AQUARIUS

Saturn is also at home in Aquarius as Saturn is the old ruler of Aquarius. Here Saturn can both organize and communicate plans. They have a strong sense of social justice. They tend to have a steady mind and high level of understanding of the laws of the universe. If afflicted, they can be cold and distant emotionally. If well aspected, they take on responsibility well and may rise in life through influential friends.

SATURN IN PISCES

Saturn in Pisces increases sensitivity and compassion. They care about the very young, very old, and those in need. If afflicted, they may take on many burdens and become depressed. Sometimes they regret the past and may feel sorry for themselves. If they cannot release the past, they become neurotic. If well aspected, they are capable of deep meditation and serious spiritual studies.

CHAPTER TWELVE

URANUS: HIGHER CONSCIOUSNESS

The ancient astrologers only had knowledge of the Sun and Moon, Mercury, Venus, Mars, Jupiter and Saturn. Uranus, the seventh planet from the Sun, was not discovered until March 13, 1781, when it was first seen by Sir William Herschel at Bath, England. Interestingly Uranus, which represents revolution, came into view about the time of both the French and American Revolutions.

Uranus has an eighty-four year cycle around the Sun and stays approximately seven years in each sign, influencing a whole grade-school generation. Uranus, Neptune, and Pluto are higher octave planets. Uranus is a higher octave of Mercury; Neptune a higher octave of Venus; and Pluto, a higher octave of Mars. While Mercury rules the rational mind, mechanics and communication, Uranus rules genius, electronics and large scale changes. Uranus can influence a whole generation. For example, many of the early baby boomers (born 1942 to 1949) had Uranus in Gemini, the sign of communication. When these people came of age in the 1960's, they ushered in the computer generation which was a merging of Uranus (genius) and communication systems (Gemini).

Uranus shows intelligence, intuition, and inner will in a chart. Often someone with will will be inventive and ahead of their times. Uranus also represents change. Transits of Uranus indicate times of sudden changes. Accidents may be seen by squares and opposition to native planets. However, good aspects bring fortuitous changes and inspiration. During these cycles dreams can come true.

URANUS IN ARIES

July 7, to October 10, 1934

March 28, 1935 to August 7, 1941

October 6, 1941 to May 14, 1942

Uranus was in Aries during the 1800's (1844 to 1851) and brought many new inventions. Elias Howe invented the sewing machine and Richard Hoe the rotary press--both in 1846. Henry David Thoreau wrote Civil Disobedience, which emphasized the

136

power of individual protest. In the United States the pioneers pushed westward, and the 49ers ushered in the California Gold Rush. In 1847, the Mormons founded Salt Lake City in Utah to ensure their individual right to worship as they pleased.

In the twentieth century, there were many new breakthroughs in technology with Uranus in Aries. In 1927 Charles Lindberg flew the Atlantic alone. This was the height of the flapper ear, with women flaunting new freedom with bobbed hair and short skirts. Art Deco became popular. Many finances shifted--the stock market in the United States crashed in October 1929. The rise of nationalism brought Hitler, Mussolini, and Stalin into power. This cycle ended in 1935, at which time civil war broke out in Spain.

Individuals born with Uranus in Aries have unusual methods of leadership, the pioneering spirit, and new ideas about art. For example, Art Deco reinterpreted the classics. If Uranus in Aries is well aspected, they may do well in their own business or if it is in the tenth house of career. If afflicted, the reverse is true and there can be losses due to speculation and lack of planning.

When these people came of age in the 1950's, they ushered in the baby boom and brought tremendous energy to the economy as they were the rebuilders of the world torn down by World War II.

URANUS IN TAURUS

July 7, 1934 to October 10, 1934

March 28, 1935 to August 7, 1941

October 6, 1941 to May 14, 1942

When Uranus was in Taurus 1851 to 1859, the Industrial Revolution prospered with inventions such as Isaac Singer's sewing machine and Henry Bessemer's steel technology. The Transcendentalists influenced writing and philosophy. Henry Thoreau published Walden in 1855 and Walt Whitman Leaves of Grass in the same year. Both books glorified nature.

Uranus in Taurus came at the time of the Great Depression. Here sudden reversal in fortunes (Taurus) and depression ruled the land. New methods had to be put into operation--the New Deal to handle these changes. The average person had to be inventive with resources just to survive.

Individuals born with Uranus in Taurus may be inventive in business and can have a strong need to achieve. There was a conservative attitude toward marriage and stable values. If well aspected, people with this sign can bring financial success due to concentrated efforts and an abundance of will power. If afflicted, they lack staying power and may experience "flash in the pan" successes." More effort is required for lasting success.

Many born with Uranus in Taurus come of age in the   they favored a conventional life style in the late fifties and early sixties. They were also in abundant supply in a strong economy.

URANUS IN GEMINI

1942 to 1949

August 8, 1941 to October 5, 1941

May 15, 1942 to August 30, 1948

November 13, 1948 to June 10, 1949

When Uranus was in Gemini 1859 to 1865, the

Civil War broke out in the United States, severely restricting travel, communication, and family life. Uranus in Gemini strongly affects the United States because the national horoscope has a Gemini ascendant. The country's whole outlook (ascendant) was transformed (Uranus) during this period.

In the twentieth century, World War II erupted during this aspect, disrupting travel and communications. The transit of Geminis in the first house of the United States chart, so as a nation we are deeply affected by its transit. On a positive note, the G.I. Bill was signed under this aspect, opening higher education to the masses.

Uranus in Gemini has increased mental energy, and is often imaginative, intellectual, or computer literate. They enjoy short distance travel. If well aspected, people are drawn to them because of their magnetic personality, gift for communication, and unusual abilities. If afflicted, these qualities are seen as "off beat." They have difficulty staying on task or they need to be more "mainstream" in thinking to expand career options.

People born with Uranus in Gemini ushered in

the computer age and revolutionized business in the late 1960s and 1970s.

URANUS IN CANCER

August 31, 1948 to November 12, 1948

June 11, 1949 to August 24, 1955

January 29, 1956 to June 9, 1956

When Uranus was in Cancer in the last century, 1865 to 1872, the United States expanded and changed since it is a Cancer nation. The United States purchased Alaska from the Russians in 1867. The Union Pacific and Central Pacific railroads joined in 1869 to form the first transcontinental railroad. In medicine, Dr. Joseph Lister pioneered antiseptic surgery. Louis May Alcott wrote the classic Little Women.

In the twentieth century, Uranus in Cancer brought a tremendous boom in housing industry as masses of GI's returned home and started families. New inventions in domestic products, such as cake mixes and appliances were marketed.

Individuals born with Uranus in Cancer may be

141

sensitive, home oriented, and have an interest in history. If well aspected, there is benefit from the intuition, real estate, and government. Sometimes an interest in cooking or antiques exists. If afflicted, they may be too dependent on parental or government support. They need to break away from and start their own traditions to increase success in life.

When young people came of age in the 1970s, there were many family struggles and runaways. Also communal living was explored.

URANUS IN LEO

August 25, 1955 to January 28, 1956

June 10, 1956 to November 1, 1961

January 11, 1962 to August 9, 1962

In the nineteenth century Uranus was in Leo 1872 to 1878. Joseph Swan and Thomas Edison were developing the incandescent bulb which would eventually add more light to the world. Royalty was exalted as Queen Victoria reigned. The United States went on the old standard. In 1876, Alexander

Graham Bell invented the telephone and Thomas Edison, the phonograph in 1877.   Both would eventfully add to the entertainment industry, ruled by Leo and enjoyed by youth who come under Leo.

In the twentieth century Leo made technology (Uranus) entertaining (Leo) with the invention of the television.   Now everyone could enjoy comedy, drama, and music in their own living room. Confidence in the economy and the stock market soared. Technicolor movies and later color T.V. heightened our entertainment pleasure. Movies about teenagers such as Rebel Without a Cause were popular.   Before the end of the transit of Uranus through the firery sign of Leo, the United States entered the space age and sent John Glenn into orbit.

Individuals born with Uranus in Leo like to play and enjoy sports, gambling, and music.   They can have a flair for romance and art.   If well aspected, leadership is strong and they may enjoy being their own boss.   Many entrepreneurs were born in this generation.   If afflicted, they are too willful and need to gain cooperation of others to be more successful.

When young people born with Uranus in Leo came of age in the 1980s, we had many corporate takeovers and new styles in the music industry with the advent of CD's, music videos and VCR's. They benefitted from the "go-go" economy of the mid 1980s.

URANUS IN VIRGO

November 2, 1961 to January 10, 1962

August 10, 1962 to September 28, 1968

May 22, 1968 to June 24, 1969

During the previous transit of Uranus in Virgo, William Croakes invented the cathode-ray tube (1878), Dr. Ivan Pavlov discovered the conditioned reflex, Dr. Louis Pasteur streptococcus bacteria which led to "pasteurization" (1880), and May Baker Eddy became the pastor of the First Church of Christ Science in Boston (1879). Mrs. Eddy, demonstrated with Christian Science, that health is ruled by the mind.

Uranus' latest transit in Virgo brought interest in urban renewal and new methods in medicine. Tranquilizers replaced straight jackets in psychiatry. Birth control pills became popular. Health was highlighted. In 1946 the United States government issued a report linking smoking and with cancer and heart disease. Concern with health extended to the environment with the publication of Rachel Carson's The Silent Spring. With Uranus in the skeptical sign of Virgo, religion was taken completely out of public schools when the Supreme Court ruled the reading of prayers in school was unconstitutional. (When Uranus is in Pisces, this ruling may be modified.)

When those born with Uranus in Virgo came of age in the late 1980s and 1990s, jobs in medicine and technology were favored. Many generation Xers became discouraged with corporate cutbacks and downsizing of the late 1980s and 1990s. Many New Age practices became big business under the direction of people born with Uranus in Virgo; for example, psychic hot lines, a boom in herbs, acupuncture, and ayurvedic medicine were popularized.

Individuals born with Uranus in Virgo may have talents in business and medicine. They may have unusual ideas about health and nutrition. If well aspected, they can prosper in business and medicine due to knowledge of new technology, methods of organization, and cost cutting modalities. If afflicted, they may be too narrow and not connect with the wider world.

Look for this trend in New Age healing to continue through 2030 while this generation is in charge. Eventually New Age modalities will be conventional.

URANUS IN LIBRA

October 29, 1968 to May 21, 1969

June 25, 1969 to December 14, 1974.

In the nineteenth century Uranus was in Libra from 1885 to 1891. Art flourished as Victorians enjoyed showing off their wealth and finery. In 1888 Eastman Kodak developed the camera and Nikola Tesla, alternating current. In England, the Fabian Society was started to achieve "the highest possible morals." In the United States huge estates were build in Newport Rhode Island and the pre-income tax wealthy, enjoyed their splendor with huge staffs.

In the twentieth century, when Uranus went into Libra, our ideas about marriage and partnerships underwent profound changes. Marriage was now viewed as an avenue for partnership. The divorce rate skyrocketed. No fault divorce was instituted in many states legislatures to insure equal rights came into play. Marriage counseling also became fashionable. Abortion was legalized at the end of this era to insure women control over their bodies. An unusual art form-pop art-was in vogue. The play Hair was on Broadway and Jesus Christ Super Star was a hit. A new idealism was dawning.

Individuals born with Uranus in Libra are partnership oriented, enjoy unusual forms of art, and have an innate sense of fair play. If well aspected, they may have artistic gifts or a creative streak. They find happiness in marriage and public relations. If afflicted, they can have problems in marriage and partnerships due to unconventional relationships. They may need to clean up their image to be more successful.

When those born with Uranus in Libra come of age in 2008 to 2015, they will once again review partnership rulings. Gay unions may be legalized, and new rights will be given to children. Mediation and parent counseling will be the norm in divorce cases. Look for some new rulings on abortion at this time as well.

URANUS IN SCORPIO

November 21, 1974 to May 2, 1975

September 8, 1975 to November 17, 1981

In the last century, Uranus was in Scorpio from 1891 to 1898. In 1895, Dr. Sigmund Freud published, "Studies in Hysteria," beginning his brilliant career in psychology. Freud's theory of psychosexual stages of development shocked Victorian society. New forms of power were founded. In 1892, Rudolf Diesel developed the internal combustion engine, and Karl Benz produced the first four-wheel car the next year.

In the twentieth century, Uranus in Scorpio brought in experimentation with sex. Unusual sex practices, living together, homosexuality, and "one night stands" flourished pre-AIDS. Interest in the occult, reincarnation, and death was explored. The economy underwent shortages with the oil embargo and crisis in Mid East. Double-digit inflation put construction and jobs on hold. Citizens revolted against high taxes.

Individuals with Uranus in Scorpio can be magnetic, strong willed, and conservative. As a group, they earn their keep. If well aspected they can have an interest in banking, corporation, portions of power and influence. They have both staying power and depth. If afflicted, they will undergo many ups and downs in finances. They need to save for a rainy day when the Sun is shining.

When people with Uranus in Scorpio come of age, look for cures for sexually transmitted diseases such as herpes and AIDS. There will be more emphasis on joint ownership of property and a new moral order.

URANUS IN SAGITTARIUS

February 17, 1981 to March 21, 1981

March 17, 1981 to December 2, 1988

In the nineteenth century, Uranus was in

Sagittarius 1898 to 1904. In 1901 Marconi developed the telegraph. In the United States the Wright brothers ushered in the age of aviation on December 17, 1903, with historic flight. While Dr. Sigmund Freud pushed psychoanalysis and wrote The Psychology of Dreams in 1901, Dr. William James of Harvard wrote Varieties of Religious Experiences in 1902. Both books explored altered states of consciousness.

In the twentieth century, when Uranus was in Sagittarius, new entertainment technology-video games, camcorders, VCR's, and C.D's came into being. Video presentations played a larger role in sales. Television was used to sell religion--PTL clubs and tel-evangelists were popular.

Individuals born with Uranus in Sagittarius enjoy their freedom and fun, and have a unique sense of humor. If well aspected, they benefit from foreign lands, the legal profession, and education. If afflicted, they may rebel for attention rather than for principles. To be more successful, they need to rebel less and stay on target.

People with Uranus in Sagittarius come of age in 2008 to 2018 and many will travel to foreign lands as we will be part of a global economy. Religion will be popular. Buddhism and Eastern religions will become mainstream.

URANUS IN CAPRICORN

December 2, 1988 to April 2, 1995

June 9, 1995 to January 12, 1996

In the nineteenth century, Uranus was in Capricorn from 1905 to 1912. This period brought the overthrow of the Czar of Russia, Albert Einstein's theory of relativity, and in the United States the Pure Food and Drug Act. Reform was a strong element. In the art world, Cubism had its day, and steel and glass building began a new chapter in architecture.

In the twentieth century, Uranus in Capricorn makes for a time of political conservativism, people were wary of change in government and a "back to basics" mentality existed. The economy cooled down. President Bush's approach brought unprecedented unemployment, as many businesses were forced to cut back. Real estate prices went down on both coasts.

Individuals born with Uranus in Capricorn have a strong need to channel their energies into concrete and constructive work. They may have unusual methods of organization. If well aspected, their good methods pay off in dividends. If afflicted, they are too conservative or narrow in focus. They may need to broaden their attitudes and scope. They basically need to have more faith in life and be willing to risk a bit more.

People born with Uranus in Capricorn when they come of age in 2015 to 2022 will usher in a new work ethnic and conservative element.

URANUS IN AQUARIUS

January 12, 1996 to 2,002

When Uranus was in Aquarius at the turn of the century, 1912 to 1919, many new inventions, such as the telephone and car came into being. Henry Ford pioneered the assembly line in 1914. World War II disrupted life. Einstein's General Theory of Relativity changed physics forever. The Music of Dixie Land was beginning to be popular. Women's rights were championed, and women in England and German got to vote.

Now, expect new technologies such as laser surgery to expand and new types of energy to come in. When both Neptune and Uranus are in Aquarius, look for tremendous advances of the medical profession and a merging of alternative and traditional medicine.

Individuals born with Uranus in Aquarius have progressive fair minds. They are willing to work in groups. Technology can greatly benefit them. If afflicted, they are too far out in ideas. If well aspected, their intelligence is increased and alliances.

People born with Uranus in Aquarius will be the leaders in the Aquarian Age and then they come of age in 2022. They will spearhead a worldwide democracy and world government which will be heavily reinforced by the new technology. We won't need a physical policeman for video police will prevail. On the plus side, these people will be citizens of the world and will lead us into the Age of Aquarius.

URANUS IN PISCES

2002 to 2011

When Uranus was in Pisces 1920 to 1927, we had the Roaring Twenties. Jazz, bathtub gin and the flappers flourished. Creativity was strong for Uranus brought new ideas to creative Pisces. Religious views were challenged by the Scopes trial in Tennessee which championed Darwin's view that we descended from the ape. Mahatma Ghandi began his passive resistance movement in India in 1926 and Hitler published <u>Meine Kauft</u>, Volume I. In 1920, Dr. Carl Jung published Psychological Types and pioneered dream analysis, myth, and creativity as part of the psychological process. Dr. Coue used the affirmation "Every day in every way, I'm getting better and better to improve health. Lesser known, Dr. Carl Wickland, wrote Thirty Years Among the Dead and advocated mediumship to help the mentally ill rid themselves of discarnate spirits.

When Uranus goes into Pisces in 2002, expect a

new revolution in medicine and psychology. Mediumship may be proven to be valid. Instead of psychic hot lines, more serious research will be done on the paranormal. In the United States, there will be an erosion of both coasts by water. Purification of drinking water will be of prime importance. On the plus side, new spiritual truths will bring greater compassion to the afflicted. Hopefully hospitals will become true temple of healing the mind and body. The prison system will be replaced by new youth reform movements with large camps set up for this purpose. The medical profession will be expanded and revised. Look for universal health care in the United States. Life after death will be a scientific fact.

Individuals born with Uranus in Pisces may have an interest in the paranormal or religion. They are often sensitive and drawn to the arts. If afflicted, they may lack faith in themselves or a Higher Power. If well aspected, they are blessed with inspiration and intuition and can be a help to the very young, very aged, and those who are ill. Often they are drawn to the medical profession.

When these children grow up in the 2028 to 2035 period, they will be more enlightened. Many talented healers, mystics, and humanitarians in this group will continue the work of those who came before them with Uranus in Aquarius.

CHAPTER THIRTEEN

NEPTUNE: SPIRIT

Neptune, the eighth planet in our solar system, was discovered in 1846 by Jean LeVerrier in Paris and John Coach Adams in England. Neptune cannot be seen by the naked eye. It has eight moons and is nebulous in color. Neptune takes 165 years to orbit the Sun and stays approximately 14 years in each sign. Like Uranus, it is a planet which influences groups of people. Neptune, name after the god of the sea, rules the spiritual and idealistic, the subconscious mind, and illusion--both glamour and fraud. It also rules chemistry, hospitals, anesthesia, asylums, prisons, drama, poetry, motion pictures, and hypnosis.

Neptune is a generational planet and as such shows the artistic and spiritual attributes of each generation. Its influence increases when it is on angle of the chart, houses one, four, seven, and ten. In the first house, Neptune adds charm to personality and mysticism. In the fourth house, intuition is strong and mystical leanings may be inherited from parents--especially the mother. In the seventh, marriage is fated and if well aspected, heavenly; if afflicted, karmic. In the tenth house, Neptune influences career. Individuals may be attracted to the medical profession, motion pictures, arts, or photography, mediumship or hypnosis. If well aspected, a successful or glamorous career can result. If afflicted in the tenth house, disappointment may come from too much idealism or one may give more than receive in a profession, or enter a profession which requires some sacrifice, such as religious life.

At the time of its discovery, Neptune was in Pisces (May 1847 to August 1847, February 1848 to April 13, 1861, October 2, 1861 to February 13, 1862. Spiritualism had its start with spirit rapping of a diseased peddler heard by Fox sisters in Rochester New York in 1848. Andrew Jackson Davis, respected clairvoyant, published his first volume of trance discourses in 1847 and established a career as a medical clairvoyant. Dr. Elliotson advance the hypnosis movement. In 1855, American

Daniel Douglas Home became famous for his seances in Europe. In 1858, the Virgin Mary appeared to Bernadette Soubirous in Lourdes, France. When Neptune was in its own sign Pisces, not only was it discovered, but the mystical and supernatural flourished.

NEPTUNE IN ARIES

April 14, 1861 to October 1 1861

February 14, 1862 to June 6, 1847

October 1, 1874 to April 6, 1875

Neptune, planet of mysticism, healing arts, and paranormal, felt the pioneering and energizing influence of Aries from 1861 to 1875. During this period interest in mesmerism, later became known as hypnotism, remained strong. Dr. Ambrose Liebeault worked with the poor of Nancy, France, using hypnosis as a cure. In 1862 Matin Charcot founded his school in France, attracting physicians such as Dr. Sigmund Freud to his clinic in Nancy. On the religious front, Allen Kardec started Spiritism, a religion based on mediumship, in South America and Europe. The following year, the Bahai faith, which preached unity of all religions, was founded. On the negative side, Ku Klux Klan was formed at the end of the Civil War in 1865. Neptune is fiery and idealistic in Aries, but must be channelled in a constructive direction. Julia Ward Howe's "Battle Hymn of the Republic" written in 1862 is a good example of the valor of Neptune in Aries which spurred many men into battle for their ideals.

NEPTUNE IN TAURUS

June 7, 1874 to September 30, 1874

April 7, 1875 to August 15, 1887

September 22, 1887 to May 25, 1888

December 28, 1888 to March 20, 1889

Neptune in Taurus brought an interest in aiding humanity. Mary Baker Eddy organized a group known as Christian Scientists, dedicated to healing body through mental attitude. The same year Madame Blavatsky started the Theosophical Society "to investigate unexplained laws of nature and powers latent in man." On July 17, 1882, the Society for Psychical research was founded to research hypnotism and the paranormal. Studying mysticism (Neptune) in the time of the nineteenth century materialism (Taurus) was not an easy matter; however the diligent efforts of the Society of Psychic Research set the standard for later parapsychologists.

NEPTUNE IN GEMINI

September 16, 1987 to September 21, 1887

May 26, 1888 to December 27, 1888

March 21, 1889 to July 19, 1901

December 26, 1901 to May 20, 1902

Neptune was in Gemini in the gay 1890s, bringing a lighter touch to heavy decorative art of Neptune in Taurus. This was an era in which there was much intelligent (Gemini) investigation of occult (Neptune). Harvard professor, Dr. William James, Sir Oliver Lodge, and Professor and Mrs. Sidgwick delved deeply into parapsychology. The Society of Psychical Research investigated two remarkable mediums, Mrs. Lenore Piper and Eusapia Pallidino.

On the religious front, the World Parliament of Religions opened in Chicago in 1893. Swami Vivekananda introduced Vendanta philosophy to the assembly, paving way for an interest in Eastern metaphysics in the West. Vivekananda who thought of all people as his spiritual brothers and sisters, worked hard to improve the welfare of women and erase bigotry, as well as share Eastern philosophy with its emphasis on mediation and discipline with West. In 1993, the Theosophical Society sponsored a second World Parliament of Religions, and this time Tibet's Dali Lama delivered a similar message of universal love.

NEPTUNE IN CANCER

July 20, 1901 to December 25, 1901

May 21, 1902 to September 22, 1914

December 15, 1914 to July 15, 1915

March 20, 1916 to May 1, 1916

In 1903, Dr. F.W.H. Myers published his two volume work, Human Personality and its Survival of Bodily Death. Christian Science, theosophy, Vedanta, and spiritualism continued to expand. In 1902 Edgar Cayce learned he was a medical clairvoyant and began his famous trance readings which he continued until his death in 1945. Since Cancer rules the unconscious mind, Neptune in Cancer increased scientific interest in the unconscious. Dr. Sigmund Freud became the father of psychology with his new technique of psychoanalysis, and astrological societies also flourished. In England, Alan Leo produced a series of textbooks on the subject. In the United States, Evangeline Adams (1864 to 1932) legalized astrology as a profession in 1914 in New York. Miss Adams was charged with fortune telling and went before a judge. To prove her point, she meticulously delineated the horoscope of a young man (whom she later learned was the presiding judge's son). Impressed with her work, the judge ruled that the "defendant raised astrology to dignity of an exact science", in 1909, Max Heindel (1865-1919) founded the Rosicrucian Fellowship in Oceanside, California.

NEPTUNE IN LEO

September 23, 1914 to December 14, 1914

July 19, 1915 to March 19, 1916

May 2, 1916 to February 20, 1928

February 20, 1928 to July 23, 1929

Neptune in the fire signs (Aries, Leo, and Sagittarius brings out a passion for art, idealism, and glory. Historically this passion fueled the overspeculation in the stock market which led to its collapse when Neptune went into the practical and skeptical sign of Virgo in the second half of 1929. By October 29, 1929, the sun fueled by Neptune in Leo was over. The arts flourished under this aspect, heralding the creative styles in music with the sound of jazz, new fashion of the flapper, art deco designs, stream of consciousness writing of James Joyce, and new art period of Picasso. The movie industry came into its own with epics, comedies, and make believes. In 1914, Sigmund Freud and Carl Jung went their separate ways--forming two separate schools of psychology. As for the mystical, Edgar Cayce's work prospered and aided by wealthy benefactors was able to build a hospital at Virginia Beach. Alice A Bailey began receiving messages from he Tibetan master, Djwhal Khul, and began the writing that was to fill twenty-four volumes from 1919 until her death in 1949.

NEPTUNE IN VIRGO

September 21, 1928 to February 19, 1929

July 24, 1929 to October 3, 1942

April 19, 1943 to August 2, 1943

When Neptune is at its fall in Virgo because Virgo is opposite Pisces, the sign Neptune rules. In the United States we had the Great Depression during this transit. Jobs were scarce; soup kitchens and bread lines were set up in many cities. Hitler was rising in power in Germany by preaching the purity of the Aryan race, while Mahatma Ghandi was admonishing India for its cast system. Both men inspired devotion--Hitler with his pomp and Ghandi with his simplicity. In 1930, Dr. J.B. Rhine began studying telepathy at Duke University. Unfortunately, these first systematic studies of the paranormal were inconclusive. Spiritual healers, Harry Edwards, Brother Mandus in England, and Oral Roberts in the United States began their work during this period. World War II, a form of mass hysteria, began at the end of this cycle.

NEPTUNE IN LIBRA

October 4, 1942 to April 18, 1943

August 3, 1943 to December 23, 1955

March 12, 1956 to October 18, 1956

June 17, 1957 to August 4, 1957

Libra is a sign that rules both war (open enemies) and peace (law). When Neptune was in Libra we had both--World War II and the Nuremberg Trials which insisted on a higher moral law than obedience to authority. The United Nations, dedicated to world peace, first met in London on January 10, 1946. Then we had the "Cold War." When Neptune was in Libra, the marriage rate increased and the number of post war births soared. Unfortunately, the divorce rate climbed as well. The glamour of the movie industry was at its peak with the classic good looks of stars such as Rita Hayworth, Cary Grant, and Clark Gable. Existentialism and Zen Buddhism became popular in the fifties. Alan Watts introduced Zen Buddhism to the West. The "beat" era was beginning with the publication of Jack Kerouac's On the Road.

NEPTUNE IN SCORPIO

December 24, 1955 to March 11, 1956

October 19, 1956 to June 16, 1957

August 5, 1957 to January 4, 1970

May 4, 1970 to May 6, 1970

Neptune in the sensual and psychic sign of Scorpio brought renewed interest in both. Movies became increasing sexual, and nude scenes were featured in Hair and Oh Calcutta! The birth control pill allowed greater sexual freedom, and the rate of veneral disease and divorce soared. The United States unwittingly became involved in the Viet Nam Conflict, creating more confusion at home. In 1956 The Search for Bridey Murphy was published, bringing a renewed interest in reincarnation and the occult. In 1966, Dr. Ian T. Stevenson published <u>Twenty Cases Suggestive of Reincarnation</u>. Yoga became popular, and Marcia Moore published <u>Yoga, Youth, and Reincarnation</u> in the sixties. The Russians heavily investigated psychic phenomena during this period.

NEPTUNE IN SAGITTARIUS

1970 TO 1984

Neptune in Sagittarius brought interest in foreign shores. Religious wars in the Mid East created problems for our economy. The 1973 oil embargo created a rise in the cost in oil and gas which made manufacturing costs spiral. Many industries such as steel, moved their operations overseas to cut costs. The economy of Japan prospered, and trade with China was initiated. Since Neptune was going through our seventh house, we had many problems with secret wars such as the Iran Contra affair and the hostage crisis in Iran. Spiritual themes became more popular in music such as "My Sweet Lord" and "Bridge over Troubled Waters". Gambling prospered. In the early 70's <u>Psychic Discoveries Behind the Iron Curtain</u> was published, and our own government became more involved with psychics, using them for remote viewing. Jimmy Carter is quoted as telling an audience that the CIA used a psychic to locate a downed aircraft. She did this by giving the coordinates. <u>Clear Intent</u> and <u>Communion</u> were published during this time, fueling interest in UFOs.

NEPTUNE IN CAPRICORN

1985 to 1997

Neptune in Capricorn brought more corporate takeovers and downsizing. The average person's wages fell. Emphasis on the environment and preserving natural resources, such as the rain forest, were initiated. As material goods became more costly, recycling efforts were put in place. The numbers of homeless people grew with the emphasis on deinstitutionalizing the mentally ill.

169

The chemical industry underwent changes besieged by high lawsuits for asbestos and silicon implant claims. Biotechnology came into its own. Religion went back to basics as many "born again" Christians proclaimed their faith. This movement also put a damper on mediation, mediumship, and New Age practices. Due to economic problems, the Berlin Wall and the Communist Bloc broke up. The 1990 conjunction of the Sun, Mercury, Venus, Saturn, Uranus, and Neptune in Capricorn ushered in an era of material despair. News concerning the economy dominated the evening news.

NEPTUNE IN AQUARIUS

THE FUTURE

1998 TO 2012

When Neptune enters the sign of Aquarius, there will be more intelligent investigation of the occult and more acceptance. More emphasis on human rights will emerge. Conflicts in the Mid East and Eastern Europe will erupt over human rights. Electronic terrorism may escalate. Many of our freedoms will be curtailed as more electronic surveillance is put in place to deal with the criminal element. When Neptune is at 18 Aquaris, 2000 TO 2001

there will be changes in the presidency, and the electoral Congress may be abolished. New technology and diagnosis in the medical profession will be emphasized. Many new branches of medicine and psychology will be founded. Transpersonal and spiritual psychology will vie with biopsychological schools. Interest in UFOs will heighten, and communication with aliens will be acknowledged. Studies of crop circles will be validated scientifically. Look to the establishment of a world government by the end of this cycle.

NEPTUNE IN PISCES

2012 TO 2026

Neptune is well placed in Pisces as it is in its own sign. Medicine will have a cure for both AIDS and cancer by then. Infectious diseases should be wiped out world wide by vast innoculation programs and a new humanitarian spirit. The paranormal will be studied in universities, many of which will be set up in New Mexico, Arizona, and Colorado. China will experience a new spirituality challenging the old Communist rule which will be weakened if not abolished. An American Indian will be president as the karmic cycle turns. Extensive programs for the environment, children, the ill, and the elderly will be founded as spiritual principles to replace the frugal economy of Neptune in Capricorn which shut down many of these programs and the retooling of the economy with Neptune in Aquarius. World religions of the East will be popular in the West as Christianity is discovered in China. New technologies discovered with Neptune in Aquarius will improve the quality of water world wide. True spirituality will also improve the quality of life as volunteerism, fueled by the retirees with their Neptunes in Libra, work to promote social justice. The mechanics of mediumship will be understood as life after death is proven, bringing comfort to many. Writings of the great psychics and mystics will be part of the new literature.

Astrologer, Marcia Moore, gives this summary of Neptune in terms of spiritual development:

NEPTUNE	MOVEMENT
Aquarius	Hypnotism
Pisces	Spiritualism
Aries	Spiritism
Taurus	Christian Science, Psychical research and theosophy
Gemini	Vedanta
Cancer	Astrology, psychoanalysis
Leo	Conscious mediumship
Virgo	Spiritual healing and telepathy
Libra	Existentialism, Zen
Scorpio	Reincarnation, Yoga
Sagittarius	A World Religion
Capricorn	A World Government
Aquarius	Age of Brotherhood

(Marcia Moore, Astrology, the Divine Science, page 277, Arcane Publications)

CHAPTER FOURTEEN

PLUTO: TRANSFORMATION

Pecival Lowell, American astronomer, discovered the planet Pluto on February 18, 1930. As the ninth planet in the solar system, Pluto has an eccentric orbit around the Sun of 228 years. In 1999 Neptune will actually be outside orbit of Pluto because of its erratic tilt to Pluto at that time. This unique astrological situation will make for an unusual year in 1999, with continued world unrest and strange weather patterns. Pluto stays usually between twenty to thirty years in one sign, but its stay can be as brief as thirteen years or as long as thirty-two years.

Pluto, named for the Greek god of the Underworld, stands for death and resurrection. A higher octave of Mars, it represents mass destruction and mass consciousness. It also rules secrets and covert government operations, such as the Secret Service, FBI and CIA.

In an individual chart Pluto gives leadership,

transformation, and intuitive energy. On the negative side, it can bring out sarcasm, competition and jealousy. People with strong Plutos can be reformers of the world or, if afflicted, sinners. In any event, if Pluto is on an angle of the chart in houses one, four, seven and ten, emphasizing resourcefulness, vitality, and increased intuition.

PLUTO IN ARIES

1822/23 to 1851/53

Pluto in Aries brought a strong sense of individual freedom and pioneering spirit. New inventions and social reforms were stressed. During this period, Marxism was born and became a reaction to oppression of the masses. In the United States, masses of people known as pioneers moved westward.

PLUTO IN TAURUS

1851 to 1882

Pluto in Aries brought a strong sense of

individual freedom and pioneering spirit. New inventions and social reforms were stressed. During this period, Marxism was born and became a reaction to oppression of the masses. In the United States, masses of people known as pioneers moved westward.

PLUTO IN TAURUS

1851 TO 1882

Pluto spent thirty-one years in Taurus creating powerful industrialists and wealth often made at the expense of masses. Victorian arts an design saw a return to ornately decorated homes and lavish displays of wealth. In the United States the discovery of oil in 1859 added to the country's wealth. Mass production of many furnishings and art made the finer things of live available for mass consumption

PLUTO IN GEMINI

1882 TO 1912

Pluto in Gemini brought changes in communications

and travel. The automobile, telephone and airplane all came into being. Dr. Sigmund Freud and Dr. William James brought in new discoveries about the mind, shattering many of the rigid ideas of Pluto in Taurus. Masses of people now have better transportation, communications, and an understanding of human psychology.

PLUTO IN CANCER

1912 TO 1938

When Pluto was discovered in 1930, the world was sowing seeds of power struggles which erupted in World War II. Domestic life improved for women with new stoves, washing machines and kitchen appliances. Child rearing practices came under the influence of psychology. People enjoyed a home complete with radio and telephone.

PLUTO IN LEO

1938 TO 1957

The entertainment industry blossomed with

romantic movies such as Casablanca. World power struggles erupted in World War II, and millions went to war. At the end of this period the entertainment industry was revolutionized with the television set and people had access to dramas, comedies, children's programs and variety shows.

PLUTO IN VIRGO

1957 TO 1971

Pluto in Virgo revolutionized the medical industry with advent of tranquilizers, barbiturates and anti-depressants. The birth control pill gained popularity. Medicine improved under this cycle as did the chemical industry.

PLUTO IN LIBRA

1971 TO 1984

Pluto in Libra revolutionized the institution of marriage. More emphasis on companionship in marriage and no-fault divorce laws escalated the divorce and remarriage rates. Individuals were free to marry and divorce, while marriage counseling also grew as a field under this aspect.

PLUTO IN SCORPIO

1984 TO 1995

Pluto in Scorpio revolutionized our views on sex as homosexuality came out of the closet and the number of births to single mothers skyrocketed. A war on drugs was declared, and AIDS made its appearance. Taxation national and global became issues as well as bank and corporate takeovers. New interest in life after death emerged with the publication of books by, Dr. Kenneth Ring, (Heading Toward Omega); Dr. Raymond Moody, (Life After Life); Dr. Brian Weiss, (Many Lives, Many Masters); John White, (A Practical Guide to Death and Dying); Dannion Brinkley (Saved by the Light); and Betty Eadie (Embraced by the Light). In addition to large numbers of publications on near death experiences, people had access to the occult through "psychic hot lines."

PLUTO IN SAGITTARIUS

1995 TO 2,008

Pluto remained in Scorpio about twelve years and will remain in Sagittarius for only thirteen years--both short periods. People are experiencing these rapid transits, creating some confusion in sexual values in Scorpio and religious values in Sagittarius. Look for many changes in religion as well as a new sense of altruism with Pluto in Sagittarius. Individuals will investigate the high mind through hypnosis, past life regression, and dreams. Jungian psychology, with its emphasis on dreams and the collective unconscious, will replace drug therapy and freudian psychology.

PLUTO IN CAPRICORN

2009 TO 2024

Pluto in Capricorn will see more of a new world order with emphasis on survival. Famine and lack of property may necessitate new tariffs and regulations. There will be more of a "Big Brother" mentality with electronic surveillance of the masses. Since Capricorn rules careers, public service, and institutions, more rebuilding in these areas will occur. New universities will come into being in the West--New Mexico, Colorado, and Arizona.

PLUTO IN AQUARIUS

2024 TO 2044

Pluto in Aquarius will bring in new aerospace technology--inventions such as cars which fly low to ground and trans that operate in a vacuum at rapid speeds. Air travel will be available on an everyday basis. A new spirit of friendship will prevail, as the average man sees his neighbor as his brother. More scientific study of the occult will lead us firmly into the Age of Aquarius. Alice Bailey predicted that there would one day be a telephone line to the other side. It could well be invented when Pluto is in the sign of Uranus. Mass consciousness will be revolutionized under this transit.

PLUTO IN PISCES

2044 TO 2064

Pluto in Pisces will bring in new age truths. Mediumship will be common place, and the truth of life after death will be accepted. Christianity will be revived, especially in the Far East. Creative forms in art and music will have a spiritual element. The new technology of Pluto in Aquarius will purify our water systems. More communal ownership of property and health care will be available for the average citizen. Masses of people will understand the truths Christ, Krishna, and Buddha as teachers like Prema Sai Baba usher in a new spirituality.

CHAPTER FIFTEEN

ASCENDANT: YOUR WINDOW TO THE WORLD

The Sun, Moon, and ascendant make up the three power points of the chart. They are the foundation on which the chart rests. If the Moon represents habits of the past, the Sun is the conscious mind, then the ascendant is the facade which the world sees. Hence it is possible to have one sign influence the unconscious mind (Moon), and another the conscious mind (Sun), and yet another the Ascendant. If these three are in harmony, the individual is congruent. If the Sun and Moon are opposite or square to each other, the person's emotional or private life is in conflict with his public life. For example, President Clinton has his Sun in Leo which gives leadership and direction, but he is emotionally held back by his earthy Moon in Taurus. Sometimes the Sun and the Ascendant will be square of opposite. Jacqueline Kennedy Onassis had her Sun in the theatrical sign of Leo, but her ascendant in the private sign of Scorpio--hence she guarded her privacy, while being a public figure (Leo). The more the public clamored for details about her life, the less she revealed of her private life. Sometimes the Moon and Ascendant are at odds. Such is the case with Dr. Maria Montessori. She had her Moon in the passionate sign of Scorpio but had a proud Leo ascendant. Known for her leadership in education she revealed little until late in her career, about her personal life, which included a son born out of wedlock.

Think of your ascendant as your window to the world. As such it shows your outlook on life and what you reveal to the world. Since it rules your first house, it governs your early childhood, your psychological environment, and your physical body. In esoteric terms, the ascendant represents the immediate lessons the soul must encounter before progressing on the spiritual path.

ARIES ASCENDANT

Aries ascendant is a man in a hurry--full steam ahead. Often he is energetic, competitive, and athletic. He hates to be ignored and has no patience with details. His courage and idealism make him a natural leader. He is willing to try anything once. Often he prefers to work alone so he can go at a faster pace than colleagues. If afflicted he can be arrogant or domineering. Physically, he is of slender build with chin thrust forward, quick moving and eyes alert. Bette Midler has the brash, fun loving, generous Aries Ascendant personality. Healthwise, they may be prone to minor accidents, migraines, or head injuries. The lesson here is to be the "captain of one's soul" without infringing on the liberty of others.

TAURUS ASCENDANT

Taurus ascendant is like his symbol the bull--is deliberate in action, has good concentration and leaves no stone unturned in his search for material comforts. Underneath the gentle facade is a stubborn streak. At times Taurus rising can be fatalistic. Ruled by Venus, he may be fair of form with a tendency to plumpness. Elvis Presley's Taurus rising good looks and sensuous voice made him a legend. He also battled his weight and a drug problem in later years. People with this ascendant love to eat, especially sweets. If afflicted, they can become indulgent, obstinate and lazy. Their lack of discipline can become their downfall. If well aspected they make a good manager and may excel in business. Healthwise they may be prone to throat problems, or diseases from overindulgence such as gout. Esoterically, individuals must earn their way in life without becoming too possessive of his material goods. Hence they need to have a ceiling on their desire nature before they can progress on the spiritual path.

GEMINI ASCENDANT

Gemini ascendant is like a butterfly flitting from place to place. They are friendly in a breezy sort of way, enjoy short jaunts, and have many interests. Often the hands and feet are moving-- even when sitting still. Often they enjoy crafts and may possess mechanical ability. John Denver had the easy-going friendliness of a Gemini ascendant, and unfortunately died enjoying his favorite hobby--flying. Ruled by Mercury, they can be quite intelligent, and enjoy reading newspapers and short publications. If afflicted, they are worrisome and may lack purpose in their life, and are content to go from job to job. If well aspected, they may possess keen intelligence and speaking or writing ability. Healthwise, the lungs may be sensitive and they may be prone to injuries of the shoulders, arms and hands. Esoterically, they need to learn to think rationally not fanatically before they can progress spiritually in life.

CANCER ASCENDANT

Cancer is a Moon child with large dreamy eyes and a gentle air. He is closely attached to family and has a protective nature. He is often patriotic and has an interest in history, including the family tree. Shy at first, he will reveal himself slowly. Ruled by the Moon, he may have a fuller or "moon" fact and a rounded build. Comedian Jonathan Winters has the round face and hostile humor of Cancer ascendant. If well aspected, intuition plays a role in his life and helps make his dreams come true. If afflicted, he may be petty and overly sensitive to criticism and his environment. Healthwise, he needs to watch his stomach. Food may play a role in depression and moodiness. Esoterically, he needs to learn to nurture others before he can progress on the spiritual path.

LEO ASCENDANT

Leo ascendant has a sunny disposition, a noble bearing, generous nature, and a bright smile. Ruled by the Sun, he has a flair for getting the spotlight and enjoys attention. In fact he can stand anything--except being ignored. He may enjoy sports, games of chance, music, and art. He is a romantic at heart. Often he is a handsome figure with broad shoulders and narrow hips. The ladies favor "big hair." Marilyn Munroe had this ascendant and was known for her bright mile, blond mane, and sunny disposition. He can be an executive or the life of the party-- sometimes both. If afflicted, he can be a party animal or petty dictator. Healthwise, he needs to watch the heart and circulation. Esoterically he needs to learn to give and forgive without any acknowledgement.

VIRGO ASCENDANT

Virgo ascendant has the quiet personality of a librarian or an accountant. He may appear younger than his years with a slender build and neat attire. Modest by nature, he is very capable of taking over when the boss is out. He favors honest work, enjoys detail analysis, and prefers to be indoors. Ruled by Mercury, he is thoughtful and polite in speech. Actress Jean March, who played "Rose" in Upstairs, Downstairs, had the prim and proper appearance of Virgo ascendant. If well aspected, he will enjoy material success won by his own efforts. If afflicted he may miss opportunities because of a lack of faith in his own abilities or a worrisome nature. Health wise, digestion and the intestines can present problems. Esoterically he is here to serve without thought of reward.

LIBRA ASCENDANT

Libra ascendant is beautiful. Ruled by Venus, he is fair of face with balanced features and lovely lips. He is courteous and has a strong desire to please others. Sometimes Libra rising is slender in youth but puts on weight in middle years. If well aspected there is great charm to the personality. If afflicted, he may be a social climber. Either way, he possesses discriminating intelligence and likes to reason things out. Both John F. Kennedy and Bill Clinton have this ascendant with its classic good looks. Healthwise he needs to watch the lower back and kidneys. Esoterically, he must learn to put the needs of others first before pursuing his own agenda.

SCORPIO ASCENDANT

Scorpio ascendant wants all or nothing. They have a strong desire nature and can be demanding. They like to be in control and prefer to keep their private life private. They have innate dignity. Physically, they are large boned with strong shoulders, back, full eye brows and a convex forehead with a line of concentration in the middle of the forehead. They are ruled by Pluto. They can be loyal friends or bitter enemies. If well aspected, they have excellent intuition and may excel in positions of leadership and have an interest in investments. If afflicted, their bossiness and critical attitude may alienate others. Healthwise, Scorpio rules the sense of smell and the sex organs. If afflicted, these can be problem areas, as well as the rectum and bladder. Esoterically, they need to learn to "let go and let God." Resentment will hinder their spiritual progress.

SAGITTARIUS ASCENDANT

Sagittarius ascendant has a wonderful sense of fun. Diana, Princess of Wales, a noble personality, was ruled by this sign. They like to be on the go and have a creative and warm personality. Physically, they tend to be tall and long legged. With Jupiter as their ruler, they enjoy helping others and make excellent teachers. However, they may lack concentration, preferring a variety of tasks to routine work. They love to travel--especially to foreign shores. If well aspected, they may benefit from travel and high education or the arts; they may possess prophetic vision. If afflicted, they can be "rolling stones." Healthwise, they need to watch the thighs and liver. They tend to ignore health problems and may overexert their energies. Esoterically, they must learn to use their vision in a responsible way to create a better world for all to see.

CAPRICORN ASCENDANT

Capricorn ascendant can hear the grass grow. They also don't let much grass grow under their feet, as they are purposefully ambitious. They are known for their serious expression high cheek bones and flat chest. They can keep a secret well. J. Edgar Hoover, Director of the F.B.I. had this ascendant. He was well known for his ambition, heard work, and ability to guard the nation's secrets. His lackluster personality and tight lip is typical of Capricorn rising. Ruled by Saturn, they have a strong sense of responsibility and duty. If well aspected, they are destined to rise in life. If afflicted, ambition can be their downfall. Healthwise they need to watch the bones and teeth. They are also prone to depression.

Esoterically they need to take responsibility for others without seeking recognition. To do this they need to cultivate a sense of faith in themselves and others.

AQUARIUS ASCENDANT

Aquarius ascendant is unique. They have a friendly, easy going personality with a zany sense of humor. Attractive and intelligent, they seek a great deal of freedom in relationships. Since their ruler is Uranus, they may dislike authority. If afflicted, they can be a "rebel without a cause." If well aspected, there can be genius--or at least unconventional creativity. Joseph Stalin and Karl Marx had Aquarius rising which gave them mass appeal as revolutionaries. Singer Billie Holliday, whose incomparable voice and unconventional life style, gave her mass appeal, had Aquarius rising. They often have refined features and may have a heart shaped face or a pointed chin, and sometimes wavy hair. Healthwise Aquarius rules the legs, ankles, and circulation. These can be problem areas if afflicted. Esoterically, Aquarius Ascendant needs to learn to love on an impersonal level--to love all mankind without seeking personal favor.

PISCES ASCENDANT

Pisces ascendant is a gentle dreamer, easy going and warm in nature. They tend to be plump with small hands and feet, large eyes and unruly hair. Singer Rosemary Clooney, with her pretty face and likable personality, has Pisces rising. They tend to see the good in everyone and enjoy children and animals. They may lack self confidence. Sometimes they turn to alcohol to bolster their confidence. If well aspected, they are known for their kindness, charm and spirituality. If afflicted, they can be messy, disorganized, and their worst enemy. Healthwise, Pisces rules the feet, which can be problematic if afflicted. Esoterically, their lesson is to be in the world, but not of it.

CHAPTER SIXTEEN

HOUSES: DEPARTMENTS OF LIFE

A horoscope is broken into twelve sections, each of which represents a different department of life. Babylonians astrologers first designated these twelve houses. The placement of planets in each sector determines the emphasis and quality of that department of life. For example, if a person has the Sun in the tenth house which rules career, they will invest a lot of their ego (Sun) in career. If the Sun is in the seventh house, the focus will be on marriage, artistic expression, and social events. Aspects to the planets in each house show the degree of ease or struggle present in that department of life. If the Sun in the tenth house has good aspects as does Elton John's chart, then fame and fortune come easily. If aspects are difficult, the same desire for success is present but it may only come after some struggle or to a lesser degree.

While your natal chart remains the same,

different departments of life are set off by transiting planets. For example, Elton John's Sun in the tenth house which is trined by Pluto, promising career success, was influenced by transiting Pluto in a positive way in 1997. Hence, his song "English Rose" dedicated to Princess Diana became a legendary best seller at the end of 1997.

Houses one (personality, four (parents), seven (marriage), and ten (career) on the angles of the chart are the strongest in influence. Houses one (self), five (children), and nine (higher mind) are the house of life. Houses two (money), six (property) and ten (career) are the financial houses. Houses three (brothers and sisters), seven (relationships), and eleven (friends) are concerned with relationships. and the psychic houses are four (intuition), eight (occult), and twelve (unconscious mind).

FIRST HOUSE

The first house, the ascendant, represents the physical body, personality, and early childhood. The ascendant is your window to the world, it shows both your outlook on life and how others perceive you. The early physical and psychological environment represented by the ascendant color the native's attitude throughout life to some degree. In terms of the physical body, the ascendant shows the size and shape as well as the general health. In esoteric astrology, it represents the immediate lesson the soul needs to master before it can progress on the spiritual path. The ascendant, Sun and Moon are the power points of any chart. transits of the benefic planets (Sun, Venus, Jupiter) are positive as they brighten, sweeten, and expand the personality. While generally positive, transits of Jupiter can put on weight. Mercury brings travel, and Mars will often take you out of the house as your energy and vitality expands. Saturn may bring some lessons of life; while the outer planets (Uranus, Neptune, and Pluto) can bring major physical or psychological changes.

SECOND HOUSE

The second house rules all wealth that is portable. Look to the fourth for real estate. It also shows what the person values. The second house indicates your finances – both your attitude toward money, ability to earn, and sources of wealth. The benefic planets (Sun, Jupiter, and Venus) tend to increase prosperity. The Moon indicates fluctuation in finances. Mercury and Mars stimulate spending; while Saturn can bring financial lessons or responsibilities. Large sums can be earned if outer planets (Uranus, Neptune, and Pluto) are well aspected in the Second house. Affliction in this house create poverty, waste, or excessive concern about finances. Under affliction by transit, protect your valuables and save a bit for unexpected expenses. When well aspected nataly or by transit, wealth is increased.

THIRD HOUSE

The third house rules the mind, communications, short distance travel, and brothers and sisters. If well aspected or benefic planets place in the third house, the native will have much to do with relatives and enjoy using their mind. Benefic planets in the third house improve quality of relationships.

The Moon enjoys a change of scene. Mercury is well placed in the third and adds to intelligence. Mars quickens the mind and speech, sometime fond of debate. Saturn makes the mind more serious, and the outer planets, if well aspected, bring out unique talents. Positive aspects to planets in the third house give good intelligence and abilities in teaching, sales and communications. Relations with family are usually pleasant. However, afflictions to planets in the third may cause family misunderstandings, confusion in communication, and losses during travel. Under affliction by transit, slow down the pace of your life, watch your luggage and read the fine print on documents. If well aspected in natal chart or by transit, the mind is stimulated and travel favored.

THE FOURTH HOUSE

The fourth house represents the foundation of life - the physical home and psychological influence of the parents. The fourth house, often referred to as the nadir, is the lowest part of the chart and indicates the end of life. Thus the sphere of life beginning with the parents comes full circle. The type of home you prefer is indicated by the sign on the cusp of the fourth house:

Aries loves a large expensive home and may overspend.

Taurus wants a comfortable home and often prefers to work at home.

Gemini enjoys a home with a library or hobby nook, but their home may also be where they hang their hat.

Cancer craves a home as a source of both psychological and financial security.

Leo loves their lair and will spend lavishly on furnishings and luxury goods. Like royalty, they prefer others to clean it.

Virgo likes a clean, neat home with good plumbing.

Libra loves to decorate and entertain in their home. Their focus is on the living room.

Scorpio wants privacy, security, and a lasting investment in a home. They may choose to redo an older home.

Sagittarius likes home to "party" in and likes

a big backyard. Like Gemini may not spend much time at home.

Capricorn looks for status in address and quality in construction. They prefer a traditional house, decorated in earth tones.

Aquarius likes a unique home with many gadgets. To a true Aquarius, friends make a house a home.

Pisces wants a "dream" house decorated in soothing colors as a place for retreat. A swimming pool makes a nice extra for the sign of the fishes.

If benefic planets are in your fourth house, nataly or by transit, real estate is a good investment, as long as there are no afflictions. The Moon enjoys domestic life in the fourth. Mercury and Mars in the fourth like to change things around. When Saturn transits the fourth, you are less likely to move. The outer planet in the natal fourth house may enhance sensitivity and intuition. By transit Uranus, Neptune, and Pluto bring long-lasting psychological changes.

FIFTH HOUSE

The fifth house rules pleasure, romance, and children. It also indicates talent and speculation. The benefic planets add charm and increase sex appeal and fertility. Children are a source of joy if well aspected. If afflicted, natives may spoil children or overwork for them. The Moon in the fifth is fond of speculation and if well aspected makes a loving parent. Sometimes it indicates fluctuations in romance. Mercury indicates intelligent children and a desire for intellectual companionship. Mars activates romance and love of sports, theatre and risk-taking. Saturn dampens the enthusiasm of the fifth house, but makes it more responsible. The outer planets may bring unique talent and/or offspring. Uranus, potential genius, Neptune, spiritual or artistic child, and Pluto dynamic pioneer. Good aspects may bring benefit through speculation or the stock market.

SIXTH HOUSE

The sixth house stands for health and service.

It shows the general health of the native, appetite, and abilities in healing. In work, both talent and work relationships are indicated by this house. Employees are ruled by the sixth house; with the tenth house indicating the boss. Planets in the sixth and the sign on the cusp of the sixth are important in medical astrology. Transits will time the illness and recovery periods. When the benefic planets are in this house, an enjoyment of good health and/or work. Nurses, cooks and homemakers may have their Moon in the sixth house. Mercury makes a good teacher but if afflicted, the native may worry too much. Mars in the sixth can indicate fevers and changes in health. In a natal chart mechanical or athletic ability may be a factor in work. The outer planets indicate unique methods of healing and/or work.

SEVENTH HOUSE

The seventh house rules marriage and partnership and legal matters. It is both the house of open enemies and peace. Moon, Venus and sometimes Mars in the seventh house indicates and early marriage. The benefic planets, if well aspected, greatly increase happiness in marriage. Mercury may indicate companionship and shared interests. Saturn takes relationships seriously. The outer planets indicate and independent mate (Uranus) a spiritual tie with mate (Neptune), or a powerful partner (Pluto). Aspects to these planets indicate success (trines and sextiles) or struggles (squares and oppositions). The seventh house is the first marriage, the ninth house, indicates the second marriage, and the eleventh house is the third union.

EIGHTH HOUSE

The eighth house rules joint property, banks, corporations, and inheritance. It rules the hidden side of life - sex, death, and the occult. Will power and intuition play a role in this house. The benefices in the eight house improve quality of life. The Mood in the eighth enhances psychic ability. Mercury in the eighth loves a mystery and Mars has added will power here. Saturn indicates lessons may come with excessive sensuality. The outer planets bring out the occult side of the eighth house.

NINTH HOUSE

.The ninth house rules the higher mind - law and philosophy. It also represents long distant travel and foreign countries. Opposite the third, it indicates your partners relatives or inlaws. If planets are well aspected in the ninth travel is indicated and success on foreign shores. Sometime they may move from their homeland. If planets are afflicted, the higher mind is narrow or fuzzy in focus, bringing difficult adjustments in life. The benefices indicate enjoyment of travel and philosophy. The Moon indicated living abroad at some time. Mercury in the ninth can be tolerant if well aspected, petty if afflicted. Mars in the ninth house is fond of debate and likes to move around. Saturn makes for a deep mind and takes legal matters seriously. The outer planets bring unusual attributes. Uranus can show invention, Neptune, psychic abilities, and Pluto passion for causes.

TENTH HOUSE

The tenth house is known as the midheaven and is the highest part of the chart. It represents our standing in the world through career or derived status. It is the public side of the native. While the fourth house represents the mother, the tenth stands for the father and authority figures. The Sun shines in the tenth house. Jupiter expands opportunities and can favor law or politics. Venus in the tenth favors the arts. The Moon is good for working with the public. Mercury in the tenth gives teaching, speaking, or mechanical abilities. Mars makes for an industrious worker capable of hard work, sometimes in technical fields. When Saturn is in the tenth, the person is ambitious, but success may come slowly or through Saturn occupations such as business or government. The outer planets with good aspects bring unique opportunities - Uranus in the electrical or engineering fields, Neptune in film, chemistry or helping professions, as well as intuitive fields, and Pluto as a leader and organizer in banks, detective work, corporations, recycling, and antiques. Watch the transit to time career moves. For example the best time to ask for a raise is when Jupiter is in your tenth house. However, one may benefit by staying put, when Saturn transits the tenth.

ELEVENTH HOUSE

The eleventh house is the house of friends, hope and wishes. Benefic planets in this house add to the success of the native. The Sun often brings powerful friends, Venus artistic people, and Jupiter benefit from friendships. The Moon may bring fluctuations in friendship and may favor female friends if well aspected. Mars brings more a male influence and may increase desire for companionship, Mercury brings intellectual friends. With Saturn in the eleventh house, old friends are best. Uranus, Neptune, and Pluto bringing unique acquaintances into your life fun-loving Uranians, spiritual Neptune types, and dynamic and powerful Pluto friends.

TWELFTH HOUSE

The twelfth house is a karmic house. It represents the unconscious mind, institutions, hospitals, prisons, hidden enemies, and the psychic. Esoterically, if you have the same sign ruling both the twelfth and the first, it is said your last lifetime was a short one and you have come back to finish where you left off. An interest in the occult, psychology, and helping those less fortunate is shown when the benefic planets are in the twelfth house. Mercury here makes a good psychic or detective if well aspected. The Moon in the twelfth is sensitive and may be mediumistic. Mars is weaker in the twelfth house. Saturn brings karmic responsibilities in the twelfth. The outer planets can trigger subconscious influences for good or ill depending on the aspects.

CHAPTER SEVENTEEN

THE SUN IN THE TWELVE HOUSES

THE SUN IN THE FIRST HOUSE

The Sun in the first house has a "sunny" disposition. Often they have a happy childhood and are confident, and sometimes willful. The Sun is strong in the first house as it is on an angle, strengthening the physical body. Psychologically, they wish to shine in life. As such they are self starters and are able to rise in life by their own efforts. If well aspected, they rise in status in life; if afflicted, their ego gets in the way.

THE SUN IN THE SECOND HOUSE

The Sun is stable in the second house and concerned with values - both moral and material. They may expend a great deal of energy making money for the creature comforts they crave. Often they are caretakers. More than anything, they like to shine at work. If well aspected, they can be generous and nurturant. If afflicted, they are too materialistic.

THE SUN IN THE THIRD HOUSE

The Sun in the third house has a bright mind and is interested in many things. They also enjoy travel and may excel in teaching or sales. They shine in communications. If well aspected, they have good powers of reasoning and are known for community involvement; if afflicted, they are too scattered for lasting success.

THE SUN IN THE FOURTH HOUSE

The Sun in the fourth house has a strong attachment to family. They like to shine in the home. Often they enjoy working from their home. They may also have an interest in real estate, cooking, children and history. If well aspected, family happiness is promised; if afflicted, family discord may erupt during sensitive transits.

THE SUN IN THE FIFTH HOUSE

The Sun in the fifth house is full of joy. They

shine in the game of life - enjoying theater, sports, games of chance, fashion, and romance. Often, they dote on their offspring. If well aspected, children are a source of pride; if afflicted, children may be spoiled by too much attention.

THE SUN IN THE SIXTH HOUSE

The Sun in the sixth house shines at work. Often they are drawn to service work, medical field, or accounting. Known for their hard work and attention to detail, they are capable employees. Health, exercise, and nutrition are of special interest to them. If well aspected, they are blessed with good health and work habits; if afflicted, delicate health and "underemployment".

THE SUN IN THE SEVENTH HOUSE

The Sun in the seventh house shines in relationships. Marriage and companionship are very important to them. Since they have a strong need to feel connected, their lives are often influenced by others. They have a strong social side and may have an artistic streak. If well aspected, a fortunate marriage; if afflicted, marriage is one of compromise.

THE SUN IN THE EIGHTH HOUSE

The Sun in the eighth house shines in enterprise. They may have an interest in banking, insurance, corporations, and recycling. Often they rise in life; as the Sun will eventually progress to the top of the chart. Intuitive by nature, they are known to play their hunches. If well aspected, they may inherit wealth; if afflicted, they "earn" their inheritance.

THE SUN IN THE NINTH HOUSE

The Sun in the ninth house favors long distance travel, philosophy, and culture. They shine in vision and can be an inspiration to many. Often they may choose to live in a foreign country or travel as a part of their job. If well aspected, they benefit from foreign lands; if afflicted, they need to use caution during travel, especially in foreign lands!

THE SUN IN THE TENTH HOUSE

The Sun in the tenth house focuses on career and status. Often they have an innate sense of leadership and a desire to shine. Politics and public speaking may be of interest to them. If well aspected, they rise in life and are popular; if afflicted, there could be a fall from grace during difficult transits.

THE SUN IN THE ELEVENTH HOUSE

The Sun in the eleventh house shines in humanitarian pursuits. Everyone is their friend since they are broad minded and tolerant. Often causes are important to them. They would rather help someone than make a sale. If well aspected, powerful friends will aid them in life. If afflicted, they may give more than they receive.

THE SUN IN THE TWELFTH HOUSE

The Sun is sensitive in the twelfth house.

Its power goes underground in this house of the unconscious mind. They are often kind and interested in helping others. While quiet, they don't miss much as they are very intuitive. If well aspected, they may make a good detective or psychologist; if afflicted, they are too sensitive and may retreat from life.

CHAPTER EIGHTEEN

THE MOON IN THE TWELVE HOUSES

The Moon governs emotions, women, and mother in the chart. When it is on an angle (houses one, four, seven, and ten), the feeling nature is strong. The house in which the Moon resides, like the planet itself, may be prone to fluctuation. The Moon is accidentally dignified in the second house which stabilizes its influence and the fourth house its natural home.

THE MOON IN THE FIRST HOUSE

The Moon in the first house is restless, kind, and sensitive. They may resemble the mother's side of the family and are close to both parents. They may have a round face and a tendency to fluctuate in weight. Femininity is strong in a woman's chart; sensitivity strong in a male chart. If well aspected, increases happiness in family life and good abilities to work before the public. If afflicted, they can be attention seeking and are prone to self pity. They may need to heal relationships especially with the mother. In either case, they are apt to be emotional. To offset this tendency, they need to "tune" in to others and focus less on themselves.

THE MOON IN THE SECOND HOUSE

The changing nature of the Moon is stabilized in the second house. There is a strong tendency to hold on the relationships and possessions. They need material possessions in order to feel secure. Sometimes they are natural collectors. There can be fluctuations in finances. Sometimes these people are sentimental about possession and may become collectors. If well aspected, they can earn money through working with public or government service. They are shrewd in finances and can maintain wealth. If afflicted, the opposite is true and there can be financial reversals. They may worry too much about money. They need to set aside some "worry" time and learn to relax the rest of the day.

THE MOON IN THE THIRD HOUSE

The Moon in the third house does not want to be still. They like short distant travel and a variety of tasks in their work, as they enjoy changing locations. They enjoy associating with different types of people and may have a flair for writing or journalism. If well aspected, the mind is imaginative and creative. If afflicted, they may lack concentration or be a dreamer. To balance this tendency, they need to concentrate on finishing one project before starting the next.

THE MOON IN THE FOURTH HOUSE

The Moon in the fourth house loves their home. They have a close tie to family for good or ill; and they don't forget their roots. Subjectivity is strong and feelings may fluctuate. They may have an interest in gourmet food, history, antiques, and older homes as they enjoy the traditions of the past. If well aspected, family ties are beneficial and their sensitivity and creative side strong. If afflicted, they need to let go of the past and start each day fresh as they have a tendency to hold resentments. Dependency issues may play a role in their life.

THE MOON IN THE FIFTH HOUSE

The Moon in the fifth house loves to take a chance. They enjoy children and romance and may experience fluctuation in these areas. They can make good parents, but have a tendency to be too emotionally involved with offspring. If well aspected the pleasures of life are increased and relationships with children a joy. If afflicted, their strong emotional nature can create blocks in relationships. They crave recognition especially for artistic talents. They may need to cultivate more will power and less pleasure-seeking.

THE MOON IN THE SIXTH HOUSE

The Moon in the sixth house makes a good nurse, caretaker and cook. Nutrition, diet and exercise may also be of interest. They make a good civil servant as they are interested in health, sanitation, and welfare. They like keeping things in good working order. If well aspected they serve others well and are nurturant and kind. These natives are well liked at work. If afflicted there can be fluctuations in work conditions and they may be prone to stomach problems due to "stuffing" their feelings. Sometimes it is helpful to talk, write, paint, or exercise feelings out of the system, rather than let them fester inside.

THE MOON IN THE SEVENTH HOUSE

The Moon in the seventh house is very emotional about relationships and may choose to marry early as a "good" marriage and a home are important to their emotional security. They may attract a sensitive partner. Sometimes they marry a "parent" or "child" or for the sake of social status. If well aspected, they are receptive to the needs of others which brings happiness in relationships. If afflicted, there can be fluctuation in relationships due to unstable emotions. They have a tendency to be moody needs to be examined. Sometimes they need to be less concerned with opinions of other and "tune in" to their heart.

THE MOON IN THE EIGHTH HOUSE

The Moon in the eighth house can be psychic and have a "nose for news". They have deep feelings and look beyond the senses in relationships. Often police or detective work is favored. If well aspected, they can "tune" into others and may experience a world beyond the material either in meditation, dreams, or hunches. They may inherit money especially from the mother's side of the family. If afflicted, fluctuations in moods can make them vulnerable. Often they need to learn to release negative feelings such as jealousy and greed. A "Let go and let God" attitude would be helpful.

THE MOON IN THE NINTH HOUSE

The Moon in the ninth house enjoys travel especially to foreign lands. Sometimes they live in foreign countries or move from their homeland. Religion and philosophy may be of interest. They enjoy sharing knowledge. If well aspected, they have a positive philosophy of life and may have vivid prophetic dreams. If afflicted, fluctuations in fall off may cause confusion. They need to use caution during long distance travel as there can be unexpected problems.

THE MOON IN THE TENTH HOUSE

When the Moon is in the tenth house personal charisma is strong. It can denote a career before the public and fame. These people may experience fluctuations in careers. Often this position favors advertising, politics, and public relations. Ties with parents remain strong. If well aspected, the father aids the native in life. In a man's chart, a happy marriage to an equal partner. If afflicted, they can be moody and experience difficult public relations. Fame and fortune do not always go together. Material success comes and goes, but spiritual values last a lifetime.

THE MOON IN THE ELEVENTH HOUSE

The Moon in the eleventh house favors female friends and group associations. Relationship with mother and woman, and friends add to happiness if well aspected. Democratic by nature, they attract many friendships. If afflicted, they may be too dependent on friendships or attract friends who "sponge" off them. Discrimination in friendships is important. Either way, they instinctively know what they send in to the lives others comes back into their own.

THE MOON IN THE TWELFTH HOUSE

The Moon in the twelfth house can be shy and somewhat psychic. They often play their hunches and may enjoy a mystery. If well aspected makes a good psychologist or detective. Their sensitivity works in their favor. If afflicted can bring fluctuations in moods and secret romances. Emotionalism needs to be curbed. Sometimes there is suffering from the mother or home life because of a karmic debt. While they may prefer to bear their cross privately, sometimes it helps to talk about it with a loyal friend or counselor. If there are no benific aspects to the Moon in the twelfth, they may experience adjustment disorders under difficult transits.

CHAPTER NINETEEN

MERCURY IN THE HOUSES

Mercury rules communication and travel. It shows the way you speak, form ideas and the manner in which you communicate with others. When Mercury is on an angle of the chart (Houses one, four, seven, and ten), it is stronger. When it is in the third or sixth, it is at home, because Mercury rules Gemini, the natural ruler of the third house and Virgo, the ruler of the sixth house. Since Mercury is exalted in Aquarius, the ruler of the eleventh house, it is favorable in the eleventh. The less favorable positions are the twelfth house or the ninth where it is accidentally in detriment - opposite its ruling house three and twelve; and the fifth house which is opposite the eleventh house of exaltation.

MERCURY IN THE FIRST HOUSE

Mercury in the first house has many interests. People with their Mercury in the first house are curious, sociable, and friendly. Often they make friends readily and enjoy short distance travel. If well aspected, the person may be interested in teaching, sales or writing. They are also intelligent and adaptable. If afflicted, they may be self centered or high strung. They may also be prone to nervous disorders.

MERCURY IN THE SECOND HOUSE

Mercury in the second house is interested in making money. Here Mercury is the second can be practical and firm in opinions. They have an interest in business and may choose to work with relatives. If well aspected, they can earn money through writing, speaking, travel and commerce. They often like to collect books and records. If afflicted, they may focus too narrowly on commercial interests or be inflexible or impractical in methods or opinions.

MERCURY IN THE THIRD HOUSE

Mercury in the third house increases

intelligence and ability to do detailed work. They may have an interest in teaching or research. If well aspected, they are fond of study and capable of obtaining advanced degrees. They also enjoy their brothers and sisters. If afflicted, they may be prone to worry or may be too superficial in thought. Relatives may present problems at times, due to poor communications.

MERCURY IN THE FOURTH HOUSE

When Mercury is in the fourth house, there is a strong interest in home and family. They love their home, but may have changes of residence. They may enjoy collecting cookbooks and kitchen gadgets. If Mercury is well aspected, they enjoy remodeling or decorating the home. If afflicted, they need to relax more in the home. Sometimes they are prone to stomach upsets or ulcers.

MERCURY IN THE FIFTH HOUSE

Mercury in the fifth house does not like to take life seriously. They are interested in having fun and are drawn to the adventure, romance, and art. They enjoy attention and love to make a point before an audience. If well aspected, they may be creative with good speaking or writing ability. If afflicted, they can be opinionated and domineering. They tend to worry about their children, often over-correcting them.

MERCURY IN THE SIXTH HOUSE

Mercury is interested in matters of health in the sixth house. If well aspected, the native may have an interest in the health field as a profession. If afflicted, they tend to worry about their health and may be prone to psychosomatic diseases. In terms of work, they can get bogged down in details which can cause nervous strain.

MERCURY IN THE SEVENTH HOUSE

When Mercury is in the seventh house, people are interested in relationships. Many with this position may choose to marry a younger partner or may marry early in life. If well aspected, marriage brings companionship and happiness. Legal matters are favored. If afflicted, there can be arguments and disagreements in marriage. It would be better to settle difficulties out of court if possible.

MERCURY IN THE EIGHTH HOUSE

When Mercury is in the eighth house the natives are persistent investigators. Their interest may include the occult, recycling, corporate life, and banking. When well aspected, they may inherit money from a relative or do well with investments. When afflicted the opposite is true. There can be problems with inheritances or joint finances. Since the eighth house is the "house of death", the lungs may be a source of concern under affliction.

MERCURY IN THE NINTH HOUSE

When Mercury is in the ninth house, natives are interested in education and philosophy. They may also have a desire to visit far away places and experience vivid dreams. If well aspected, this is a good position for teaching and counseling young people; or business which involve travel or the field of law. If afflicted, the interest is in travel is strong, but less opportunity. Sometimes they can be fanatical in thinking and preach rather than teach. Since this is also the house of in-laws, there can be disagreements under affliction. It might be wise to allow some space in the relationship.

MERCURY IN THE TENTH HOUSE

When Mercury is in the tenth house, natives are interested in career, public speaking, writing, or mechanical pursuits. Mercury is strong in the tenth house since it is culminating at top of chart. If well aspected, people with this position rise in life and enjoy a good reputation. They have a variety of talents which can be combined to their advantage. When afflicted, there can be problems in communication or unfavorable changes in career. Sometimes there is a tendency to overachieve which can create nervous strain.

MERCURY IN THE ELEVENTH HOUSE

When Mercury is in the eleventh house, there is an interest in friendships based on common interests. They enjoy joining clubs and group association. Since Mercury rules eleventh house, it is well placed here. They value ideas of others and can see issues from different viewpoints. If well aspected, friends aid individual in obtaining goals in life. If afflicted, there can be losses through friends and a tendency to just get by rather than achieve life's goals.

MERCURY IN THE TWELFTH HOUSE

Mercury is weakened in the twelfth house. People with this position may lack confidence and can be secretive or shy. If well aspected, intuition and compassion are strong. They would make a sensitive counselor or minister. If afflicted, they are too sensitive. Sometimes relatives may be out of sync with the native, which can create a lack of empathy or support.

CHAPTER TWENTY

VENUS IN THE HOUSES

Venus is the planet which rules love - both the way one relates to others and the feminine principle of attraction. In a man's chart, Venus is the wife or lover. In a woman's chart, Mars represents, the husband or lover. Venus also rules finances and the beautiful and sweet things of life. If Venus is on an angle (houses one, four, seven, and ten), it is more prominent in the chart. Venus in the first house gives physical beauty and grace. In the fourth house Venus can bring a happy family life and love of home. In the Seventh house, Venus sweetens the marriage and brings a happy union. In the tenth house Venus can indicate a career before the public or artistic talent. Since Venus rules Taurus, the natural ruler of the second house and Libra, the natural ruler of the seventh house, it is well placed in those houses. Venus is weaker in the eighth and first houses since it is opposite its rulership houses.

VENUS IN THE FIRST HOUSE

Venus in the first house is considered lucky. The Personality is sweetened, making the native friendly and charming. They have a knack for getting what they want. Here Venus represents a love of beauty. If well aspected the person is good looking and can attract many material comforts in their life. Their artistic nature is strong and they do their best work in peaceful and harmonious surroundings. If afflicted they can be lazy or self indulgent.

VENUS IN THE SECOND HOUSE

Venus in the second house is lucky in finances. They can often earn through luxury occupations such as beauty culture, art, gift shops, and fashion. Here Venus represents a love of wealth. If well aspected, money may come easy or they may inherit money. Business partnerships are favored. If afflicted they may be extravagant or wasteful with resources. They may need to settle down in order to acquire material success.

VENUS IN THE THIRD HOUSE

Venus in the third house likes art poetry and music. They prefer harmonious communications and avoid arguments. Here Venus represents a love of brothers, sisters and relatives. They are able to communicate well and may show artistic talent. If afflicted, they may become "people pleasers" or lazy in communications. They may need to guard against gossip.

VENUS IN THE FOURTH HOUSE

When Venus is in the fourth house, they want a home of their own, and will spend generously on furnishing and decorating it. Their home is often a place of social gatherings and fun, as they have a talent for making people feel welcome. Venus truly loves their home in this house. If well aspected, good relationship with the mother and family. The end of life is peaceful, surrounded by family and friends. If afflicted, there can be problems with the relationship with the mother or father and a tendency to overspend on the home itself or furnishings.

VENUS IN THE FIFTH HOUSE

When Venus is in the fifth house, love of romance, art, and children is strong. Often they have a playful nature. If well aspected, they may gain through speculation, romances, and creative endeavors. Here Venus loves romance and adventure. Children are a source of pride. If afflicted the opposite is true. They may be too indulgent with children or loved ones or there could be losses through speculation.

VENUS IN THE SIXTH HOUSE

When Venus is in the sixth house, health and work relationships are favored. Law, mediation, and social work may be of interest. They have high standards of health and beauty care. Here Venus loves work. If well aspected, they have good earning power and enjoy good health. They often make social contacts through work. If afflicted, they may have health problems due to neglect or overindulgence. For example, to much sugar can lead to diabetes; or too much "high living" may cause gout. Problems may crop up in relationships due to a critical attitude or a tendency to overwork at the expense of intimacy.

VENUS IN THE SEVENTH HOUSE

Venus, the love planet, is well placed in this house of relationship, as Venus loves relationships. When Venus is in the seventh house, opportunities for marriage and partnerships are many. If they choose not to marry, it is by choice. If well aspected, marriage brings happiness and often improvement in finances and sometimes health improves as well. If afflicted, there can be a tendency to indulge the partner or to be too dependent in the relationship. Sometimes there is a tendency to " remake" their partner if Venus is afflicted.

VENUS IN THE EIGHTH HOUSE

When Venus is in the eighth house, they often benefit from joint finances or inherit money. The natives love mystery and the occult. Often they are good at appraising the values of property and objects. They can be sensual and enjoy material security. Since this is the house of death, Venus "sweetens" death or makes an easy end to life. If well aspected they acquire wealth and security as they go through life, often from the marriage partner. If afflicted they can be too sensual or materialistic. They may lack discipline or have a temper when crossed. Jealousy can get in the way of intimacy if afflicted.

VENUS IN THE NINTH HOUSE

Venus in the ninth house loves to travel. They enjoy philosophy, religion and may have a talent for law or writing. They may live in a foreign land. If well aspected, marriage is happy and they enjoy good relationships with in-laws. If afflicted, they may promise more than they can deliver or spend too much on travel or cultural pursuits. Sometimes they may assist in-laws.

VENUS IN THE TENTH HOUSE

Venus in the tenth house loves the limelight. They do well in life and enjoy a good reputation. They may be socially ambitious. If well aspected a career in before the public, singing, or in the arts, or business is favored. People work with them in business not against them. Often they are financially successful. If afflicted their halo is tarnished. They may be lazy or lack motivation in work. Manipulation may get in the way of intimate relationships.

VENUS IN THE ELEVENTH HOUSE

Venus in the eleventh house is very friendly. Natives love groups and friendships. They can put people at ease with their relaxed manner. If well aspected, their friends aid them in life and may be of an artistic or wealthy nature. Group associations are favored. If afflicted, they need to be more discriminating in friendships, as there can be losses due to a tendency to be lax with friends.

VENUS IN THE TWELFTH HOUSE

Venus in the twelfth house is compassionate and kind. They have a strong spiritual side. Sometimes they devote their life to helping others in a hospital, prison or religious setting. Natives love to serve with this position. If well aspected, marriage brings spiritual happiness as well as emotional satisfaction. If afflicted, they can suffer through secret love affairs or platonic romances.

CHAPTER TWENTY-ONE

MARS IN THE HOUSES

Mars is the planet of energy, physical stamina, sexual nature. This is the motor of the chart. When Mars is in the first or tenth houses, the native may have athletic ability or a Mars career such as military, construction, engineering, or mechanics. Mars will energize the house, but it can also be disruptive. Aspects to Mars will show which direction the energy is headed. Mars likes the first and eight houses which it rules and is accidentally exalted in the tenth house, making it the best placement for Mars in the chart. Mars is less favorably placed in the seventh, fourth and second houses.

MARS IN THE FIRST HOUSE

Mars is strong in the first house. Here the fiery nature of Mars is expressed in high energy and athletic ability. Love of debate and competition are strong. If well aspected, they have a strong physical body and confidence runs high. They may excel in sports, debate, or leadership. If afflicted, they have a temper and may be rash in judgment. Sometimes they are accident prone or may run high favors.

MARS IN THE SECOND HOUSE

The firey nature of Mars is settled down in the second house. Often the native can be quite sensual and enjoy the material pleasures of life. If afflicted too sensual and can be lazy at times or stubborn. If well aspected, they are workers, but like to go at their own pace. They can excel in business and may have an interest in collecting.

MARS IN THE THIRD HOUSE

When Mars is in the third house, it stimulates the intellectual nature. Often fond of travel and naturally curious, they make good traveling companions. If afflicted, they may be sarcastic in speech or impulsive in actions. If well aspected, they have a strong investigative nature. They may have an interest in "tinkering", teaching, or travel. They usually like to be out and about.

MARS IN THE FOURTH HOUSE

Mars is weaker in the fourth house as it is opposite house of exaltation, the tenth. Mars may be slower to react and more emotional in this position. If afflicted, the native may experience emotional losses or problems with parents. Sometimes, there is a tendency to stomach troubles under affliction. If well aspected, emotional side is strong and compassionate. Relations with parent and family remain strong.

MARS IN THE FIFTH HOUSE

Mars can be playful in their fifth house. They may enjoy children, romance, gambling, and sports. If afflicted, they can be wasteful or extravagant. There may be disagreements with children or loved ones due to a combative approach to relationships. If well aspected the romantic nature is strong. They are "young at heart" and enjoy children and young people. Often they have a flair for creativity and art.

MARS IN THE SIXTH HOUSE

The fiery nature of Mars is toned down by the detailed-oriented sixth house. Often there is an interest in health and fitness. If afflicted, the general health and stamina may be weak. Sometimes there are problems with intestines or digestion. If well aspected, their health habits are good. The native is a hard worker and will rise in life through his own efforts when Mars is well aspected in the sixth house of work and health.

MARS IN THE SEVENTH HOUSE

When Mars is in the seventh house it is weaker because it is opposite the first house which it rules. Mars in the seventh house has a strong desire for marriage and partnerships. Often they choose to marry early in life. If afflicted, there can be separations, due to disagreements. If well aspected, the union is a vital one which benefits the person. Often fond of debate and may have an interest in law or art when Mars is well aspected.

MARS IN THE EIGHTH HOUSE

Mars is strong in the eighth house as it is the old ruler of the eighth house. Here Mars is strong and ambitious. These people often rise in life as Mars reaches the top of the chart by progression. When Mars is afflicted in the eighth house, the native may be too ambitious or ruthless. Sometimes they can let passions get out of control or be domineering. When Mars is well aspected in the eighth house, health and longevity improve. They may have good intuition and may inherit as the eighth house rules legacies. Good aspects here add to the overall success of chart making it favorable for rising in life through their own efforts.

MARS IN THE TENTH HOUSE

The best placement for Mars is in the tenth house. Here it is accidentally exalted by house position. These people are ambitious, hard working and purposeful in their activities. They always have a method to their work or a plan behind their decisions. If afflicted, their ambition works against them. They may have a temper or be accident prone. If well aspected, they rise in life. They are natural leaders and may have an interest in politics or Mars professions such as engineering, sports, and the military.

MARS IN THE ELEVENTH HOUSE

When Mars is in the eleventh house, friends are important. They often like group associations and may obtain leadership in one. If afflicted, they may tend to be too much of a "joiner" or friends may "sponge" off them. If well aspected, they are popular and enjoy many friendships. Friends will aid them through life.

MARS IN THE TWELFTH HOUSE

Mars can be weak in the twelfth house as it loses some of its fire. Generally, it is compassionate and sensitive in this house. If afflicted their energy may be siphoned by carrying the burdens of others. If well aspected, they may be interested in the "helping professions" such as nursing, teaching, prison work. Intuition is increased, as they access and understand the unconscious mind under strong aspects.

CHAPTER TWENTY-TWO

JUPITER IN THE HOUSES

Jupiter is the planet of good fortune. It is the largest planet in our solar system, and in astrology it is termed the greater benefic. The house in which Jupiter is placed is the department of life where you can expect the most good luck. Jupiter is strongest in the first house, where it is a born leader and in the tenth house where it bestows status. Since Jupiter rules Sagittarius, it is well placed in the ninth house, giving positive vision and a noble mind. It is weaker in the third and sixth houses which are considered to be detrimental by house position.

JUPITER IN THE FIRST HOUSE

When Jupiter is in the first house, it expands personality, making natives natural leaders. They are expansive in personality. Since they believe in themselves, others also believe in them. If well aspected, they rise in life and have a sense of abundance. If afflicted, they can have a sense of entitlement which works against them. For example, they may be argumentative or lazy.

JUPITER IN THE SECOND HOUSE

When Jupiter is in the second house, it expands material success. People with this placement have a strong sense of values and enjoy their creature comforts. They may have an interest in environment, real estate or gardening. They respect "Mother Earth". If well aspected, money keeps flowing and is circulated wisely. If afflicted, abundance comes, but may slip through their fingers.

JUPITER IN THE THIRD HOUSE

When Jupiter is in the third house, it expands mental interests. People with this position may enjoy teaching and travel, and usually get along well with relatives. They have many interests and good intelligence. If well aspected, there is gain from relatives, friends, and mental pursuits. If afflicted, there can be a tendency to let things slide or promise more than they can deliver. They may overspend on travel or education.

JUPITER IN THE FOURTH HOUSE

When Jupiter is in the fourth house, family life is expanded. Relationships with parents, particularly the mother, go well. If well aspected, the family aids them throughout life. They may inherit or gain through real estate holdings. If afflicted, the family may be taken for granted and profits from real estate squandered. They need to appreciate the source of their abundance.

JUPITER IN THE FIFTH HOUSE

When Jupiter is in the fifth house, love of life is strong. Their sense of romance and adventure is expanded. Relationships with children and young people are positive. If well aspected, children are a source of pride. They can gain through creativity or speculation. If afflicted, much is spent on children. There can be losses through extravagance and overconfidence in speculation or gambling.

JUPITER IN THE SIXTH HOUSE

Jupiter in the sixth house loves to work. Both health and work are expanded. Their job is more than just a pay check. If well aspected, they have excellent methods of organization and may benefit from the health professions. Jupiter also increases their own good health. If afflicted, health problems may come from neglect or overindulgence. There may be a tendency to be bossy with others at work or have difficulty working under supervision.

JUPITER IN THE SEVENTH HOUSE

When Jupiter is in the seventh house, marriage is expanded. These people know how to get along with others. Legal affairs, partnerships and marriage are improved. They often gain financially through marriage if well aspected. If afflicted, there can be losses due to extravagance or a tendency to overindulge the beloved.

JUPITER IN THE EIGHTH HOUSE

When Jupiter is in the eighth house, matters of the eighth house - sexuality, inheritance, death, and intuition - are expanded. These people are sensual and enjoy their sexuality. Joint finances are expanded. If well aspected, they may inherit from their parents or partner. They can use their intuition to gain financially. Often death, when it comes, is an "easy" passing. If afflicted, they may be too sensual, and joint finances including inheritances may be wasted. Death may come because of neglecting health or being too indulgent.

JUPITER IN THE NINTH HOUSE

Jupiter is at home in the ninth house of philosophy and law. They enjoy travel, religion, and culture. Their sense of vision is expanded. If well aspected, they succeed in law, travel, writing, or lecturing. There is benefit from foreign cultures. If afflicted, they may have difficulty settling into one profession. They may waste resources on unnecessary travel or overspending on cultural pursuits.

JUPITER IN THE TENTH HOUSE

Jupiter in the tenth house confers success. People with this placement may be attracted too prestigious professions, such as law or finance. If well aspected, they excel in leadership and have an abundance of confidence to inspire others. They gain financially through career or marriage. If afflicted, they may be too smug about their success or too extravagant. Success may still come, but power and prestige may be misused.

JUPITER IN THE ELEVENTH HOUSE

When Jupiter is in the eleventh house, friendships are expanded. Generally, they will obtain their hopes and wishes in life. If well aspected, these people are popular and may benefit through wealthy or influential friends. They do well in joint ventures. If afflicted, they may expect too much of friends or may give too much to their friends.

JUPITER IN THE TWELFTH HOUSE

Jupiter in the twelfth house expands the subconscious mind, making natives sympathetic and sensitive to others. Like the "Good Samaritan," they like to help for sake of being of service. Often there is an interest in psychology or mysticism. If well aspected, their intuition is their best friend. If afflicted, they may give too much and need to have some boundaries to generosity.

CHAPTER TWENTY-THREE

SATURN IN THE HOUSES

Saturn represents our lessons of life. Just as Jupiter expands, Saturn constricts. Saturn rules construction, limitations and the solid realities of life. From a psychological point of view, Saturn shows where we need to do the most emotional work. On a spiritual level, Saturn shows our soul's lesson for this lifetime. The sign it is in shows how we approach this work. For example, Saturn in Cancer feels deep emotional responsibility. The house Saturn falls in your chart, shows the department of life which needs the most work. For example, if a woman has Saturn in Cancer in the seventh house of marriage she will learn many lessons through partnerships and/or marriage. Intuitively, she knows she must take responsibility for relationships she has set in motion in order to progress on a soul level. Emotionally, it may be hard for her to give up on a relationship. She may be attracted to a Saturn-type of mate, an older, more stable person or a businessman. The sign of the cusp of the seventh house tells more about the partner. If Cancer is on the seventh house cusp, she is attracted to sensitive, home-loving men who may be emotionally dependent on her. Will the marriage be a happy one? Look to the aspects to Saturn in the seventh house. Trines and sextile bring fulfillment; squares and opposition bring difficulties. As to when these events will be set in motion, watch the transiting planets, especially the Saturn transits.

Saturn is best placed in the tenth house which it accidentally rules or the seventh where it is accidentally exalted. Saturn is weaker in the fourth opposite its house rulership or the first opposite it "exalted" house. However, Saturn in the first house can add stamina and staying power to the chart.

SATURN IN THE FIRST HOUSE

People with Saturn in the first house take life seriously, sometime there are limitations in childhood. Often these people are shy. If well aspected, they can be industrious, moral and ambitious. If afflicted, they may lack confidence and can be easily depressed. Life may have many lessons for them to overcome. Sometimes there is a tendency to overwork or be unsympathetic. Through grit and determination people with Saturn in the first house often succeed. Those with good aspects enjoy the fruits of their labor, while those under harsh aspects may achieve at the price of physical or mental well being.

SATURN IN THE SECOND HOUSE

When people have Saturn in the second house. they take matters of finance quite seriously and values quite literally. Due to their willingness to work hard and stay with projects, they are often successful in business dealings. If well aspected, they share their success which brings even greater benefit into their life. If afflicted, they may be miserly with their goods. Like Scrooge in "A Christmas Carol", they may find in the end that money is a poor substitute for love.

SATURN IN THE THIRD HOUSE

When people have Saturn in the third house, they tend to have a serious mind, and are apt to take on responsibility for their brothers and sisters. They may have an interest in science, math, or business. If well aspected, their organizational and research skills are strong. They tend to gain from teaching, writing, or sales. If afflicted, they tend to worry and may lack confidence in their own abilities. Sometimes, they are prone to depression and nervous disorders. In order to succeed, they need to cultivate a more positive and progressive attitude.

SATURN IN THE FOURTH HOUSE

When Saturn is in the fourth house, relatives, particularly the father, play a strong role in the native's life. They take matters to do with family seriously. If well aspected, the father or an older relative will aid the native through life. If afflicted, older relatives and the father may need the native's help. Family responsibilities may weigh heavily on his shoulders.

SATURN IN THE FIFTH HOUSE

When Saturn is in the fifth house, matters of pleasure, romance, and children are taken seriously. There is a great desire to do what is right in terms of lovers and children. Sometimes the first child is more serious or Saturn-like in personality. If well aspected, children bring benefits, especially later in life. These people do well in long term investments. Sometimes they may make a business of a fifth house occupation, such as dating service or a children's store. If afflicted, speculation is not advised. Children may be a source of concern and responsibility. Sometimes breaks and separations in relationships with loved ones occur. To counteract this, the native needs to be more expressive in affection and less worrisome.

SATURN IN THE SIXTH HOUSE

When Saturn is in the sixth house, matters of work and health are taken seriously. Sometimes there is an interest in the health professions for work or as a business venture. If well aspected, Saturn brings stable health and work conditions. These people make loyal employees and often enjoy gainful employment. If afflicted, health needs to be watched especially under Saturn cycles. The native may have difficulty staying with a job and the work record can be spotty. Often there is a need to improve organizational skills and to learn patience with others.

SATURN IN THE SEVENTH HOUSE

When Saturn is in the seventh house, people take marriage quite seriously. Sometimes they may marry later than average or may choose a partner for stability and industry. When Saturn is well aspected, the marriage is lasting and an aid to the individual. Partnerships are often beneficial and legal matters favored. If afflicted, the marriage can be rocky at times due to misunderstandings and clashes of wills. Legal matters are best settled out of court if at all possible.

SATURN IN THE EIGHTH HOUSE

When Saturn is in the eighth house, investments are taken seriously as are matters to do with inheritance and the occult. If well aspected, death may be due to old age. Often these people will live to inherit money from relatives. If afflicted, death may be prolonged or the result of a long illness. There may be difficulties surrounding inheritance or joint finances. It is best to get all promises in writing and not rely too much on financial help from others.

SATURN IN THE NINTH HOUSE

When Saturn is in the ninth house law, education, culture and philosophy are taken seriously. Often these people have a strong moral code. If well aspected, they may do well in law, teaching, writing or the ministry. They may have an interest in foreign lands and may assist those in Third World countries. Often, they wish to be of service in a practical way. If afflicted, they may have a tendency to a melancholy view of life or loss through foreign ventures. Legal matters should be settled out of court if at all possible. To counteract the negative aspects, a less provincial viewpoint and more progressive philosophy of life is needed.

SATURN IN THE TENTH HOUSE

When Saturn is in the tenth house, natives work hard for their living. Career is very important, and there may be an interest in business, construction, or government occupations. If well aspected, they achieve self-earned success. Often they continue to work to their benefit late in life. Sometimes this placement gives leadership and stability in work. If afflicted, their work is routine, mechanical or lackluster. There may be problems with the father and authority figures in general. Sometimes there is the proverbial "chip on the shoulder." To counteract this, natives need to be more communicative and personable so others will be willing to consider their position.

SATURN IN THE ELEVENTH HOUSE

When Saturn is in the eleventh house, people take both dreams and friendships seriously. Often they are willing to work very hard on behalf of groups or causes. If well aspected, there is benefit from older, more traditional friends. There may be an interest in working for political groups and older friends give them a step up in life. If afflicted, friendships can be draining. Either the native is too dependent on friends or vice versa. Discrimination in friendship is advisable.

SATURN IN THE TWELFTH HOUSE

When Saturn is in the twelfth house, secrets and the subconscious mind are taken seriously. Sometimes there is an interest in working in prisons or hospitals. If well aspected, the mind is deep, stable and capable of psychological and intuitive study. They are not easily fooled. If afflicted, resentment is strong, and there is a tendency to secret fears and illnesses that are hard to diagnose. To counteract these tendencies, the person needs to "air out" grievances.   Psychotherapy may be needed to alleviate physical ailments.   They are prone to depression under difficult transits.

CHAPTER TWENTY-FOUR

URANUS IN THE HOUSE

Uranus is a planet of generation since it stays about seven years in each sign. While astrologers consider the Sun, Moon, Mercury, Venus, and Mars our personal planets, and Jupiter and Saturn the karmic influences of society, Uranus, Neptune and Pluto are transpersonal planets. Dr. Gregory Bogart in his book, Astrology and Spiritual Awakening, explains the effect of the transpersonal planets:

Uranus, Neptune, and Pluto are called the "transpersonal" planets. Physically, they are outside the orbit of Saturn and symbolically they operate beyond the laws of Saturn - defined by family, tradition, and cultural institutions. These planets are often felt to disrupt and transform the structures developed by Saturn. Uranus impacts the life through rebellion, defiance, and unconventional behavior, expression of uniqueness, scientific pursuits, progressive or radical politics, and sudden changes of direction. (Gregory Bogart, Astrology and Spiritual Awakening, Dawn Mountain Press, Berkeley, CA, page 8)

Uranus is the transformer. It represents change, rebellion, and that which is unique. Uranus is strongest in the first and tenth houses, and is well placed in the eleventh house which it rules accidentally. It is weaker in the fifth which is its house of accidental fall.

URANUS IN THE HOUSES

Uranus in the first house creates an original personality. Independence and personal freedom are important to these people. If well aspected, leadership and intuitive abilities are enhanced. Good aspects indicate mechanical, engineering, or scientific abilities. If afflicted., they may be too opinionated or outspoken. Sometimes they are high strung.

URANUS IN THE SECOND HOUSE

When Uranus is in the second house, people have original ideas about finance and unique values. If well aspected, large sums of money can be made through original ideas or speculation. They may earn through Uranus trades - science, engineering, the media or astrology. If afflicted, this can lead to get rich quick schemes or financial losses.

URANUS IN THE THIRD HOUSE

Uranus in the third house makes for original minds and ones that are fond of new ideas and unusual places for travel. If well aspected, their original ideas verge on genius. Often their advice is sought, and they may excel in writing, teaching or communications. If afflicted, their ideas lack practical substance and may not be of benefit. They may cook up crazy schemes or day dream too much.

URANUS IN THE FOURTH HOUSE

When Uranus is in the fourth house, the feeling of nature is strong. They may like an original home with gadgets or antiques. If well aspected, the opposite is true. Family life may be unconventional, but it is fun. Real estate investments may benefit them. If afflicted, there can be family separations or misunderstandings. Often the natives break away from home early.

URANUS IN THE FIFTH HOUSE

Uranus in the fifth house likes to make changes. They have original ideas about having fun. They may have a high octane romance or unique children. If well aspected, their children are intelligent, independent in nature, and may possess great talent. Romances and creative endeavors flourish. If afflicted, romances may end suddenly and there can be separations from children.

URANUS IN THE SIXTH HOUSE

When Uranus is in the sixth house, health and work may fluctuate. These people do not like 9 to 5 jobs. Often they have an interest in alternative health regimes. If well aspected, they do well in Uranian occupations - science, engineering, technology, astrology, and alternative health fields. They usually maintain good health through original methods. If afflicted, they may have difficulty keeping a job because of their off beat attitude or independent nature. Illnesses may be hard to diagnose or ill health may be due to accidents or falls.

URANUS IN THE SEVENTH HOUSE

People with Uranus in the seventh house have original ideas about marriage or may be attracted to Uranian mates. They have a need for breathing space in relationships. If well aspected, partnerships flourish on their own terms. Often they marry a friend. They can have a flair for creativity and a thirst for social justice as well. If afflicted, their need for independence or an unreliable mate may lead to divorce.

URANUS IN THE EIGHTH HOUSE

When Uranus is in the eighth house, ambition is intensified. They may inherit from a friend or in an unusual way. Often they have an unorthodox approach to death and dying. If well aspected, their intuition is "on the money." Inheritance and joint finances are favored. Death, when it comes, is mercifully sudden or consciously understood and therefore not to be feared. If afflicted, death may be due to accidents or falls. There can be squabbles over inheritance. Sometimes they are attracted to unusual occult groups.

URANUS IN THE NINTH HOUSE

When Uranus is in the ninth house, the higher mental life is stimulated with unique ideas, philosophy, or cultural interests. They can be tireless in their search for truth. If well aspected, they make an excellent professor, writer or inventor. Sometimes they are not always appreciated in their time, just as prophets are not honored in their own country. If afflicted, they are too "far out" in their thinking.

URANUS IN THE TENTH HOUSE

People with Uranus in the tenth house are attracted to Uranus occupations such as science, invention, engineering, astrology, and the media. They always seem to attract attention. If well aspected, they attract positive attention and admiration. They do well in public life and may rise in life due to group associations, friends, as well as their unique talents and abilities. If afflicted, the attention may be more notoriety. Often there are changes of career as the native may be too creative or original to stay in one field or position for long.

URANUS IN THE ELEVENTH HOUSE

When Uranus is in the eleventh house, friends are important. These people are often attracted to unique or Uranian friends. If well aspected, friendships and group associations are beneficial. This increases the natives' chances of obtaining their hopes and wishes. If afflicted, friendships may not be long lasting. There can be losses through groups or clubs.

URANUS IN THE TWELFTH HOUSE

When Uranus is in the twelfth house, the subconscious mind is stimulated. Often unusual ideas and sensitivity are strong. If well aspected, the opposite is true. They may make excellent psychologists or diagnosticians. Their creative ideas may be viewed as poetry or genius. Often they have a sixth sense. If afflicted, some of their ideas may seem a little crazy to others. Illnesses may be of psychosomatic nature. Under severe afflictions, their erratic nature can put them on hold for a while in either a hospital or prison!

CHAPTER TWENTY-FIVE

NEPTUNE IN THE HOUSES

Neptune is a transpersonal planet. According to Dr. Gregory Bogart in <u>Astrology and Spiritual Awakening</u>, "Neptune operates through expansion, transcendence, religion, spirituality, development of intuitive or psychic capacities or through avoidance and escapist behavior." A well aspected Neptune brings spirituality and enlightenment; an afflicted one, escapism and suffering.

The house shows what department of life will be affected by Neptune's energy. Neptune is the strongest in the first and tenth houses and best placed in the twelfth house because Neptune is the accidental ruler of the twelfth house. Conversely, it is in its fall in the sixth house.

NEPTUNE IN THE FIRST HOUSE

Neptune in the first house brings out mystical tendencies. It makes for a sensitive, intuitive nature. If well aspected, these people make excellent physicians, nurses, ministers, psychologists, chemists, or social workers. They may have artistic or musical abilities and often are protected by their sixth sense. When it is afflicted, too much sensitivity is present which can make people prone to allergies or immune system diseases. Sometimes they are too trusting and need to do more reality testing. They may also have a tendency to avoid reality through the use of alcohol or drugs

NEPTUNE IN THE SECOND HOUSE

When Neptune is in the second house, the area of finance is a sensitive one. If well aspected, large sums of money can be earned through speculation or investment. They are often interested in charities and will use their resources wisely. If afflicted, there can be a tendency to avoid responsibility or get involved in financial schemes. There needs to be more reality testing in this area.

NEPTUNE IN THE THIRD HOUSE

When Neptune is in the third house, the mind is

sensitive and impressionable. If Neptune is well aspected, their intuition is favored. They may be creative in communication and artistic expression. Hence art, music, theater, creative writing, and psychology are favored. They just "know" when something will happen. If afflicted, they can be too sensitive and have impractical ideas about life. They may either be to fatalistic or fearful of the future. Either way, they need to learn to do some reality testing before making decisions.

NEPTUNE IN THE FOURTH HOUSE

When Neptune is in the fourth house, the area around family is a sensitive one. These people may prefer to live near water or more private locations. Their home is their sanctuary. If well aspected, the opposite is true and the parents are sensitive to the child's needs and the tie is a happy one. Family life may be idealized or intuition strong. If afflicted, there can be losses of family members through death or emotional distance. Sometimes the mother or father is lacking in emotional or financial support. If not counteracted by another caring adult or psychotherapy, these issues can leave emotional scars.

NEPTUNE IN THE FIFTH HOUSE

When Neptune is in the fifth house, areas of children, romance, and creative enterprises are sensitive ones. There may be a karmic tie to a lover or the first child. If well aspected, the opposite is true and there is benefit from art, music, theater, and poetry. Children are quite close and the romantic nature is strong. If afflicted, there is a tendency to give much to children and loved ones to the natives' detriment. Often it is hard for them to articulate their creative urges, or if creative, they may not personally benefit from their gifts.

NEPTUNE IN THE SIXTH HOUSE

When Neptune is in the sixth house, the area of health and work is a sensitive one. If well aspected, there is some glamour or inspirational nature behind work. They may have an interest in theater or medical field or photography. Often health is good and illnesses may respond to faith and nontraditional methods of healing. If afflicted, health may be delicate. They may not benefit from jobs or have unrealistic expectations of work. Often they will serve rather than lead others.

NEPTUNE IN THE SEVENTH HOUSE

When Neptune is in the seventh house, the area of marriage and partnerships is a sensitive one. Often they crave a soul mate. If well aspected, the opposite is true and marriage and partnerships are beneficial. They may marry a dream lover and often idealize the relationship. Sometimes, they are attracted to people in the medical field or of a Neptune nature. If afflicted, they may be attracted to unconventional unions. Sometimes, marriage may be one-sided, or they may be attracted to one who is not free to be with them because of previous commitments. They may suffer in relationships until they do some reality testing before they commit.

NEPTUNE IN THE EIGHTH HOUSE

When Neptune is in the eighth house, sex is romanticized and sensitivity strong. If well aspected, their romantic nature received gratification because they are sensitive and tender lovers. They may benefit through joint financial ventures and may inherit from a partner or parents. If afflicted, they may have unusual ideas about sex - either too erotic or too romantic. They may also run into trouble in terms of joint finances such as taxes or inheritances

NEPTUNE IN THE NINTH HOUSE

When Neptune is in the ninth house, the higher mind is sensitive. Often these people are vivid dreamers. If well aspected, they are prophetic in vision. Writing, philosophy and foreign travel are favored. Their creative nature is strong, as is their desire to help others. If afflicted, they may be too philosophical and lack practicality. Sometimes there are losses through foreign travel or legal matters.

NEPTUNE IN THE TENTH HOUSE

Neptune's influence is strong, as it culminates in the tenth house. Here the mystical nature is strong. Often they are attracted to Neptune's occupations which utilize their sensitivity. Many psychics and mediums have this position, as do medical people, dramatists, photographers, and artists. If well aspected the positive side of Neptune which includes compassion, spirituality and creativity, is emphasized. Natives benefit from Neptune occupations are apt to seek spiritual or artistic success over material gain. If afflicted, they may be too idealistic for the real world. Sometimes this leads to avoidance behavior such as substance abuse, retreating from reality, or emotional escapism of a guru or commune. Reality testing is important as well as seeking good psychological advice.

NEPTUNE IN THE ELEVENTH HOUSE

When Neptune is in the eleventh house, friends are a sensitive issue. They may be attracted to unusual or Neptunian friends. Often they idealize their friends. If well aspected, friends are a source of emotional support and may aid natives to achieve their hopes and wishes. These people truly can wish upon a star for success. If afflicted, the friends may be a source of concern. Either they are unreliable at times or can be a financial or emotional drain. Best advice: Offer your help once or twice, and then release them to a Higher Power.

NEPTUNE IN THE TWELFTH HOUSE

Neptune in the twelfth house is well placed in terms of house rulership. However, it gives an extra dose of sensitivity to the unconscious mind. If well aspected, their sensitive subconscious mind is a source of inspiration and help to natives. They may be attracted to the occult or the arts. Often they have a creative imagination. They may have psychic abilities and often have good psychological insight into the motives of others. People often seek their opinion. If afflicted, this can lead to mental instability and neurosis. Good Saturn aspects can offset this tendency.

CHAPTER TWENTY-SIX

PLUTO IN THE HOUSES

Pluto is the planet of transformation. Dr. Greg Bogart in <u>Astrology and Spiritual Awakening</u> explains, "Pluto transforms through catharsis, purgation of outmoded attitudes or behaviors, and the elimination of psychic impurities such as hatred, greed, resentment, or jealousy." Wherever Pluto is placed is a department of life in which there may be a tendency to be compulsive. Pluto is strongest in the first and tenth houses, and it is well placed in the eighth house, which it accidentally rules, and is weakest in the second house. Astrologers do not really know exactly where it is exalted, since we have only studied its influence since 1931. Wherever Pluto is placed, we find the finger of fate.

PLUTO IN THE FIRST HOUSE

Pluto is strong in the first house. Here, the personality takes on an intense, Scorpio nature.

They may have a sense of intuition and guarded behavior. It takes a while to get to know these people. If well aspected, they may prefer to be in charge and are often resourceful and reliable in judgment. Sometimes they make good detectives or researchers. Fate plays a strong role in their lives. If afflicted, they may be "lone wolf" types, preferring their solitude out of fear of rejection.

PLUTO IN THE SECOND HOUSE

When Pluto is in the second house, there is a compulsive nature in regard to money. If well aspected, they manage finances well. They may earn through investments and sound business practices. Fate is on their side financially. If afflicted, there can be financial losses due to poor management or a tendency to hoard money so it brings no one any happiness

PLUTO IN THE THIRD HOUSE

The mind is intense and detailed when Pluto is

in the third house. Relationships with siblings are karmic in nature. If well aspected, they enjoy research, psychology, and have a probing mind. Relationships between brothers and sisters are loyal. Good aspects promote a positive belief in fate - faith. If afflicted, these people can be sarcastic or distrustful of others. Brothers and sisters may be a source of concern

PLUTO IN THE FOURTH HOUSE

When Pluto is in the fourth house, relationships with the parents are often deeply emotional and private. If well aspected, the parents are more dutiful. Often people with well aspected Plutos in the fourth house are intuitive and may do well with real estate ventures. They believe in fate and listen to their inner voice. If afflicted, these people have disruptive childhoods and emotional insecurities

PLUTO IN THE FIFTH HOUSE

When Pluto is in the fifth house, matters of

children and romance are taken to heart. If well aspected, the opposite is true, and children and loved ones are a source of emotional benefit. In either case, they are hard to forget. If natives are without children, their intense nature may go into creative endeavors. Speculation or the stock market may be a source of wealth. They believe in Lady Luck. If afflicted, romances and relationships with children take on a compulsive or intense nature. There may be old debts to settle here, requiring time and resources.

PLUTO IN THE SIXTH HOUSE

When Pluto is in the sixth house, there may be a deep commitment to work. If well aspected, their strong work orientations bring good results. Health is improved to some extent because good aspects here strengthen the immune system. They may have an interest in Pluto occupations like psychology, prisons, recycling or research. They may feel a "calling" to their work. If afflicted, they may be compulsive about work or health, due to past difficulties

PLUTO IN THE SEVENTH HOUSE

Fate plays a role in marriage when Pluto is in the seventh house. These people may be possessive or attracted to obsessive mates. In any event, they believe in "until death do us part". For good or ill, the marriage is karmic in nature. If well aspected, the opposite is true, making the union a warm and lasting one. Marriage may bring a step up financially. Sometimes the partners seem to be able to read each other's minds. If Pluto is afflicted, there can be jealousy and suspicions which may break down the union. Often the resentment will go underground and come out in controlling behaviors.

PLUTO IN THE EIGHTH HOUSE

Pluto is at home in the eighth house. Matters of death, joint finance and intuition are taken seriously. If well aspected, the reverse is true. Often they live long and productive lives due to a good immune system. They may be resourceful and have good ideas regarding recycling, joint finances, or banking. Inheritances are favored and intuition is strong. They believe in fate and may have experiences with deja vu, precognition, or mediumship. If afflicted, these people may fear the end, making death a protracted affair. They may have to fight for their inheritance. Often there will be bouts of loneliness due to a distrustful nature. It would be best to try to resolve differences without bitterness.

PLUTO IN THE NINTH HOUSE

When Pluto is in the ninth house, there may be a destiny on a foreign shore or a strong religious or philosophical nature. If well aspected, they may benefit from other cultures and travel. Often their intense religious and philosophical views inspire others. They can have vivid dreams which may indicate their fate in life. If afflicted, people with Pluto in the ninth house may be fanatical in their ideas. Often, they have difficulty accepting new ideas or adapting to foreign countries.

PLUTO IN THE TENTH HOUSE

Pluto culminates in the tenth house. Here fate plays a strong role in their career and reputation. The need for power is intense. Often these people are executives or self employed as they do not like to work under the influence of others. If well aspected, their career is a lasting one. Power is used judiciously. Politics, corporate work, and management are favored. If afflicted they are hard workers, but lack lasting success. There can be a fall from fate. Richard Nixon's fall from grace is an example of Pluto's finger of fate.

PLUTO IN THE ELEVENTH HOUSE

Pluto in the eleventh house can bring powerful friends or lasting enemies. Friends seem fated in influence. If well aspected friends will aid them in life, often "nudging" them into power. If afflicted, friends may be a source of conflict. Often there are political rivalries. It is important to be above board in relationships. Differences of opinion are a matter of debate, not a threat to the relationship. In either case, fate plays a strong role in choice of friends.

PLUTO IN THE TWELFTH HOUSE

Here, Pluto's influence is behind the scenes. They can attract secret admirers or hidden enemies. Sometimes, they can be paranoid or suspicious. If well aspected, the opposite is true. Their sense of intuition is beneficial. They can use it as a source of protection. Often they have an interest in studying the motives of others. They could be interested in reforming others through counseling or prison work. Sometimes they not only believe in fate, but rely on it! If afflicted, they can be paranoid or suspicious. Often their behavior is compulsive in nature. Good aspects to Saturn will help stabilize their emotions.

CHAPTER TWENTY-SEVEN

NODES OF THE MOON: KEY TO THE SOUL

The nodes of the Moon represent the karmic lessons of life. The south node shows the direction the soul took in his past life. If the soul is to grow in the present life, he must pursue the opposite path, shown by the north node of the Moon. Since each lifetime is an opportunity to balance the karmic scales, an esoteric astrologer examines the nodes, including their sign, house, and aspects in order to understand the spiritual potential of the chart.

When the personal planets Venus, Mars and Mercury aspect the nodes of the Moon, the karma is usually a personal one. For example, one with Venus conjunct the north node may be popular; while a native with Venus conjunct the south node may find relationships to be more problematic. However, when the outer planets, Jupiter and Saturn, the talents are more substantial and the lessons deeper. For example, natives with Jupiter conjunct the north node may have great optimism, which can motivate groups of people to purposeful action. When Uranus, Neptune, and Pluto are involved, the karma is one of generation. For example, from the fall of 1946 to June of 1947, children were born with Neptune, the mystical planet, trine the lucky north node. This would signify a very idealistic, romantic and spiritual group coming in. Many of these children were known as "flower children", when they came of age in the late 1960's. Their placard was, "Make love, not war!"

Often souls show the influence of the south node more in their youth and only gradually grow into the influence of the north node. Those who had their south node in Sagittarius, were into philosophy and politics in their youth, but matured into the north node in Gemini. Hence many born with the north node in Gemini also had the opportunity to benefit from the new computer age of technology and communication. World opportunities often propel souls in the direction of the north node. The Moon's nodes have a cycle of 18.6. After the first nodal return, about age eighteen, childhood ends, as the native takes on the legal status of an adult. Astrologically, the native is ready to begin his soul cycle indicated by the north node.

To understand the soul cycle, look first to the sign the nodes are placed in. Later review house placement and aspects to the nodes. As a general rule, the north node, known as the dragon's head, enhances the planetary influence. The south node, called the dragon's tail, drains the energy of the planet. For example, one born with Mercury conjunct the north node would tend to be optimistic; while a native with Mercury conjunct the south node would tend to be pessimistic. Natives with Mercury conjunct the north node enjoy learning and are friendly. In opposition, those with the south node conjunct Mercury tend to be more suspicious and argumentative. Hence they can drain others around them.

As a general rule, aspects between the nodes and the Sun have an influence on the ego and personal power and vitality of the native. The north node adding to one's confidence; and the south node bringing into play negative ego forces of conceit and pride. The father or his side of the family should be close to the native, if the Sun conjuncts or trines the north node. When the Sun conjuncts or squares the south node, the opposite is true. The north node conjunct the Moon adds to the sensitivity of the native. Often they enjoy their creature comforts and pampering. When the Moon conjuncts, sextiles or trines the Moon, the mother or mother's side of the family may be close to the native. When the south node conjuncts the Moon, the native may be restless and drained emotionally. Often the relationship with the mother or the mother's family is difficult, when the south node conjuncts or squares the Moon.

The north node conjunct Venus adds to the native's popularity; while the south node conjunct Venus makes him more indulgent and sensual. Often there is a tendency to rely too much on others. When the north node conjuncts Mars, the native will have courage and leadership. However, the south node often drains Mars of its vitality and creates misplaced optimism. The north node adds to the enthusiasm of Jupiter; the south node may create a "doubting Thomas". In the case of Saturn, the north node adds to the wise deliberation and careful planning of Saturn, while the south node makes natives more fatalistic.

When nodes are conjunct any of the three outer planets, Uranus, Neptune, and Pluto, remain in place for many months. At this time whole groups will incarnate for a specific purpose. For example, when the north node joined Uranus from October 1946 to about June of 1947, a whole group of advanced souls with superb Atlantean technology energy were born. When they came of age, they brought in the computer age. When Uranus in Cancer conjoined the south node in Cancer, November 1953 through the summer of 1954, many children incarnated who had karmic relationships with their parents. Since they did get along with their families, we had an epidemic of runaways in early 1970's.

When the nodes conjunct, trine, or sextile Neptune, they enhance spiritual qualities of generations. For example, many "flower children" were born with the lucky north node trine Neptune. Children born from April to December 1991, had the north node conjunct Uranus and Neptune. Many in this group will have unusual healing and occult powers as well as enhanced spiritual awareness. When the south node conjuncts Neptune, groups may suffer from harsh world conditions. Such is the case from July 1999 to March of 2,000.

Like Neptune, Pluto influences masses of people. When the north node conjuncts Pluto, optimism prevails. However, the south node conjunct Pluto creates more pessimism and destruction. The last time Pluto joined the north node was March through August of 1994. It will conjunct the south node in March 2,002 through October 2,002 signaling mass destructions such as earthquakes and tidal waves!

North Node in Aries, South Node in Libra

Here the soul has leaned on others in the past (Libra) and now with the north node in Aries, the direction of soul growth is through individual effort. While sensitive to others, there would be a shift to a more independent attitude. In order to advance spiritually, these natives must be willing to forge a new path and become self-reliant. The personality is often strong and creative. If the north node in Aries is afflicted, the ego needs to be held in check.

North Node in Taurus, South Node in Scorpio

Natives with the south node in Scorpio have resourcefulness and passion. Their focus has been beyond the mundane. Now in this life, they must grow into their Taurus north node. The reformer soul now has to be satisfied with the status quo and learn to deal with the practical affairs of life. The north node in Taurus has solid values which lead to commercial and material success. If the north node in Taurus is afflicted, greed and sensuality can be a downfall.

North Node in Gemini, South Node in Sagittarius

In the past, these natives have had fiery Sagittarius standards. Often there has been a religious or legal lifetime dedicated to ideals. In this life, the native gains by communicating on the mundane level. Teaching, sales and writing are favored, along with mechanical abilities. Often they are interested in community affairs and happy to share their knowledge. Many of the pioneers of the computer age such as Bill Gates were born with this nodal position. If the north node in Gemini is afflicted, the soul may scatter his forces, accomplishing little in this life.

North Node in Cancer, South Node in Capricorn

The focus in the past life has been on the outer world, career and public standing. In this life he needs to be part of a family. The soul progresses by achieving emotional harmony, rather than material success. Hence, family takes precedence over career. If the north node is in the house of career, they will even tend to treat coworkers as family. Their motto is "think globally, but act locally". Often they extend their nurturance to the community. If the north node is afflicted, the family relationships may require patience and sacrifice.

North Node in Leo, South Node in Aquarius

Here the soul has been part of an Aquarian group effort in a past life. In this life, the laws of karma are balanced by expressing his personal power. The pleasures of life romance, art, and children are important to these natives. They have a firm grip on reality and can be possessive. Often these souls are born to lead. However, if the nodes are afflicted, they may lead at the expense of others or their own undoing.

North Node in Virgo, South Node in Pisces

With the south node in Pisces, attraction to mysticism and spirituality has been strong in a past life. In this life, their task is to make their vision a reality. Hence there is a strong drive to perfect ideals through work. Those with the north node in Virgo do well in business, medical field, technology, and research. Material success is enhanced with this nodal position, as they are willing to adapt to their circumstance of life. If the north node in Virgo is afflicted, the soul may find serving others has few rewards.

North Node in Libra, South Node in Aries

The soul has tended to "go it along" in past lives, as indicated by the south node in Aries. In this lifetime, soul growth comes from partnerships and group associations. They may be attracted to the legal profession, the arts or politics. Often they benefit from marriage. They wish to bring more harmony into the world around them. If the north node in Libra is afflicted, the partnerships may entail sacrifice.

North Node in Scorpio, South Node in Taurus

Here the soul enters with a background of maintaining the status quo. The last lifetime may have been centered on material comforts. In this life, the native seeks beyond every day existence. Often there is a sixth sense and a desire to reform the world. Their desire in nature is strong, making them ambitious and capable of succeeding in corporate life. If the north node in Scorpio is afflicted, the soul is quite ambitious, but receives little recognition.

North Node in Sagittarius, South Node in Gemini

This soul has been heavily involved with their immediate environment and brothers and sisters in past life. In this lifetime, the world becomes their neighborhood.

Foreign travel is favored by the north node in Sagittarius. If other aspects of their chart concur, they may even live in a foreign land for part of their present incarnation. Religion, law, philosophy and culture are important to these natives. As a fire sign, they can be quite independent and like the north node in Aries and Leo, they crave recognition. If the north node Sagittarius is afflicted, the soul may desire foreign travel and spiritual life, but will have to work for it.

North Node in Capricorn, South Node in Cancer

The south node in Cancer indicates strong family ties from a past life. Here is one who may have given much energy to the person side of life in the past. In this incarnation, soul growth comes from the outer world as indicated by the north node in Capricorn. Government, politics, and executive positions are all favored. They are able to stand alone and rule by delegated authority. If the north node in Capricorn is in the fourth house of family, they may direct their influence to become head of the family or neighborhood politics. As an earth sign, they have material success, much like the north node in Taurus or Virgo. If the north node in Capricorn is afflicted, success has its price.

North Node in Aquarius, South Node in Leo

The south node in Leo indicates one who has expressed personal power in a past life and may even have had connections with royalty. In this life the soul gains from putting aside personal expressions of power and working for the common good. The north node in Aquarius can be very democratic and idealistic. As they advance through group associations, the natives learn to "love all, serve all." Along with the north nodes in Gemini, and Libra, they value relationships. If the north node in Aquarius is afflicted, group associations may require much time and effort.

North Node in Pisces, South Node in Virgo

The south node in Virgo has had lived involved in work and service. These natives have gleaned knowledge through experience. Hence in this lifetime, the soul is given some respite, and has a deep sense of connection with the cosmic world. Often there is a desire for creative or spiritual success, rather than material pursuits. Along with the north node in Cancer and Scorpio, they value emotions and can be intuitive. If the north node in Pisces is afflicted, good deeds may be overlooked. The houses in which the nodes of the Moon are placed indicate where opportunities present in this life via the north node. The north node, which looks like a horse shoe, represents good luck. The south node represents lessons of life. With its cup-like shape, think of it as your cup of sacrifice. Usually there is a draw to affairs ruled by the house the south node is placed in. For example one with the south node in the eleventh house, the native may be fascinated by groups. However, group endeavors or friends may drain him. From a reincarnation view, he may have given much to groups and friends in the past and his destiny is to grow individually. Hence with the lucky north node in the fifth house (one of the best placements for the north node), his talents unfold through individual endeavors, artistic abilities, speculation, and children. The north node shows the direction of the soul's growth in this lifetime.

North Node in the First House, South Node in the Seventh House

This placement indicates one who was very partnership oriented in his past life. Hence in this lifetime growth is indicated in matters of the first house. Leadership, confidence, and a positive spin on life are indicated, when the nodes are well aspected. These natives are generally popular and well-liked. However, if the nodes are afflicted, there may be a tendency to rely too much on others or to give too much in relationships. This holds natives back until they learn the lesson of self-reliance. Sometimes they are inclined to marry later, or more financially secure partners.

North Node in the Second House, South Node in the Eighth House

This placement indicates one who may be very sensual or too reliant on the resources of others in a past life. Often they adopt a cautious attitude toward occult practices and may be conservative in their approach to joint finances. Soul growth in this lifetime comes from being grounded and practical. Money, strong values, and practical matters are favored when these nodes are well aspected. However, if the nodes are afflicted, natives may acquire money, but there may be financial losses or tax difficulties.

North node in the Third House, South Node in the Ninth House

This placement indicates one given studies of the higher mind - religion, law or cultural affairs. They may well have had a religious or idealistic past life. Often they feel compelled to help others acquire a deeper understanding of moral values. Soul growth in this life time comes from working with the lower or intellectual mind. These natives are good communicators, teachers, writers, or salesmen. They keep up with current events and maintain an interest in local matters. When the nodes are well aspected they are known for their abilities and enjoy good relationships with siblings. However, if the nodes are afflicted, in-laws (ninth house) may present problems. Care should be taken in foreign travel.

North Node in the Fourth House, South Node in the Tenth House

This placement indicates a public past life.

They may have been strongly involved in career, politics, or status. In this life time there may be little interest in accommodating the public by compromising on professional principles. While they may obtain success in the long run, soul growth in this life time comes from energy spent on home and family. If the nodes are well aspected, relationships with parents, especially the mother is warm and helpful and often indicates happiness through family life. Their home may be a meeting place for social activities. However, if the nodes are afflicted, there may be an interest in career at the expense of family. Home matters may become draining. Their reputation may suffer under difficult transits, as they may experience a fall from grace.

North Node in the Fifth House, South Node in the Eleventh House

This placement indicates one who has given a great deal to group endeavors and lived through others. These natives may have had idealistic or religious past lives. In this lifetime, the direction of soul growth is through individual growth. If the nodes are well aspected, the natives are talented, creative, and inventive. Matters of the fifth house - romance, children, and the arts - are lucky for them. They enjoy keeping up with the arts and current trends in entertainment. Often children, especially the first child is a source of pride. However, if the nodes are afflicted the opposite is true. Children, while dearly loved, may be a source of concern. Friends and groups may drain the native. They need to examine carefully the purpose and intent of groups, they join.

North Node in the Sixth House,
South Node in the Twelfth House

This placement indicates one who has had a contemplative past life or one away from the world. In this life, there is a strong draw to business and interest in health. When the nodes are well aspected, natives are successful due to hard work and enjoy good health habits. They are often popular with their boss. During illness, they reach out for good medical treatment. However, if the nodes are afflicted, there may be periods of worry and disillusionment from relying too much on others. Severe afflictions to the south node in the twelfth house without any aspects to Saturn may indicate mental instability.

North Node in the Seventh House, South Node in the First House

This placement indicates one who had a strong sense of self in a past life. Often there is a tendency to be a bit pessimistic at times as the south node may devitalize the ego. They tend to be cautious and somewhat reserved in manner. Women with this nodal position may be slow to adopt the hottest fashions, preferring to see what remains in style for the long season. Often natives are tactful and diplomatic. Marriage and partnerships seem fated. When the nodes are well aspected, natives marry well and benefit from group association. However, if the nodes are afflicted, there is a tendency to take partnerships for granted.

North Node in the Eighth House, South Node in the Second House

This placement indicates one who has been too concerned with money and personal power in a past life. In this life time growth comes relying on others, inheritance and joint finances, as well as those matters beyond the material plane. When the nodes are well aspected, these natives may be quite intuitive. Work in banking, recycling, and corporations may be favored. Often they gain from inheritances. However, if the nodes are afflicted, joint resources such as inheritances may be hoarded or a source of concern. These natives may also be prone to extravagance, conceit, or excesses.

North Node in the Ninth House, South Node in the Third House

This placement indicates one who has been involved with the lower, intellectual mind, siblings, and neighborhood affairs. In this life, soul growth come from expanding his horizons. Hence religion, foreign countries, and relationships with in laws are favored. They are interested in current philosophies or cultural trends. When the nodes are well aspected, natives may benefit from, foreign travel, even residing in a foreign land. While intellectual, their minds are stimulated by philosophy and religion, especially as they mature. However, if the nodes are afflicted, there can be too much intellectual pride or difficulties with siblings. Care should be taken to read the fine print before signing documents.

North Node in the Tenth House,
South Node in the Fourth House

This placement indicates one who has been very much involved with home and family in a past life. There are often karmic ties to the parents. In this life soul growth may come from the outer world, with success with the public. These natives are often well-liked in their community. They will rise in life through their own efforts when the nodes are good aspects to the nodes. There may be a step up in status due to marriage or a prestigious career. However, if the nodes are afflicted, they may become reclusive.

North Node in the Eleventh House, South Node in the Fifth House

This placement indicates one who has been very much involved in developing their personal life in a past life. Often there are frustrations with children and or romantic ties - karmic debts. In this life time soul growth comes from giving impersonally to others. These natives find it easy to gain rapport with others. When the nodes are favorably aspected, groups and friendships are favored. Often friends will go out of their way to assist them. However, if the nodes are afflicted, they receive help from others, but do not reciprocate, creating losses in relationships.

North Node in the Twelfth House, South Node in the Sixth House

This placement indicates one who has been involved in practical work and health in a past life. In this life time, soul growth comes from contemplation. Often these natives are very compassionate. When the nodes are well aspected the spiritual subconscious mind is strengthened giving them intuitive insight. Since they have worked hard for others in the past, they will receive help from spiritual sources in this life. Often they have a "guardian angel" watching out for them. However, if the nodes are afflicted, they need to guard against health, as they may neglect exercise and diet regimes. They may also experience a lack of popularity at work during stressful transits.

CHAPTER TWENTY-EIGHT

ASPECTS TO THE SUN

The Sun is the basic life force, which psychologists call the ego. The life force represents authority and the male principle - the father, male energy or the husband in a woman's chart. They are all interrelated. for example, a man may model his male energy after his father. A woman may unconsciously choose a husband who is like her father. Often both men and women relate to authority figures in the same way they related to their parents.

The Sun also represents pride, honor, leadership, physical strength and vitality. In terms of health, the Sun shows the basic life force and the heart. Negative aspects can foreshadow cardiovascular diseases. Negative aspects may also signal lower vitality, accidents, or poor metabolism. For example, the Sun opposite or square Jupiter shows a tendency to overdo or to be lazy at times. In either case, the energy is out of sync.

Often the person likes rich foods such as ice cream or French fries, but does not metabolize fat well. Overindulgence in these foods can add weight, clog the arteries, or cause gout. Eventually, without intervention such as a positive change in diet and exercise, more serious ailments such as heart disease can develop. Astrologically, the antidote to Jupiter affliction is Saturn - discipline.

In terms of health, afflictions to the Moon may cause worry and emotional disorders. Afflictions to Mercury may cause mental or nervous disorders. Mars afflictions can result in overdoing, which leads to muscle strain or accidents. With Venus afflictions, sugar or "sweets" can lead to health problems, and the person may neglect proper diet and exercise. Often Saturn ailments are chronic and more serious in nature. Since Saturn rules the bones and teeth, they should be watched carefully. Depression is often a key factor in Saturn ailments. Saturn also indicates blockages of some kind.

With the higher octave planets, like Uranus, diagnosis may be more difficult. Look to the glandular system for imbalances. Uranus afflictions often curb the ego in some way. Sometimes accidents force the native to be more reflective. Since there is a tendency to overdo, adrenal glands and kidneys should be watched. When the Sun (heart) and Uranus (circulation and electrical system of the body) are out of balance, watch the transits for times when a person may be prone to stroke or heart attack.

With Neptune afflictions, sensitivity can be an issue. Watch for allergies, poisoning, or addictions. Often the vitality of the body is being sapped. Dr. Edith Fiore, leading psychotherapist, feels possession may be a factor in energy leaks. With Neptune affliction without stabilizing Saturn aspects, mental illness, addictive behavior, and "out of body" experiences may afflict the native. With Neptune secret fears abound. Antidote: reality therapy and a sober lifestyle.

Pluto is the trickiest planet to diagnose. Afflictions to Pluto could be due to obsessive-compulsive characteristics, glandular imbalances often resulting from over drive, or secret vices. Sometimes the native may be a victim of a crime or has criminal tendencies. Here possession

313

may play a role - if there are no stabilizing aspects. More common, is the need to put one's life in balance and work with destructive emotions of anger, hate, and greed. An excellent psychology book on this subject is You Can't Afford the Luxury of a Negative Thought. Here hope and optimisim is given as an antidote to diseases caused by stress and negative thought.

Aspects to the Sun will either strengthen or weaken its influence. In general, conjunctions add strength. With the opposition aspect, there is tension. With the square, obstacles are present. The best aspect is the trine which gives the most efficient and positive flow of energy. The next best is the sextile which is rally half a square. Opportunity is waiting with the sextile, but you have to open the door.

Esoterically, negative aspects teach what we did not learn in previous incarnations. In this sense, our enemies really do become our teachers. Positive aspects, rewards for having used the energy judiciously in past lives, give a sense of faith. For example, a native may have the Sun opposite

Neptune, indicating the father's influence is weak or absent. Later in life she may attract a husband who is weak or too dependent on her. If the lesson is still not learned, she may have a son who is weak, perhaps an alcoholic. The universe will keep providing opportunities to learn the lesson of the Sun opposite Neptune until the native looks deep inside and makes changes. The universe is insisting she stand up for herself. Once this lesson is learned, she can do some reality testing and may decide to forgive her "lost" father, not allow her husband to sponge off her, or her son to manipulate her empathic nature.

Positive aspects make us strong if we use them. For example, if a man has the Sun trine Jupiter, he has a sense of optimism, takes pride in his work, and may be a leader in his field. This many may have been a monk in a past life and helped others, so in this life other people will give him a step up. Often his father and brothers are a help to him in life.

Most people have a mix of positive and negative aspects in the chart. For example, a man could have both the Sun opposite Neptune and the Sun trine Jupiter and both aspects would apply. He may lose his father emotionally through divorce when he is ten (Sun opposite Neptune), yet an uncle may step in to raise him (Sun trine Jupiter) and help him to obtain an education. To understand the particulars, look at the house place and signs the planets are in as well as the aspects they make. Then the transiting planets will time the events such as the time of the parents' separation.

SUN AND MOON

SUN CONJUNCT THE MOON

This is a very important aspect. The Sun is the basic self, and the Moon is the emotional principle. Their combined influence is quite beneficial unless it is an "old Moon". If it is an old Moon - the Moon has not made the conjunction or is lower in degree than the Sun, then there is unfinished business. Esoterically, it could be the person's last life was cut short.

The new Moon conjunction is beneficial. Here

the outer (the Sun) and the inner (the Moon) are merged, giving strength of purpose. Here the individual feels integrated and "ready to go". Initiative is strong and he may be a pioneer or self starter. Basically, he knows himself and is able to go forward without internal conflicts.

SUN OPPOSITE THE MOON

This is a full Moon aspect. Just like the full Moon, these people attract attention. They may have a dramatic side to their personality. Their inner nature (Moon) may be quite different from their outer side (the Sun). Mediation, journal keeping or psychotherapy may be helpful to get in touch with the inner nature.

SUN SQUARE THE MOON

Here the Sun (ego) is in conflict with the inner nature (the Moon). These people find it hard to know themselves. Often they think they want one thing and then realize they are not satisfied. They may have to find a way to give both the Sun and the Moon some expression. For example, a woman with the Sun in Aries may have the need to exert leadership in the outer world, yet with Moon in Cancer want to be home to nurture her family. She could choose to work from her home or work part-time.

SUN TRINE THE MOON

This is the best position. These people know what they want and can be successful in their effort. They are at peace with themselves. Often they have a sense of themselves which translates into leadership or executive ability.

SUN SEXTILE THE MOON

Like the trine, this aspect promotes inner harmony and self love. It is not as charismatic or dynamic as the trine.

SUN AND MERCURY

SUN CONJUNCT MERCURY

The Sun conjunct Mercury strengthens the mind.

Often these people have a good mind, but may lack objectivity since the Sun, the ego, is on top of the mind, Mercury. They are too close to the forest to see the trees. Often they are quick to form opinions. To counteract this tendency they must train their minds to listen carefully to others before forming opinions.

SUN OPPOSITE MERCURY

When the Sun is opposite Mercury, people may lack tact in some aspects and may be argumentative or lack concentrated effort. Sometimes they are scattered or talkative.

SUN SQUARE MERCURY

Here ego gets in the way of good judgment. These people are opinionated and quick to judge. Often they are sure they are right and they like to argue the point. Since "pride goeth before a fall", they need to think before they speak.

SUN TRINE MERCURY

Leadership and reason go hand in hand. The mind is reasonable and optimistic in nature. These natives are good communicators and may have teaching, sales, or writing ability. People often look to them for advice.

SUN SEXTILE MERCURY

Sun sextile Mercury is similar to the trine and as powerful. They have good logical minds, but not as much charisma.

SUN CONJUNCT VENUS

Venus gives refinement to the Sun, making it artistic and interested in beauty. Often these people enjoy dressing well. The Sun is the ego and Venus is love, so their motto is "I like me". They also have gentleness and kindness to their nature.

SUN OPPOSITE VENUS

Here the ego (Sun) and Venus (love) are at odds. Often these people do not feel loved and may have an excessive need for attention, money, or jewelry to feel loved. Until they love themselves, relationships may suffer. Either they are too dependent or too demanding. Often there is genuine artistic talent, but they lack the discipline to develop it.

SUN SQUARE VENUS

These natives feel unloved and may be "thumb suckers". They are prone to tantrums and complaints to get attention. The problem is within them. They desperately need to feel loved, yet they push people away by their behavior. For example, they may wear too much perfume or be theatrical in speech. Self esteem issues need to be addressed. They may have an interest in the arts and are often generous to friends.

SUN TRINE VENUS

This is a lucky aspect - the two benefic planets, Sun and Venus in trine. These natives have talent and charm. Often their pleasant personality will draw many friends. They tend to see the good in others and wish them well. Music, art and theater may be of interest. People are drawn to them and love relationships are favored. They may excel in Venus occupations such as the arts, public relations, and retail.

SUN SEXTILE VENUS

This is similar to the trine but not as strong. Artistic talent is present, but they may have to cultivate it more. Often they must work to achieve harmonious relationships and financial success. They enjoy the "sweet" things of life.

SUN CONJUNCT MARS

The Sun conjunct Mars confers stamina and athletic ability. Often there is a strong determination and leadership. Sometimes these people can be strongwilled or aggressive, characteristics of athletes or leaders.

SUN OPPOSITE MARS

Here the two fiery planets work opposite each other, creating friction. Often there is temper and rashness. These people are in a hurry and can attract minor mishaps. In a woman's chart, she may be attracted to strong, but temperamental, men. Like the conjunction it can give athletic ability.

SUN TRINE MARS

When the Sun trines Mars, the vitality is strong. Often athletic ability, including dance and physical fitness is present. These natives make good leaders as they are decisive. Often health is good. In a man's chart, he may prefer to work with other men. In a woman's chart, she is attracted to strong men in her life.

SUN SEXTILE MARS

This aspect is similar to the trine, but not as strong. For example, athletic ability is present, but people must work at maintaining it. They have strength of purpose, but are not as strong in leadership as the trine.

SUN CONJUNCT JUPITER

Here two benefices meet. The Sun's vitality and confidence is expanded by Jupiter. Often there is an ennobling influence. These natives are helpful, optimistic and tolerant by nature. They enjoy life and often like to indulge in the good things of life. Usually they are well liked.

SUN OPPOSITE JUPITER

These natives want to be popular and often will go out of their way to help others. However, they may try too hard or promise too much. They like to do things in a big way and have a lot of pride. They may either do too much or too little. While they are well liked, they may not always get the attention or the respect they truly desire, unless they come to terms with their inner insecurities.

SUN TRINE JUPITER

This is one of the luckiest aspects people

could have in a chart - two benefic planets in trine. These natives "feel" lucky. Often they have confidence and are willing to work with those in authority to improve themselves and others. They are generous and wise in giving. When they climb the ladder of success, they do not neglect those on the rungs beneath them. Leadership, executive, or political ability may surface as they go through life. In a woman's chart, men may aid her in life.

SUN SEXTILE JUPITER

This aspect also gives luck, but not as much. The natives are positive and willing to work for their goals. They are kind to others and can work well with those in authority. Often they rise in life through their own efforts.

SUN CONJUNCT SATURN

Saturn puts the brakes on the Sun. Often it makes for a more serious outlook on life. These people take their responsibilities seriously and work hard to achieve their goals. Sometimes, they are too serious and need to "lighten up" a bit.

SUN OPPOSITE SATURN

Here Saturn blocks the Sun's natural vitality. Often there can be disappointments due to struggles with the father or people in authority. These natives are very sensitive to rejection. They may desire success but fear of failure stands in their way. They need to have a game plan before they begin a project and more faith in themselves and others to counteract the negative influence of Saturn.

SUN SQUARE SATURN

When the Sun squares Saturn, there is an inner lack of confidence. Sometimes this is due to a poor relationship with the father or a lack of encouragement in early life. These people tend to see life as a struggle. They may be sober or judgmental in nature and lack vitality. Sometimes they attract demanding or unsympathetic parents or bosses. Other times the demands may come from within. Often they feel guilty about enjoying themselves or believe themselves unworthy of success. This lack of confidence can lead to depression. To counteract this tendency, they need to pace themselves, get plenty of rest and exercise, and practice positive thinking, then their innate discipline will be an aid to them in life.

SUN TRINE SATURN

These natives are serious, hard working, and have a strong sense of duty. They dislike wasting your time or theirs. Often they accomplish much in life through willpower and determination. Older people (Saturn) may aid them in life. They are capable of deep study and may have an interest in science or math.

SUN SEXTILE SATURN

The influence is the same as the sextile, but not as strong. They are determined and disciplined, but they need to work more at maintaining it. This aspect acts as a stabilizing force.

SUN CONJUNCT URANUS

Uranus livens up the Sun with its electrical energy. Often the Sun takes on an Aquarian flavor, making it more tolerant, friendly, and inquisitive. People with the Sun conjunct Uranus are noticed because of their unique nature. They definitely have their own style and enjoy it. These natives make an impression on others!

SUN OPPOSITE URANUS

When the Sun is opposite Uranus, people can be egocentric and demanding. They sometimes attract attention through negative means. They can have a sense of entitlement and at times a temper. In a man's chart, the male energy may be too strong. In a woman's chart, she may be too assertive or attract aggressive men who can become a source of conflict. To soften this aspect they must pick their battles careful. Some things are just not worth fighting over - even if these natives feel they are right!

SUN SQUARE URANUS

The Sun square Uranus gives the same high energy of the conjunction and opposite, but there is more tension. Here the ego may be out of control or inflated. Leadership is still strong, but others may resent the native. Sometimes they can be tyrants. Hasty actions and temper work against these individuals. They should count to ten or better yet a hundred before speaking!

SUN TRINE URANUS

When the Sun trines Uranus, it brings out a zest for life and a sense of purpose. These people have an abundance of energy. What others see as a problem, they see as a challenge to be mastered. Their positive attitude makes them natural leaders, explorers, and inventors. They are fun to be around and make friends easily.

SUN SEXTILE URANUS

The Sun sextile Uranus is similar to the trine,

but not as strong. They are creative and inventive, but have to work to sustain their efforts.

SUN CONJUNCT NEPTUNE

Neptune softens the influence of the Sun, making it less focused and more gentle. Often these people are idealistic and creative. They prefer the softer side of life and may be attracted to the helping professions or the arts. Sometimes they need to have more confidence in themselves.

SUN OPPOSITE NEPTUNE

Karmic issues are played out with the father or male influence when Neptune opposes the Sun. Sometimes the father is physically or emotionally absent. Natives can have a tendency to lose faith in men or take on too much responsibility for others with this aspect. Often these people have suffered some in life and are kind hearted. They need to learn to control their sensitivity by doing some reality testing before placing their trust in others, otherwise, they can be victimized by others. Creativity and kindness are important to them.

SUN SQUARE NEPTUNE

These people are often shy and sensitive like the opposition, but more so. They need to be more objective. In man's chart, he may need to work on leadership and assertion. In a female chart, she may attract men who are not what they seem. Advice from objective friends, some reality testing or psychotherapy can help with this aspect. Often these people are gentle and kind, but may give more than they receive.

SUN TRINE NEPTUNE

The Sun trine Neptune makes for a gentle soul. These people are idealistic, kindly, and sensitive. They prefer dealing with others in a non-confrontive manner. They can be visionaries, poets, musicians, and actors. Often they are interested in meditation and spiritual practices. They are natural caretakers and may be attracted to professions such as social work or the ministry. Their intuition is strong, and they are rarely wrong in their first impressions. Often they have a mystique about them which makes them memorable.

SUN SEXTILE NEPTUNE

The Sun sextile Neptune is similar in energy, but not as intense in mystique or intuition. These people are gentle and kindly, often doing small favors for others. They are artistic and creative, but need to work at developing their talents.

SUN CONJUNCT PLUTO

Whatever Pluto touches, it intensifies for better or worse. Here the Sun takes on a Scorpio influence, with passion intensity, and willfulness. Often they take an all or nothing position on matters, preferring either to work hard or not at all. Pluto heightens the Sun's energy and makes it more compulsive in nature.

SUN OPPOSITE PLUTO

When the Sun is opposite Pluto, the compulsive

nature of Pluto works against the Sun. For example, they may have a father who is too demanding. Often they are trying to prove themselves. These people are overdoers. Their compulsive and rigid behavior works to distance them from others, and sometimes they feel isolated and use overwork to fill their lives. They need to be more flexible in attitude and learn to tune in more to others in order to avoid the trap of isolation and compulsive behavior.

SUN SQUARE PLUTO

Pluto is even more compulsive and intense with this aspect. Often isolation and compulsive behavior bring out a combative attitude. These people are "from Missouri". They can also isolate themselves and have a suspicious streak. Often they are "lone wolves". To overcome these tendencies, they need to be more flexible, less suspicious, and willing to listen more carefully to others. They don't really want to be alone, but they are afraid of the pain of exposure, ridicule, or rejection. Often this goes back to a "toxic" parent. A supportive grandparent, friend, or therapist can help overcome their lack of trust.

SUN TRINE PLUTO

This is a second chance aspect. Here the Sun (ego) gets a cosmic gift from Pluto. They are prophetic and have an excellent sense of timing. Since they like to be thorough and have an abundance of energy, they often rise as they go through life. A mentor may come in to assist them. These natives make excellent psychologists, diagnosticians, psychics, scientists, detectives, and researchers, as they love to probe the unknown.

SUN SEXTILE PLUTO

Like the Sun trine Pluto, it gives a second opportunity, but the person has to ask for it. This is less dynamic in energy, but just as protected as the trine aspects. They also do well in Pluto profession psychology, research, and detective work. When in doubt, they should sleep on the matter, for their dreams are prophetic.

CHAPTER TWENTY-NINE

ASPECTS TO THE MOON

If "the Sun and Moon are the eyes of God", the Moon represents the receptive side of the Soul while the Sun is its active nature. Thus, the ancients termed the Moon's energy feminine and the Sun's energy masculine. In terms of precious metals, the Moon rules silver and the Sun gold. The Moon also governs pearls in a man's chart, the Moon governs his relationship with his wife as well as his mother and daughter. In a woman's chart, it shows her feminine nature and her relationship with her mother, as well as her own mothering nature. If the Moon is well aspected, nuturance will be natural. For example, if a woman has the Moon trine Jupiter, her relationship with her mother will be a warm and happy one. Later, she will take on a warm feminine nature and be able to mother her own children well. On the other hand, if she has the Moon square Saturn, relations with her mother will be problematic. Her mother may be emotionally absent or a resentful parent. This may cause the young woman to question her own worth and become defensive. Later when she has children of her own, she's likely to duplicate her own childhood, unless there has been some therapeutic intervention by a warm father, wise grandmother, a mentor, or a therapist.

In addition to the feminine nature, the Moon represents the subconscious mind and habit patterns. Often we are not even aware of many of our internal emotions, such as hidden guilt or anger. If individuals wish to grow, they need to weed out these destructive emotions. It is important to look at your childhood. What messages did your parents give you growing up? How happy were your mother and father? Did they love and value each other? Did you feel loved and valued as a child? It is normal to have mixed emotions, as few had a perfect childhood. In fact, John Bradshaw, author of Healing the Shame that Binds Us, says the majority of us grew up in dysfunctional families. Look at the Moon's aspect to see how you deal with these feelings. By studying the aspects to the

Moon, you can be more aware of subconscious habit patterns - the first step in dealing with them.

The Moon also represents the public. If people are to be recognized by the public, there must be a favorable aspect to the Moon, or the Moon on the ascendant or midheaven. Individuals with well aspected Moons can deal well with the public because they are naturally expressive. People whose Moons are negatively aspected may be shy or distrustful of the public.

In terms of health the Moon represents emotions, the stomach and the breasts. Affliction can bring problems in these areas. Watch the transits to see when these issues are most likely to manifest. The Moon also rules the astral body. When an amputee feels pains in his "phantom" limb, he is picking up distress in the astral body. When the Moon is afflicted, astral disturbances may apply - such as phantom pains, possession, and emotional imbalances. Alternative therapies, such as acupuncture, herbs, Reiki, and hypnosis may provide a cure.

With Moon-Mercury affliction, the mind is the key factor. Often the memory and nervous system are

337

involved. Sometimes the mind is in one place and the body in another, making it difficult for people to remember appointments or focus on a treatment plan. With Moon-Mars or Moon-Uranus afflictions, there is a tendency to overwork the emotions. Rest, mental and physical, should be part of the treatment. Often with Moon-Venus afflictions, histrionics, sugar or indulgence may play a role in the problem. Since the patients usually enjoy attention, they are more than interested in seeking advice. Following through is another matter.

More chronic illnesses are seen with Moon Saturn afflictions. When the Moon squares or opposes Saturn, the negative effect is enhanced because the Moon chases Saturn by progression as well. Here depression, lack of vitality, and fear may lead to physical or mental deterioration. Often good aspects to Saturn from other planets will give the discipline needed to stay with treatment. Faith and positive affirmations are also helpful.

With Neptune Moon afflictions, stress, imagination, fear, and, in severe cases, possession may be a factor. This is a classic indication of a tendency to addictions - using food, alcohol, lovers, drugs, or cults to fill up their lives. Watch also for glandular imbalances. When people have Moon Pluto afflictions, they may also have glandular imbalances. However, they need to express their feeling side more. Their suspicious nature makes it difficult to trust others. This leads to emotional armoring and obsessive behavior, and addictions. Their ailments may be chronic or difficult to diagnose. Watch also for manipulation and control issues to surface in treatment. The flip side is these people can also be reformers. Once they are "cured", they will often dedicate their lives to helping others.

MOON CONJUNCT VENUS

Here Moon is sweetened by the influence of Venus, making it more refined. There is an interest in domesticity, decorating, and homemaking. Venus also can bestow beauty on the Moon Sometimes the Moon can be indulgent in nature when combined with Venus.

MOON OPPOSITE VENUS

When the Moon is opposite Venus, natives may feel unloved or deprived of attention. Hence, they often seek more than their share of attention. Their cloying sweetness detracts from their personality, and they are apt to feel jealous if slighted. Sometimes, they turn to sweets for comfort when under emotional distress. This may have a negative impact on their waistline and health.

MOON SQUARE VENUS

This aspect is similar to the opposition but more intense. Natives with this aspect may feel unappreciated. Their mother may have had difficulty in expressing affection. Low self esteem may cause them to overdo with sweet things - sugar, jewelry, or cologne. Often people would like them better if they were just themselves.

MOON TRINE VENUS

The relationship with the mother is usually a happy one. In a man's chart, the wife is attractive and loving. These natives express affection and kindness to others. They are often well liked, creative, and good with the public. Careers in retail, real estate, beauty and health care, as well as music, art, and the stage, are favored with this aspect.

MOON SEXTILE VENUS

This aspect is similar to the trine, but not as fortunate. Often there is a good relationship with the mother, wife or women in general, but not as much charisma or financial success.

MOON CONJUNCT MARS

The gentle Moon conjunct fiery Mars can create a strong emotional nature. In fiery signs, this can give a temper. In water signs, these people are too sensitive and sentimental. They often worry about loved ones. When the conjunction is in earth signs, they worry too much about material concerns. In an air sign, there is a tendency to be very opinionated. In general, the Moon is strong in feeling nature, but may lack some subtlety or discretion.

MOON OPPOSITE MARS

Here the emotions (Moon) are at odds with actions (Mars). Often natives are moody and restless. They may be on the move a lot but with few results. These people are sensitive to criticism, yet ready to go to battle on minor matters. They need to choose their battle and control their tempers.

MOON SQUARE MARS

When the Moon is square Mars, emotions (Moon) get stirred up (Mars). Natives may be argumentative or too emotional. Often this is an attention-seeking ploy. Often they can be moody or restless in nature.

MOON TRINE MARS

Here the emotions and energy of the body are in sync. Often natives have an interest in health routines and can make good nutritionists or cooks. They utilize intelligent planning to reach their goals and are hard workers. This aspect often shows mechanical or writing ability.

MOON SEXTILE MARS

When the Moon sextiles Mars, the energy is similar to the trine, but not as powerful. Mechanical and writing ability may be present with proper study. Health habits are usually good.

MOON CONJUNCT JUPITER

Here the emotional nature of the Moon is expanded. These people can be fun to be with for they are warm and enthusiastic. Usually their relationship with their parents, particularly the mother is a good one. They also get along well with women. If anything is negative about this aspect, it is they may overdo.

MOON OPPOSITE JUPITER

The Moon or emotions are too inflated with Jupiter's leadership and positive energy. This can lead to pride. These natives like to be right and are willing to argue the matter. Often they are naturally generous and like the conjunction, they may be overdoers. Generally, little harm comes from this aspect.

MOON SQUARE JUPITER

Jupiter expands and stirs up the Moon's feeling nature. These individuals are natural entrepreneurs. Often they have an ego and may be controlling. They need to learn to delegate responsibilities more and lessen "strong arm" tactics which only give limited results. They are usually well likes, if they watch their opinionated nature. Blood pressure may run high due to stress of overwork. Sometimes, the opposite is true, and the native may lack motivation and be lazy about his health.

MOON TRINE JUPITER

Happy relations with family especially with the mother, is often seen with this aspect. These individuals are nature "people people." They enjoy good public relations and may excel in sales, publishing, corporate work, real estate, and dealings with the public, such as advertising. Natives enjoy entertaining especially in their homes, which are apt to be large.

MOON SEXTILE JUPITER

The Moon sextile Jupiter is similar to the sextile, but not as strong in energy. The native is likable and good with people, but may not benefit as much from the public as the one with the trine.

MOON CONJUNCT SATURN

Here the emotions are suppressed by Saturn. These natives tend to take life seriously and may put a damper on the enthusiasm of others. Sometimes they are depressed themselves, but do not realize it. Positive aspects to other planets can give them the vitality they need. The mother or father may have been sick or demanding, making them feel life is hard work. They need to cultivate a more optimistic view of life.

MOON OPPOSITE SATURN

When the Moon is opposed by Saturn, emotions are blocked. Often the native is shy or too restrained in expression. Sometimes, the mother is lacking emotional support. For example, a parent may die or is emotionally unavailable. Often the native wishes to be close to others but is afraid to get close. Social isolation can lead to loneliness.

MOON SQUARE SATURN

The Moon square Saturn is similar to the opposition, but more chronic because the progressed Moon "chases" Saturn. Here the emotional restriction is internalized rather than left in childhood. The mother may lack sympathy with the child who has Moon Square Saturn, which in tern makes the child take on more than his share of responsibility. Often natives are shy, lonely, or isolated emotionally. They want others to be close, but emotionally push others away. Continued isolation can lead to depression. A more optimistic or flexible attitude can counteract this tendency. They may need some help in "reparenting" themselves.

MOON TRINE SATURN

When the Moon is trine Saturn, the mother was usually a good, but conservative, parent. Often the upbringing included a structure, disciplined environment which the person internalized to her benefit. If She chooses to become a mother or wife, she will be a dutiful one. In a man's chart it attracts a helpful and loyal mate. Often these natives are conscientious and well organized. They may have executive ability and will slowly make their way to the top. Their strength lies in their ability to finish and stay with their projects, so they get the benefit of their labors.

MOON SEXTILE SATURN

This is similar to the trine, but not as beneficial. These people work hard and are organized, but may not be as disciplined or dedicated to the work or family. However, as with the trine, if they stay with their projects, they will get results.

MOON CONJUNCT URANUS

When the Moon (emotions) conjunct Uranus (dynamic energy), people like to be noticed. They are often friendly, but in a detached manner. Uranus increases their emotional independence. However, they are quick to react and may have a temper.

MOON OPPOSITE URANUS

When the Moon is opposite Uranus, the mother may be too independent or detached at times. These natives need attention. If they do not get it in a positive way, they will resort to negative behavior. At times their temper may get out of hand. They have a strong need for adventure and are often restless. Domestic relations may be unstable until they can learn to settle down. They need to be more aware of the needs of others. Men with this aspect attract dynamic, independent women.

MOON SQUARE URANUS

Emotions run high when the Moon squares Uranus. There may be problems with the mother or family.

These natives may run high favors and are prone to nervous disorders. They also have a temper when crossed. They need to pace themselves, as they are prone to accidents. Often they are too self centered, and they need to work on their listening skills and really try to put themselves in the other person's place. Women with this aspect tend to be high strung. Men with this aspect may exhibit a " macho" streak, taking unnecessary risks.

MOON TRINE URANUS

The Moon trine Uranus gives a vibrant personality, capable of attracting attention in a positive way. These natives get noticed without any special effort on their part. They are naturally friendly and often have a sense of humor. They enjoy change and find travel relaxing. The relationship with the mother is usually good. Women with this aspect are interested in their children's education and are encouraging mothers. Men with this aspect often attract women who are helpful to them and make independent, but loving mates.

MOON SEXTILE URANUS

The Moon sextile Uranus is similar to the trine, but not as beneficial. These people are friendly and enjoy travel to some extent. Women are helpful to them. Women with this aspect have an independent streak, while men with this aspect may attract a "helpmate".

MOON CONJUNCT NEPTUNE

Neptune increases the sensitivity of the Moon, making it gentle and receptive in nature. Often these people are intuitive and will play their hunches. They may be dreamers, focusing on the ideal, rather than the details at hand. If this Conjunction is well aspected, natives have charisma.

MOON OPPOSITE NEPTUNE

When the Moon is opposite Neptune, the relationship with the mother and family is karmic in nature. These natives feel guilt when they don't give to others what they feel is fair. Since they are so sensitive, they are prone to take on the suffering of others. They need to be more objective about family and to learn when to serve and when to remain silent, as they are easily manipulated. If life gets too painful, they may try to escape with alcohol or medications. Often they delude themselves about relationships. It is important for them to go slowly and work on the relationship in stages. Women with this aspect tend to be martyrs. Men with this aspect may attract a gentle, but somewhat impractical, mate. Sometimes, females are a source of extra responsibility for these men.

MOON SQUARE NEPTUNE

This may indicate an emotionally absent or difficult parent. Often the mother is a source of concern. As children, they may have felt vulnerable. While these people are kind to others, they may neglect their own emotional needs. Like the opposition, they need to be more realistic in relationships and do some reality testing. In extreme cases, there can be emotional disturbances. In a woman's chart, motherhood may be draining. In a male chart, the wife may lack stamina.

351

MOON TRINE NEPTUNE

These people are gentle and love to nurture. Home is important to the, and they often have good relationships with their families. Women, mothers, sisters, daughters are generally good to them. Women with this aspect often enjoy motherhood, as they have strong maternal feelings and are willing to make adjustments for their family. Men with this aspect may attract a soul mate. People with the Moon trine Neptune enjoy music and travel and may have an artistic side to their personality. Domestic happiness is favored.

MOON SEXTILE NEPTUNE

This aspect is similar to the trine, only less beneficial. Here women are still helpful, but not quite as forthcoming. These people are kindly and willing to help others. They also enjoy travel, music, and art. Like the trine, family is important to them.

MOON CONJUNCT PLUTO

Moon conjunct Pluto often feel a sense of destiny to their lives. They can be passionate, but private, individuals. Pluto may make them seem distant on the surface, but they had an intense emotional nature. Sometimes, they can be demanding and their intuition is strong.

MOON OPPOSITE PLUTO

These natives may be distrustful of others and tend to keep their distance. Sometimes this is due to childhood scars. They may have experienced family problems early on in life. Often they see change as a negative. They are emotionally insecure and may be prone to jealousy or rage when crossed. Sometimes the opposite is true and they are victims of abusive relationships. trust is a big issue with these people. To avoid traps in relationships, they need to learn to choose wisely and take relationships in stages.

MOON SQUARE PLUTO

Like those with the opposition, these natives find it hard to trust. Emotionally, they can be fearful or rigid. Often there were breaks or separations in childhood, sometimes due to divorce. They may have had a lot to contend with as a child. As adults, they internalize strife. They need to learn there is nothing more fearful that fear itself. They must learn to trust in small states. If their ineffectual emotional habits persist, psychotherapy may aid these natives in understanding themselves better. Once unconscious fears are rooted out, they can be "reformer" types.

MOON TRINE PLUTO

When Moon trines Pluto, the mother is often a source of insight and support. Intuition and psychological insight is strong. These natives enjoy helping others change, and they see change as positive and enjoy working with the public. They can make good detectives, psychologists, or dynamic leaders. This aspect strengthens the immune system which can add years to the natives' life.

MOON SEXTILE PLUTO

This aspect is similar to the square, but not as powerful. These people are intuitive and have strong feelings. They enjoy some change, but are not as dynamic as Moon trine Pluto.

CHAPTER THIRTY

ASPECTS TO MERCURY

Mercury rules the mind, thoughts and speech. Mercury also controls practical, logical, and sequential thinking. Genius, or the higher mind, is ruled by Uranus. Mercury also rules the nervous system. Medically, nervous disorders are governed by Mercury; mental disorders by Mercury and the Moon.

Mercury is a neural planet, so any aspect to Mercury is better than none at all. Isabel Hickey gives this advice on handling Mercury's energy:

If you wish to improve your thinking in order to create happier circumstances for yourself, notice the position of Mercury in your blueprint. What is the quality, fixed, active or mutable? Are you too set or rigid in your thinking? That is an afflicted Mercury in a fixed sign. Are you apt to be too impulsive and talk before you think? That is Mercury in a cardinal sign that is not manifested rightly. Mercury is well placed in mutable sign if you have some fixed sign to back it up to give you will and purpose, for the mind is adaptable and versatile. However, a virtue carried too far becomes a vice - and this position can make you will-of-the-wisp; too vacillating and too great a tendency to be swayed by every breeze that comes to your mind.

(Isabel Hickey, Astrology: The Cosmic Science, 1992, CRCS Publications, Sebastopol, CA, page 152)

Positive aspects to Mercury add to the intelligence of the native. Negative aspects may indicate problems in thinking, speech, or communication. For example, Mercury trine Uranus gives logical and mechanical abilities. These natives are friendly and communicate well. They enjoy figuring things out or tinkering with things. This mechanical aspect enhances the intelligence and every-day problem solving, and organization. When Mercury squares Uranus, natives are just as intelligent, but they tend to overwork the mind and may become frustrated easily. They may be disorganized and impatient at times, making communications more difficult and straining the nervous system. The antidote is to slow down and take things in sequence. Often the natives are too worrisome to do this and hence their Mercury-Uranus energy works against them, rather than for them. In extreme cases, this stress can cause a nervous breakdown or what psychologists term an adjustment disorder.

Knowing your energy patterns, maximizing positive aspects and compensating for negatives is the basis for good astrology. Constructive thoughts should be nourished and implemented; negative thoughts should be turned away. Surround any negative thoughts with white light and release them to a Higher Power. In terms of mental health, it is crucial to understand your Mercury by sign, house, and aspects. According to astrologer Isabel Hickey, "Mercury is the messenger of the gods flying between Heaven (Spirit) and earth (personality) carrying messages between them". (Astrology: The Cosmic Science). She continues, "When this link is broken the automatic body processes go on, the soul has lost control over the instrument". Modern physicians such as Dr. Bernie Seigle and Dr. Depak Chopra view the mind or attitude as playing a crucial role in mental and physical health. Our thoughts today create our future reality. It takes just as much energy to formulate negative thoughts of fear and hate as it does to create thoughts of peace and love - the difference is the result. Constructive thoughts bring a positive future; negatives ones spoil future happiness. With this in mind, examine the aspects to Mercury with care.

MERCURY - SUN ASPECT

Refer to Sun - Mercury aspects.

MERCURY - MOON ASPECTS

Refer to Moon - Mercury aspects.

MERCURY CONJUNCT VENUS

Venus sweetens Mercury, giving a pleasant speaking or singing voice, and social grace. Often these people are interested in art and music. They enjoy travel for pleasure and like to collect mementos. They dislike coarse language or discord of any kind.

MERCURY OPPOSITE VENUS

Here Venus becomes saccharine. Many times these natives overdo in dress, jewelry, or cologne in an attempt to please others. Sometimes they lack sincerity or discretion in speech. Often they tend to let things slide. Mental discipline may be lacking.

MERCURY SQUARE VENUS

Mercury square Venus is similar to the square. Often these natives have a tendency to be extravagant in speech or gestures. They may be fickle in likes and dislikes. They like their creature comforts and like to show off their finery. Basically, they seek attention and can be quarrelsome when it is not forthcoming. In a woman's chart, she may be fickle. In a male chart, he may have difficulty understanding what a woman wants.

MERCURY TRINE VENUS

When Mercury trines Venus, the artistic and social side is stimulated. These people are usually well liked. They often have a pleasing personality and a good voice. Women may be helpful to the native and partnerships are favored.

MERCURY SEXTILE VENUS

This aspect is similar to the trine, but not as beneficial. The mind is agreeable and may have social or artistic interests. Often natives have a good voice or pleasant manner.

MERCURY CONJUNCT MARS

Here Mars energizes the mind, making it more active in nature, for the mind is restless and eager. Often natives are argumentative and sure they are right. These people notice everything and have endless opinions. It is hard for them to admit it, when they are wrong. They need to slow down and be sure of their facts before they speak.

MERCURY OPPOSITE MARS

These natives seem to go in two directions at once. They like to be busy and frequently overcommit themselves. They form opinions quickly and often resist compromise. They need to stop, look and listen before they act. If not, they can be accident prone.

MERCURY SQUARE MARS

When Mars squares Mercury, the mind is too active, causing arguments and slips of the tongue. Natives need to watch where they place their feet, as their mind (Mercury) can be in one place and their body (Mars) in another. This aspect is similar to the opposition but more intense.

MERCURY TRINE MARS

Here the mind and body are in sync. This aspect gives good mental and mechanical ability. Natives make good writers and orators. Often their intelligence and investigative ability is good. They enjoy travel and change in general. Since they are not easily upset by other people's hangups, these people are popular.

MERCURY SEXTILE MARS

This is similar to the trine in positive energy, but not as strong. Here mechanical, speaking, or writing ability is seen; however, more training is needed to bring this ability out.

MERCURY CONJUNCT JUPITER

When Jupiter conjuncts mercury, it expands the mind. These natives are intelligent and communicate well with others. They can be natural teachers or salesmen. They may have a sense of humor and make learning fun. Because they see the value in an education and their ambitious streak, they are successful in their careers. Publishing, public relations, teaching, sales, law, and politics are all favored.

MERCURY OPPOSITE JUPITER

When Jupiter opposes Mercury, the mind is too expansive, restless, or ambitious. These people are out of sync - either overworking or "goofing" off. Often they promise more than they can deliver or exaggerate their importance. On the positive side, they do have a sense of humor and are well liked, as long as they keep their ego in check.

MERCURY SQUARE JUPITER

Mercury square Jupiter is similar to the opposition, but more intense. Sometimes these natives have ego problems. They tend to over-commit and often promise more than they can deliver. When under stress, they may become couch potatoes. In order to compensate for this aspect, they must keep the ego in check and learn to really listen to the other person's point of view.

MERCURY CONJUNCT SATURN

Saturn puts a damper on Mercury, making the mind more serious and practical. These people work hard to keep their promises and are ethical. However, they may be too serious or rigid. Sometimes they are shy. Often they are perceived by others as a wet blanket, putting a damper on the party. Basically, they need to loosen up and see the possibilities in life, rather than the problems.

MERCURY OPPOSITE SATURN

Here Saturn works against the mind by creating limitations. Natives have a tendency to be pessimistic or may feel alone. Their defensive behavior makes it hard to get close to them. While these natives are often moral and hard working, they are lacking in communication.

MERCURY SQUARE SATURN

Mercury square Saturn is similar to the opposition, but more severe. Here the tendency to depression is more pronounced. Often they have to fight against "black moods' and may be shy and inarticulate. Communication can be a problem. They may need to read the fine print. Sometimes they prefer to work alone. Once they get over feeling negative about everything, these natives can work purposely toward an idea, since they make painstakingly hard workers.

MERCURY TRINE SATURN

Here the disciplined nature of Saturn improves the mind (Mercury), giving it depth and concentration. These natives like to solve problems and may have interest in science or math. These people remain calm under pressure. They have integrity and set realistic goals for themselves and others.

MERCURY SEXTILE SATURN

This aspect is similar to the trine, only not as strong. Discipline, integrity and concentration are present. They are mature in thinking and willing to work hard.

MERCURY CONJUNCT URANUS

When the higher mind (Uranus) meets the lower mind (Mercury), natives possess an awakened mind. People with Mercury conjunct Uranus have progressive ideas and are able to think on their feet. They are mentally courageous and willing to stand up for their beliefs. Since they are inventive, they may excel in creative or technical writing. Computers, technology, psychology, and philosophy may also be of interest to them.

MERCURY OPPOSITE URANUS

Uranus may work against the logical Mercury

mind, pushing it to its limits. Often people with Mercury opposite Uranus demand too much of themselves or others. For example, they may overwork or over-tax their nervous system, causing ill health. Often they are abrupt or demanding with others - many times without realizing their behavior is offensive. They may also eat or talk too fast. Basically, they need to make time to "chill out", organize their life, and learn the art of "win-win" compromise.

MERCURY SQUARE URANUS

Mercury square Uranus is similar to the opposition, only more intense. People with Mercury square Uranus are often intelligent, but with a know-it-all attitude. They are premature in their thinking. They need to organize their thoughts and just about everything else around them! Often they are keyed up, and they need to make time to relax. Since they are so independent, personal relationships will not last long, unless they learn the art of compromise. They can have a temper. When angry, they should practice time out and learn to walk away from confrontations. Later when the adrenaline has subsided, these natives have the mental brilliance to handle any crisis.

MERCURY TRINE URANUS

Here the mind gets the advantage of higher wisdom, making it intelligent and prophetic. The spiritual values are highly developed, and natives may be drawn to mathematics, psychology, philosophy, or social work. They may even have an interest in astrology and the occult. Since they like people, they are good communicators and attract friends. Engineering, mechanical ability, and logic are above average.

MERCURY SEXTILE URANUS

Mercury sextile Uranus is similar to the trine in nature, but not as strong. These people are intelligent and friendly. Often they may be drawn to psychology or social service. They have good communication ability. Mechanical ability and logical thoughts are good.

MERCURY CONJUNCT NEPTUNE

When Neptune (the planet of spiritual love) touches the mind (Mercury), natives are compassionate. People with Mercury conjunct Neptune are often spiritual, kindly, and compassionate folk. They may enjoy music, theater, the arts, or photography. Often their intuitive nature is strong, and they are drawn to mystery, magic, and romance.

MERCURY OPPOSITE NEPTUNE

Here the mind is too impressionable and naive. Often people with Mercury opposite Neptune find their compassion works against them, for they allow other people to manipulate their emotions. Often these kind-hearted people are wishful thinkers. They need to do some reality testing to dispel their fuzzy thinking. They avoid challenges because they do not like competition or confrontation. These natives need to be willing to take on some challenges if they wish to succeed in life. While confrontation may be unpleasant, sometimes it is a necessary last resort.

MERCURY TRINE NEPTUNE

Here Neptune enhances the mind by adding a creative dimension. People with Mercury trine Neptune may be musical, artistic, spiritual or imaginative in nature. These natives can easily tune in to others, making for a warm social life. Since they are refined and sociable, others enjoy their contact with them. People with Mercury trine Neptune can be an inspiration with their talent for art, design, music, theater or psychology, or the occult and detective work.

MERCURY SEXTILE NEPTUNE

This aspect is similar to the trine, but not as beneficial. People with Mercury sextile Neptune are sympathetic, warm, and intuitive. They may have musical or artistic abilities, but not to the extent of the trine. Often they are interested in psychology, social work, and the occult.

MERCURY CONJUNCT PLUTO

When Pluto (the planet of higher energy) touches the mind (Mercury), the mind is sharpened and focused. People with Mercury conjunct Pluto have good concentration and insight. They can also be assertive in communication and can be demanding in personal relationships. Natives may look for hidden meanings and can be suspicious of people's motives. Often, they make tireless researchers and investigators, and criminology, psychology, financial analysis, recycling, and exploring may be of interest to people with Mercury conjunct Pluto.

MERCURY OPPOSITE PLUTO

Here Pluto's intensity works against the mind. People with Pluto opposite Mercury are often combative or suspicious in nature. They can be intense, demanding, and impatient. They cannot rest until everything is done. When challenged, they can be arrogant. Without diplomacy, their hard work may be of little value. They may be drawn to the field of pathology, criminology, research, and financial analysis.

MERCURY SQUARE PLUTO

This aspect is similar to the opposition but more intense. People with this Mercury are suspicious and impatient in nature, and may be abrupt or demanding in speech. Sometimes they are pessimists, sure the world is out to get them. Often they are lonely until they learn to give a little in relationships. Fearless in nature, they may take too many risks or be accident prone. They are drawn to fields of pathology, criminology, research, financial services.

MERCURY TRINE PLUTO

Here the penetrating nature of Pluto illumines the mind. People with Mercury trine Pluto are intuitive and use intelligent discrimination. They are excellent judges of character and are seldom fooled by facades. They enjoy research, problem solving, and reform. When they give a talk, they speak with both authority and conviction. They may be drawn to work for the betterment of mankind in prisons, hospitals, courts, laboratories and institutions. Often they enjoy speculation and have an interest in the stock market.

MERCURY SEXTILE PLUTO

This aspect is similar to the trine, but not as beneficial. Natives with these aspects are as intelligent, resourceful, and hardworking as the trine, but they do not benefit as much. They may be drawn to professions which involve reform, research, or recycling. Like the conjunction and trine, they are courageous in exploring new ideas and may have a wealth of knowledge to share.

CHAPTER THIRTY-ONE

ASPECTS TO VENUS

VENUS

Venus, named after the goddess of love, rules

love and romance. It also rules all the other "sweet" things of life including art, music, poetry, money, and sugar. Venus adds harmony and beauty to the planets it conjuncts. In terms of relationships, it is the most essential element in the chart. Aspects to Venus indicate how one relates to others on a personal level. Hence personal happiness is seen in charts with good aspects to Venus.

When natives have their Venus trine Jupiter they often find happiness in marriage, as they see the innate good in partnerships. Health and happiness go hand in hand. If good health exists, it may well improve after marriage. This aspects improves finances as well. However, when Venus squares Jupiter, the opposite may be true. The natives waste their resources and may experience ill health as rich diet or lack of attention to health. While strongly attracted to the opposite sex, they may be flirtatious or lax in their standards. Good aspects to Saturn can mitigate this aspect, as it would have a restraining effect.

Venus conjunct the Sun

Refer to Sun conjunct Venus.

Venus trine the Sun

Refer to Sun trine Venus.

Venus sextile the Sun

Refer to Sun sextile Venus.

Venus square the Sun

Refer to Sun square Venus.

Venus opposite the Sun

Refer to Sun opposite Venus.

Venus conjunct the Moon

Refer to Venus conjunct Moon.

Venus trine the Moon

Refer to Venus trine the Moon.

Venus sextile the Moon

Refer to Venus sextile the Moon.

Venus square the Moon

Refer to Venus square the Moon.

Venus opposite the Moon

Refer to Venus opposite the Moon.

Venus conjunct Mercury

Refer to Venus conjunct Mercury.

Venus trine Mercury

Refer to Mercury trine Venus.

Venus sextile Mercury

Refer to Mercury sextile Venus.

Venus square Mercury

Refer to Mercury square Venus.

Venus opposite Mercury

Refer to Mercury opposite Venus.

Venus conjunct Mars

When Venus, planet of love, conjuncts Mars, planet of sex, expect great passion. These natives are "in love" with love. When Mars gets the upper hand, the senses may need to be controlled. Often natives are driven by love and lust! With strong personal magnetism, they may succeed at both. Both Mahatma Ghandi and Hitler had this conjunction. Both had the magnetic personalities of Venus conjunct Mars. However, Ghandi disciplined his senses and used his charisma for the welfare of others. Hitler on the other hand, chose to be indulgent and use his charisma for personal gain. Look to aspects this conjunction forms to the outer planets to see its potential. If this conjunction is trined by outer planets, happiness in personal relationships is indicated. When squared by outer planets, many lessons are learned through relationships.

Venus trine Mars

Here love rules. Venus and Mars work in harmony

with each other. Since these natives value love, they are willing to wait for the right partner. Confident and optimistic in nature, they draw others to them. Often they attract many friends and creature comforts. They may also show an interest in the arts and may enjoy working with the public. This aspect also improves finances.

Venus sextile Mars

This aspect is similar to the trine, but has less magnetism. Love is important to these natives as well as the arts. They also have love luxury.

Venus square Mars

Here the passion of Mars works against love relationships. These natives are too impulsive in love. Often the sensual side of love takes precedence. Jealousy and passion may rule. Men with this aspect need to cultivate patience and tact. Women with this aspect may attract aggressive or dominating partners. They need to be more discriminating in relationships. It is best to take time to form a relationship before becoming intimate. However, there is little patience with this aspect. There is a tendency to squander money on luxuries. Maturity and strong Saturn aspects will counteract some of the above tendencies.

Venus opposite Mars

Like the square there is a tendency to have difficulties in relationships. Women with this aspect may attract aggressive mates and men with this aspect may be too erotic and aggressive. These natives may be pushy and have a tendency to spend impulsively.

Venus conjunct Jupiter

When these two benefic planets conjunct luck is in the ethers. Here the love of Venus is ennobled by Jupiter. Jupiter's effects become more personal and immediate. Opportunities for love and wealth abound. People respond favorable to these natives and wish to give to them. The only negative is sometimes in their good fortune, they may become indulgent.

Venus trine Jupiter

Like the conjunction, this is one of the luckiest aspects one can have. Here love and abundance go hand in hand. Often these natives marry well, gaining both financially and socially. They have an innate respect for marriage and attract loving mates. Often they rise in life and enjoy many creature comforts. Religion and cultural activities appeal to them and are generous with their resources. Law and finance are also favored. Since they enjoy people, careers which take them before the public are favored.

Venus sextile Jupiter

This aspect is similar to the trine, bringing love and abundance, but with less ease. The native loves his creature comforts and has personal magnetism. Interest in law, religion and culture are present.

Venus square Jupiter

Here the indulgent and sensual side of Venus is emphasized. These people crave attention and the "sweet" things of life including a rich diet, love, and success. However, they may lack the discipline to obtain their desires or may squander their resources. Often they are warm hearted and affectionate. Discipline, organization, and willingness to work hard are needed to counteract the lax nature of this aspect.

Venus opposite Jupiter

Like the square, these natives are prone to be lazy and indulgent. Still they have warm and fun loving natures, often giving generously to others. John Denver, a performer greatly loved by his audience, had this aspect. However, his zest for the life on the road led to the break up of his first marriage. More discipline is needed as these people tend to let things slide.

Venus conjunct Saturn

Saturn cools the warm nature of Venus. These natives may marry later or be attractive to older, more mature partners. They are tactful and disciplined in love. Wealth is obtained through their own efforts. Often they are shy or cautious in relationships. They make loyal partners who prefer a conventional marriage, and are willing to make the sacrifices necessary for the good of the union.

Venus trine Saturn

Here Saturn works well with Venus, favoring marriage and finances. Often there is a draw to marry someone who is mature and settled in life. Marriage may bring a step up socially or financially. These natives are loyal and disciplined in love, attracting a lasting union. They may have some ability in the arts and appreciate fine art, antiques, and culture.

Venus sextile Saturn

This aspect is similar to the trine, but not as beneficial. It favors a traditional union and makes open trustworthy in love. Finances are improved. While not as artistic as the trine, these people appreciate fine art and antiques.

Venus square Saturn

Venus square Saturn brings many lessons in love. Often there is a materialistic streak and a tendency to marry for money. Sometimes the opposite is true and the native may be called on to make sacrifices to balance the karmic scales. Often these people are prone to depression and loneliness. To counteract this, they need to overcome their fear of rejection and criticism; while cultivating a more open, flexible, optimistic attitude. Often their self-defeating negativity turns away the affection, they ardently desire.

Venus opposite Saturn

This aspect is similar to the square, but not as severe. Problems in relationships may arise due to others more than psychological issues. However, they may be materialistic and cold in love. They need to guard against too much ambition and selfish desires.

Venus conjunct Uranus

These natives are unforgettable. They make an impression on others for good or ill, as Uranus adds sparkle to Venus. These natives can be the life of the party. Independent by nature, they are quite attractive to the opposite sex. They can be interested in science and the media, as well as the occult. They can earn and spend big. Often they make their own luck with their sense of leadership and entitlement.

Venus trine Uranus

These natives sparkle. They love life, attract happiness in romance and marriage, and are often lucky financially. In relationships, they need a certain amount of freedom to be happy, but they are also willing to share the spotlight with others. Even changes in relationships tend to work in their favor. Often they are attracted to the arts (Venus) or the media (Uranus). Since they are spontaneous by nature, they can captivate the minds and hearts of others. Their happiness is contagious. They attract friends of both sexes, and maintain many life-long friendships. Science and philosophy may appeal to them, as well as the occult. In an advanced chart, they will use their talents to aid humanity, sensing correctly, they are here for a higher purpose. During favorable transits, they may find sudden recognition or financial success.

Venus sextile Uranus

This aspect is similar to the trine, but not as beneficial. Natives are popular, but not as charismatic. Love life, artistic endeavors, and intuition are all improved by this aspect.

Venus square Uranus

These natives have strong likes and dislikes which may turn others off. They need to be more tactful and less defensive. Both relationships and finances fluctuate, often at the native's expense. On the positive side, they are magnetic and exciting. Their impulsive, and emotional nature works against them in love. They need to cultivate tolerance and patience to avoid breaks in relationships. In a woman's chart, she may attract a dominating mate. In a male chart, he may be overly aggressive in relationships. There is a tendency for both sexes to be highstrung and demanding. Hasty actions may be regretted later.

Venus opposite Uranus

This aspect is similar to the square, but not as harsh. Here the native attracts those who may be demanding or unavailable. Lessons may be learned through others. There may be breaks and separations in relationships and fluctuations in finances. Patience is needed to overcome restless and/or demanding qualities that occur when Uranus blocks the innate tact and harmony of Venus and is demanding and impulsive in love.

Venus conjunct Neptune

Venus is refined by Neptune's rays, making it more ethereal and spiritual in nature. These natives believe in love and are willing to make many sacrifices to maintain relationships. They crave a story-book romance. Idealistic by nature, they can close their eyes to the more realistic side of life. They may need to do some reality testing before they commit to marriage. Often kind to others, they have a gentle nature. Sometimes there is confusion or bisexuality in love relationships, especially if this conjunction is squared by the outer planets. If the conjunction is well aspected, relationships benefit the individual and artistic and mystical qualities may be present.

Venus trine Neptune

Fate plays a lucky role in their lives. Here

love and spirit merge. Often these natives attract a soul mate. They are idealistic and gentle in love, but innately sensual as well. Intuitive by nature, they are attracted to the arts, healing, and psychology. Karmically, they have given of themselves in past life and in the present life, much is given to them. Marriage and partnerships are strongly favored. However, some may choose religious life instead. This is one of the most favorable aspects for personal happiness. The only drawback is sometimes they may be too loving or giving in nature.

Venus sextile Neptune

This aspect is similar to the trine, but not as beneficial. These natives are idealistic and refined by nature. However, there is not as much charisma or material benefit. Often they are drawn to the art or occult.

Venus square Neptune

Fatal attractions may occur under this aspect. Unfortunately, these natives may be attracted to lovers who are unavailable or unreliable. Since they are very emotional in romance, it is hard for these people to break off destructive relationships. There is a strong tendency to be a victim or martyr. They need to read the fine print in contracts and shun "get rich quick schemes". Women with this aspect need to be especially vigilant. Men with Venus square Neptune may be effeminate or bisexual, or inclined to suffer through relationships. They need to adopt a more assertive nature to attract the opposite sex. Sometimes, natives seek to avoid harshness of reality with use of drugs or alcohol. Addictive tendencies are strong for both sexes and people, without some positive aspects to Saturn. Their gentle nature may find a more acceptable outlet in creative and spiritual pursuits such as meditation.

Venus opposite Neptune

These gentle souls often suffer through the actions of others. Like the square there is a deficit in relationships making them sensitive to loneliness. Finances can also be a source of concern. Get rich quick schemes and shady characters can leave a shadow on their reputation. Often they give more than receive love.

Venus conjunct Pluto

Pluto makes Venus more passionate and fanatical! Love is black and white with these natives. Inclined toward sexual expression, they may need to be less intense. Love does not flourish on command! While these natives are sensitive to love, they are also jealous and vulnerable. They may be attracted to people with Scorpio qualities or powerful individuals. They may also have a strong intuition and some inventive or artistic qualities.

Venus trine Pluto

Here love is all. Pluto makes Venus passionate,

intense, and powerful with this aspect. Marriage is favored by this aspect and may represent a step up in life. Often these natives are gifted with artistic or financial abilities. They have a healthy libido and enjoy life. Leadership and charisma come naturally to them. Intuitive by nature, they have excellent timing and a knack for surrounding themselves with the right people.

Venus sextile Pluto

This aspect is similar to the trine, but not as charismatic. Love is favored and fate may play an aspect in relationships. These natives are also attracted to the occult and are progressive in ideas.

Venus square Pluto

Here Pluto brings out the most sensual and unfavorable qualities of Venus. Fatal attractions can be their downfall. They must guard against misplaced affections, addiction, and theft, especially during negative Pluto transits. Even in a more advanced soul, petty jealousy and power struggles may manifest. In those of insufficient morality, obsessions, compulsions and in extreme cases a life of crime. Females are more likely to become victims. They may also be prone to miscarriages and female reproductive problems. In many even, passions need to be curbed and strict morality observed to overcome these negative qualities.

CHAPTER THIRTY-TWO

ASPECTS TO MARS

Mars represents energy - raw sexual energy, athletic ability, mechanical thinking, and construction, and war. Whatever planet conjuncts Mars receives energy according to the sign. In water signs, there is steam - passionate feelings. In air signs, the intellect, particularly the critical mind is stimulated. In the fire sign, the temper is strong. And in earth signs, Mars can stir materialism. While trines to Mars indicate constructive energy; squares and oppositions require restraint!

Positive aspects, such as Mars trine Uranus, channel the raw energy of Mars constructively with Uranus. This aspect indicates organization and ingenuity. Often these natives are self starters and may do well in their own enterprise. They work quickly, but accurately. When Mars squares Uranus, the opposite is true. While the person works just as hard, but many errors are made.

These natives are prone to accidents, often due to haste. Their tempers work against them, causing misunderstandings. They may be self employed more through lack of opportunity than by choice. However, patience and attention to detail can overcome many of these obstacles if they are willing to listen.

Mars conjunct Sun

Refer to Sun conjunct Mars.

Mars trine Sun

Refer to Sun trine Mars.

Mars square Sun

Refer to Sun square Mars.

Mars opposite Sun

Refer to Sun opposite Mars.

Mars conjunct Moon

Refer to Moon conjunct Mars.

Mars trine Moon

Refer to Moon trine Mars.

Mars square Moon

Refer to Moon square Mars.

Mars opposite Moon

Refer to Moon opposite Mars.

Mars conjunct Mercury

Refer to Mercury conjunct Mars.

Mars trine Mercury

Refer to Mercury trine Mars.

Mars square Mercury

Refer to Mercury square Mars.

Mars opposite Mercury

Refer to Mercury opposite Mars.

Mars conjunct Venus

Refer to Venus conjunct Mars.

Mars trine Venus

Refer to Venus trine Mars.

Mars square Venus

Refer to Venus square Mars.

Mars opposite Venus

Refer to Venus opposite Mars.

Mars conjunct Jupiter

Jupiter expands Mars giving leadership and athletic ability. There is a constructive outgoing nature. Often these natives have a zest for life, fortified with a good sense of humor. If this conjunction is well aspected, they will rise in life. If afflicted, the aspect not as successful, as natives are apt to be too opinionated and bossy. Either way, they can be a good showmen, as they are high in confidence and optimism!

Mars trine Jupiter

Mars is made more graceful, and enthusiastic by Jupiter. Many athletes, dancers, and performers have Mars trine Jupiter. These natives can also excel in politics, laws, and public relations. They believe in themselves and can inspire others. Lucky by nature, they enjoy sports, games of chance, and the stock market. At work they are a team player, gaining the respect of their colleagues.

Mars sextile Jupiter

This aspect is similar to the trine, but not as beneficial. Mars is still as purposeful, but not as lucky. Opportunity is there, if they make the effort to open the door! They may also excel in sport, dance, and performing, but to a lesser acclaim.

Mars square Jupiter

Mars is made more indulgent and arrogant by the square to Jupiter. Unless there are some positive aspects to Saturn, Mars can procrastinate. They may be lazy and lacking in motivation. Their passive-aggressive attitude can cause problems at work or in relationships. Sometimes the opposite is true and their energy gets out of sync by overdoing. Either way, these natives need to follow a well-paced schedule and avoid excesses.

Mars opposite Jupiter

This aspect is similar to the square, but not as draining. Often there is a tendency to over or under work. However, it is less ingrained and more easily modified. They may find partners demand too much of them or alternately, they depend too much on others.

Mars conjunct Saturn

Mars conjunct Saturn is a "Stop and Go" aspect. Mars gives the "go ahead", while Saturn puts the brakes on. Often the native starts a project, only to stop midstream, then go ahead once again. Basically, they are being cautious. Often this aspect slows them down for a good reason. When they do complete the assignment, it is well done. Since Saturn rules the father, they may have difficulties with their father. There is also a tendency to be pessimistic, especially if the conjunction is poorly aspected.

Mars trine Saturn

This aspect gives good reasoning, logic, and mathematics ability. There may also be interest in mechanics, engineering, or science. Will power, organization, and discipline are strong. While ambitious, they set realistic goals. They are willing to put in the time and effort needed to do the job well.

Mars sextile Saturn

This aspect is similar to the trine, but not as hard working or successful. Often they possess mechanical skills, organization, and discipline.

Mars square Saturn

Mars can be his own worst enemy, when squared by Saturn. Often these natives have difficulty with authority, stemming from a poor relationship with their own fathers. They can be pessimistic and may procrastinate to their detriment. Sometimes, they take an alternative tactic and over work trying to please their boss. Either way, these natives feel frustrated, and may scape-goat others or become a petty dictator. Since resentment is strong, they need to work on forgiveness and self love in order to overcome any masochistic tendency which may be buried in their past. Many times these natives suffer intensely or may cause pain to others by their thoughtlessness.

Mars opposite Saturn

This aspect is similar to the square, but not as detrimental. They tend to overwork or to procrastinate due to insecurity. Often they have difficulty with authority. Like the square, they need to learn to be less judgmental and harsh.

Mars conjunct Uranus

Uranus stimulates Mars, making it more independent, impulsive, and hyperactive. High energy and an independent spirit could make them capable leaders. However, they prefer to be their own boss and brook no criticism. While they would benefit from some constructive feedback, they are apt to go it alone. If this conjunction is well aspected by the outer planets, these natives are charismatic leaders. If the conjunction is afflicted, they can be petty dictators. Like the opposition and the square, they also need to watch out for accidents!

Mars trine Uranus

Uranus trine Mars is an aspect of genius. These natives are original, progressive, and humane in endeavors. They are true pioneers. Because of these qualities, they can excel in whatever field they choose! Health and vitality remain strong throughout life. While opinionated in nature, others respect their views.

401

Mars square Uranus

Mars square Uranus is unpredictable, also makes natives accident-prone. They are over-doers! Often they are too impatient and have a reluctance to take time to rest and relax. When crossed, they can have a temper. Men with this aspect may be too aggressive in relationships. Women with this aspect may attract "macho" type males. In either case, these people are demanding. To counteract the above qualities, they need to cultivate patience, good listening skills, and tolerance.

Mars opposite Uranus

This aspect is similar to the square, but not as harsh. These natives are prone to impatience, zealous ambition, and accidents, but more from outside circumstances. Abrupt in nature, they need to cultivate tact and tolerance.

Mars conjunct Neptune

Neptune waters down the fiery nature of Mars.

While it makes Mars more sensitive and artistic, it may also drain it of vitality. The native may be more gullible or confused. On the positive side, there is more compassion and intuition. Rest is a must, as these individuals tire easily. Reality testing may also help counteract some of the above qualities.

Mars trine Neptune

This aspect confers musical or artistic abilities. The native is sensitive to others and would excel in psychology or medical fields. There is a genuine compassion. While emotions run deep, the native is flexible in dealing with people and more than willing to hear the other side of the story. The gift of prophecy may also be present.

Mars sextile Neptune

This aspect is similar to the trine, but not as beneficial. Musical, artistic and intuitive abilities may be present. However, more training is needed to bring these talents out. Innate kindness is also present. Like the trine, the sextile signifies a gentle soul.

Mars square Neptune

Mars square Neptune creates a great deal of confusions, unless there are some strong Saturn aspects. The native is overly sensitive and may try to escape the harsh realities of life through alcohol or drugs. Caution is necessary with prescribed medicine, due to extreme sensitivity, their system may absorb too much of the medicine causing side effects. Often these natives suffer because of their sensitivity. If either planet is in the twelfth house, there may be a tendency toward mental illness. Caution in matters of imagination and the senses is also advised. Do some reality testing before making decisions. Meditation, exercise, and social connections are better methods of releasing stress than alcohol or drugs! Gentle in disposition, these people can do much to help others.

Mars opposite Neptune

This aspect is similar to the square but not as severe. Confusion and disorganization can hinder the native; as well as retreating from reality. Try to relax without chemical tranquilizers or alcohol. While natives are often kind to others, they may lack self assertion.

Mars conjunct Pluto

Pluto intensifies Mars, increasing drive and determination. These natives tend to go to extremes. If the conjunction is well aspected, they can be a strong reformer and force for good in the community. Afflicted, they can be their own worst enemy, with the proverbial chip on their shoulder. In this case, temper and hypersexuality need watching. Often they want to have their way at any price. Either aspect, they are human dynamos!

Mars trine Pluto

Mars is made even more powerful and resourceful by the trine to Pluto. These natives may be known for their athletic ability and leadership. These people will go where "angels fear to tread", their courage and intuition forging a path before them. They make excellent diagnosticians, detectives, and psychologists, as little goes unnoticed by them. Both their sex drives and their egos are healthy and in check.

Mars sextile Pluto

This aspect is similar to the trine, but not as powerful. These natives have courage and stamina. They are willing to go in first, when necessary. Often intuition and confidence are strong.

Mars square Pluto

Here the negative side of Pluto affects Mars. Coercion and manipulation are strong. Often there are strong desires and a tendency to bend the rules in order to get their needs satisfied. The sex drive is intensified. In extreme cases they may associate with criminal elements or become cruel to others. In a woman's chart, it attracts a dominating or intense partnership. In a male chart, there is a need for humility and the fine art of compromise. Both sexes can have a temper.

Mars opposite Pluto

This aspect is similar to the square in sexual intensity and thirst for power, but not as cruel. Often these natives find it hard to compromise and can be their own worst enemy. While they may not like playing by the rules, they need to be respectful of the law of the land.

CHAPTER THIRTY-THREE

ASPECTS TO JUPITER

Jupiter is the greater benefic in our solar system. It brings good luck to all it touches. With this planet, sometimes even negative aspects can be beneficial, for Jupiter is expansion and growth. In terms of society, it represents education, law, philosophy and religion - all agencies which are working to improve social conditions. Jupiter increases our aspirations, hopes, and dreams, individually and collectively.

When natives have their Jupiter trine the Sun, they enjoy working for the good of all and may prosper in Jupiter occupations - teaching, law, and religion. Often they are seen as pillars of society. When Jupiter is opposite the Sun, they may be enthusiastic workers, but they are out of sync either overworking or slacking off. They may rebel against the establishment. Hence, they are not likely to receive the financial and social recognition of the Sun trine Jupiter, but may have many of the same qualities.

Jupiter conjunct the Sun

Refer to Sun conjunct Jupiter.

Jupiter trine the Sun

Refer to Sun opposite Jupiter.

Jupiter sextile the Sun

Refer to Sun square Jupiter.

Jupiter opposite the Sun

Refer to Sun trine Jupiter.

Jupiter square the Sun

Refer to Sun sextile Jupiter.

Jupiter conjunct the Moon

Refer to Moon conjunct Jupiter.

Jupiter trine the Moon

Refer to Moon opposite Jupiter.

Jupiter sextile the Moon

Refer to Moon square Jupiter.

Jupiter opposite the Moon

Refer to Moon trine Jupiter.

Jupiter square the Moon

Refer to Moon sextile Jupiter.

Jupiter conjunct Mercury

Refer to Mercury conjunct Jupiter.

Jupiter trine Mercury

Refer to Mercury opposite Jupiter.

Jupiter opposite Mercury

Refer to Mercury square Jupiter.

Jupiter square Mercury

Refer to Mercury trine Jupiter.

Jupiter square Mercury

Refer to Mercury trine Jupiter.

Jupiter conjunct Venus

Refer to Venus conjunct Mercury.

Jupiter trine Venus

Refer to Venus opposite Jupiter.

Jupiter sextile Venus

Refer to Venus trine Jupiter.

Jupiter opposite Venus

Refer to Venus sextile Jupiter.

Jupiter square Venus

Refer to Venus square Jupiter

Jupiter conjunct Mars

Refer to Mars conjunct Jupiter.

Jupiter trine Mars

Refer to Mars opposite Jupiter.

Jupiter sextile Mars

Refer to Mars square Jupiter.

Jupiter opposite Mars

Refer to Mars trine Jupiter.

Jupiter square Mars

Refer to Mars sextile Jupiter.

Jupiter conjunct Saturn

Saturn adds to Jupiter's potential for success by stabilizing Jupiter. These natives can be solid as a rock, yet assertive. They are willing to gamble, but only a fixed amount. They are hopeful, but realistic. Often they enjoy traveling for work, reading self help books, and improving society.

Jupiter trine Saturn

When Jupiter trines Saturn, the natives believe in the value of hard work. They are disciplined, structured, and enterprising. They intuitively "know" they will eventually succeed. Before they start a project, they do their homework. Older people may aid in their success. Education, government, and management may appeal to them. This is one of the best aspects people can have for lasting success.

Jupiter sextile Saturn

This aspect is similar to the trine, but not as beneficial. They may have to work harder to achieve the same result; however they are disciplined and dedicated to improving their lives and the lives of those around them.

Jupiter opposite Saturn

Here the established order (Saturn) is opposite the individual enthusiasm. These people rebel against authority and may be at odds with the current political system or corporate structure. They need to have a better plan, though, before they trash the old system. Sometimes they fluctuate between giving in to the establishment and resenting it or rebelling against it and feeling left out in the cold.

Jupiter square Saturn

Often they learn the hard way. For these natives, hard work and no play is the path to success. They may rebel against the established order or lack the discipline to learn its rules. These natives may have a problem with their egos, either being egotistical or low in self esteem. Moderation and balance is important to overcome this aspect.

Jupiter conjunct Uranus

Jupiter (abundance) conjunct Uranus, is an aspect of crazy abundance, otherwise known as "good luck". People know the value of an education and have many opportunities. They are enthusiastic and like to be busy.

Jupiter trine Uranus

When Jupiter trines Uranus, people have a

sense of expansion and abundance. They are high on life. Often education, religion, and working for causes appeals to them. This helpful aspect adds to creative abilities and leadership. These natives are alert to the opportunities life has to offer and their lives are filled with abundance.

Jupiter sextile Uranus

Similar to the trine, but not as dynamic. Often these natives take pleasure in life and may possess creativity or leadership.

Jupiter opposite Uranus

Here Jupiter is too expansive, idealistic, or rebellious for the established order. These people may prefer to be their own boss and do things their way. They can be very enthusiastic and are willing to do battle for what they feel is right. However, the boss may not always appreciate their candor!

Jupiter square Uranus

Like the square, these natives are apt to be

at odds with the established order. They would like to start at the top, but would do better to learn the ropes first. What these people lack in patience, they make up for in enthusiasm. They are interested in politics, law, education, and public relations.

Jupiter conjunct Neptune

Natives with Jupiter conjunct Neptune have tremendous faith and belief. However, sometimes it is blind faith. They can be schemers or dreamers and sometimes a little of both. They can be quite charming, but may promise more than they can deliver. They need to be cautious about taking on responsibilities. They can be impractical romantics. They need to learn to accept others with all their flaws, not just the beautiful ideal.

Jupiter trine Neptune

When Jupiter trines Neptune, spirituality expands. Here faith is justified. Often they are a great inspiration to others, serving as model for unselfish service and devotions. They draw inspiration from religion, art, and philosophy.

Jupiter sextile Neptune

This aspect is similar to the trine, but not as beneficial. Their faith is strong, as is their interest in religion, art and philosophy.

Jupiter opposite Neptune

When Jupiter is opposite Neptune, the natives are apt to be too religious or too idealistic. Sometimes in their enthusiasm, they bite off more than they can chew. They may challenge others before they know all the facts. Sometimes they have to watch out for accepting too many unpaid positions. While their intentions are good, they may later feel taken advantage of by others.

Jupiter square Neptune

When Jupiter squares Neptune, religion and philosophy may be extreme. These natives tend to overextend their energies. They may buy too much on credit or take on too many responsibilities. They need to be more realistic and less idealistic. Often creativity and compassion are strong.

Jupiter conjunct Pluto

Jupiter conjunct can add to people's success, as it expands their horizon and their enthusiasm for life. They believe in themselves and can encourage others. Jupiter expands the discipline and power of Pluto. Sometimes they can be a bit demanding, especially if they feel any manipulation. They may also have psychic powers.

Jupiter trine Pluto

When Jupiter trines Pluto, the natives have a stimulating and creative attitude toward life. They see the good in education and cultural practices. Often they are tolerant of others and have good psychological insight. Their intuition is their best friend, and their faith encourages others around them. They have excellent leadership potential.

Jupiter sextile Pluto

This aspect is similar to the trine, but not as beneficial. These natives are creative and inspirational. Some intuition and leadership may also be present.

CHAPTER THIRTY-FOUR

ASPECTS TO SATURN

Saturn is the most karmic planet in our solar system. It represents our most serious lessons. Whatever Saturn touches, it restricts. For example, Saturn conjunct the Moon puts "wet blanket" on emotions. Saturn conjunct Mercury makes for a serious student. When Saturn conjuncts Venus, one takes romance seriously. When Saturn, the brakes of the zodiac, meets Mars, the accelerator; the native experiences an alternating "stop and go" flow of energy.

Fortunately, Saturn is a just planet giving rewards as one merits them. Positive aspects to Saturn add strength and stability to the chart. Saturn trines the Sun makes for a stable and hard working individual. Often these natives will succeed through patience and determination.

Negative aspects indicate lessons the native has refused to address in past lives. Now he has no choice. For example, Saturn squares the Moon brings karmic relationships with the mother. Often the child's early environment lacks warmth and support. Later in life, this can become a prototype for a defensive coping style or depression, unless the child receives some attention from a kind relative or sensitive counselor.

Saturn conjunct the Sun

Refer to Sun conjunct Saturn.

Saturn trine the Sun

Refer to Sun trine Saturn.

Saturn sextile the Sun

Refer to Sun sextile Saturn.

Saturn opposite the Sun

Refer to Sun opposite Saturn.

Saturn conjunct the Moon

Refer to Moon conjunct Saturn.

Saturn trine the Moon

Refer to Moon trine Saturn.

Saturn sextile the Moon

Refer to Moon sextile Saturn.

Saturn opposite the Moon

Refer to Moon opposite Saturn.

Saturn conjunct Mercury

Refer to Mercury conjunct Saturn.

Saturn trine Mercury

Refer to Mercury trine Saturn.

Saturn opposite Mercury

Refer to Mercury opposite Saturn.

Saturn square Mercury

Refer to Mercury square Saturn.

Saturn conjunct Venus

Refer to Venus conjunct Saturn.

Saturn trine Venus

Refer to Venus trine Saturn.

Saturn sextile Venus

Refer to Venus sextile Saturn.

Saturn opposite Venus

Refer to Venus opposite Saturn.

Saturn square Venus

Refer to Venus square Saturn.

Saturn conjunct Mars

Refer to Mars conjunct Saturn.

Saturn trine Mars

Refer to Mars trine Saturn.

Saturn sextile Mars

Refer to Mars sextile Saturn.

Saturn opposite Mars

Refer to Mars opposite Saturn

Saturn conjunct Jupiter

Refer to Jupiter conjunct Saturn.

Saturn trine Jupiter

Refer to Jupiter trine Saturn.

Saturn sextile Jupiter

Refer to Jupiter sextile Saturn.

Saturn opposite Jupiter

Refer to Jupiter opposite Saturn.

Saturn square Jupiter

Refer to Jupiter square Saturn.

Saturn conjunct Uranus

Saturn gives structure to Uranus' creative energy. These natives can transform society with their drive, ambition, and resourcefulness.

They instinctively understand the need for self discipline. Often they are attracted to research, science, math, and the occult.

Saturn trine Uranus

Saturn encourages the creative energy of Uranus, making its inventions a reality. These natives can come up the ladder of success the hard way, as they are resourceful and hard working. Often inspired by the mundane, they make good mentors, artists, and researchers.

Saturn sextile Uranus

Similar to the trine, but not as beneficial. Discipline and hard work are innate, but they may not be as successful. Natives are inspired at times and are resourceful.

Saturn square Uranus

When Saturn squares Uranus, natives may be emotionally sensitive and harbor neurotic anxiety about finances or their human potential. Sometimes they are treated harshly by a parent or boss. Often they resent authority and bend the rules more than they should. They need to learn the art of "win-win" compromise.

Saturn opposite Uranus

This aspect is similar to the square. When Saturn is opposite Uranus, changing (Uranus) to the established order is (Saturn) problematic. Either the natives are too rigid in their views, too competitive, or too idealistic. Partnerships may be difficult until they learn the art of "win-win" compromise.

Saturn conjunct Neptune

Saturn makes Neptune's idealism a reality, while Neptune softens Saturn's nature. These natives are not easily fooled. With their realistic intuition, they can deal well with every day affairs. Often they are interested in photography, psychology, or the occult.

Saturn trine Neptune

When Saturn (structure) trines Neptune (the spiritual), miracles can happen. These natives are motivated by a "higher" power. They enjoy the creativity of the film industry, the stock market, or worlds of art and entertainment. Idealistic to the hilt, they work hard to make these ideas reality.

Saturn sextile Neptune

This aspect is similar to the trine, but not as successful. These people are idealistic and creative, but may not have as many opportunities or rewards as the trine position.

Saturn square Neptune

Like the opposition, these natives are too idealistic and commit before doing their homework. Often disillusioned, they may retreat from others. They may also have unrealistic fear and worry excessively. Sometimes they are given to compulsive behavior. People with Saturn square Neptune may need to work on their self esteem. Often they give more than they receive - then feel cheated.

Saturn opposite Neptune

While these natives are sensitive to a fault, they will endure many struggles because of their beliefs. Just as idealistic as the trine, but without the structure and prudence to be successful. Naturally cautious and fearful, they may not inspire the confidence of others. Others may take advantage of them. They need to commit in stages with a good dose of reality testing. Otherwise, they are apt to feel unappreciated, which does little for their self-esteem.

Saturn conjunct Pluto

Pluto strengthens Saturn's discipline, ambition, and determination. These natives are resourceful and willing to work hard to achieve their goals. Often they prefer to work alone or in secrecy. Power and control are important to them. They are well suited to criminal justice, research, finance, and psychology as they can "read between the lines" and easily understand people's motives.

Saturn trine Pluto

When Saturn trines Pluto, both determination and concentration are strong. Often they prefer to be in control, but are not threatened by change, which they seek as necessary to progress. Government, research, and the environment may present opportunities for their talents.

Saturn sextile Pluto

This aspect is similar to the trine only not as beneficial. These natives work hard and are organized. Opportunities come - when they seek them out.

Saturn square Pluto

Saturn may create struggles against those in power. There are feelings of persecution or lack of trust. Finances or world conditions may pose a problem.

Saturn opposite Pluto

Like the square, this aspect creates a feeling of victimization. They may resent the established order or be held back in some way by it. Sometimes they are devious to compensate from a fear of ridicule or loss of finances.

CHAPTER THIRTY-FIVE

ASPECTS TO URANUS AND NEPTUNE

Aspects to the trans-Saturn planets are beyond our conscious control and the scope of everyday events. According to Stephen Arroyo, aspects to Uranus indicates a desire for freedom:

All aspects of Uranus to personal planets, indicate areas of our lives wherein we have a strong urge to obtain freedom of expression without restraint and where we feel the need for constant excitement and experimentation. It is in those areas of life where we want to be different from everyone else, where we want a broad scope of independence from binding traditions and past conditioning, where there is often a marked capacity for originality and inventiveness, and broad minded objectivity.

(Astrology Karma, and Transformation CRCS Publications, Vancouver, Washington, Page 116)

While positive aspects between Uranus and the personal planets energize in a strong, creative, independent mode, negative aspects between Uranus and the personal planets are just as strong but may lead to impatient, premature, and willful behavior. For example, the Sun trine Uranus may indicate executive ability and leadership qualities. These natives have an innate genius and are able to inspire others. When Uranus squares the Sun, natives may have just as much leadership and energy, but their timing is off. They may be demanding, tyrannical, or petty with others. Instead of leadership, they inspire fear, until they are willing to look inside and make some changes. Aspects between Uranus, and the two outer planets, Neptune and Pluto, influence large groups of people and are predictors of world conditions.

Uranus conjunct Neptune

Refer to Moon sextile Uranus.

Uranus opposite the Moon

Refer to Moon opposite Uranus.

Uranus square the Moon

Refer to Moon square Uranus

Uranus conjunct Mercury

Refer to Mercury conjunct Uranus

Uranus trine Mercury

Refer to Mercury trine Uranus.

Uranus sextile Mercury

Refer to Mercury sextile Uranus.

Uranus opposite Mercury

Refer to Mercury opposite Uranus.

Uranus conjunct Venus

Refer to Venus conjunct Uranus

Uranus trine Venus

Refer to Venus trine Uranus.

Uranus sextile Venus

Refer to Uranus sextile Venus.

Uranus opposite Venus

Refer to Venus opposite Uranus

Uranus square Venus

Refer to Venus square Uranus.

Uranus conjunct Mars

Refer to Mars conjunct Uranus.

Uranus trine Mars

Refer to Mars trine Uranus.

Uranus sextile Mars

Refer to Mars sextile Uranus.

Uranus opposite Mars

Refer to Mars opposite Uranus.

Uranus square Mars

Refer to Mars square Uranus.

Uranus conjunct Jupiter

Refer to Jupiter conjunct Uranus.

Uranus trine Jupiter

Refer to Jupiter trine Uranus.

Uranus sextile Jupiter

Refer to Jupiter sextile Uranus.

Uranus opposite Jupiter

Refer to Jupiter opposite Uranus.

Uranus square Jupiter

Refer to Jupiter square Uranus.

Uranus conjunct Saturn

Refer to Saturn conjunct Uranus.

Uranus trine Saturn

Refer to Saturn trine Uranus.

Uranus sextile Saturn

Refer to Saturn sextile Uranus.

Uranus opposite Saturn

Refer to Saturn opposite Uranus.

Uranus square Saturn

Refer to Saturn square Uranus.

Uranus Conjunct Neptune

This aspect occurred in Capricorn from 1992 to 1994. Children born with this aspect will have great leadership. When the idealism of Neptune combines with the freedom-loving Uranus, this generation will tolerate no abuse of power. They will also have many visionaries and inventors who can utilize the Capricorn earth energy and collective power to invent new forms of energy and a one world government. These young people will be the rebuilders of the world!

When the conjunction took place in 1992 and 1994, there were tremendous corporate take-overs and changes in our government. More awareness of the environment and organic farming became popular. While President and Mrs. Clinton, both born with Neptune in Libra, tried to bring in universal health care for Americans, they proved out of step with the new corporate mentality of the bottom line.

Uranus trine Neptune

Here technology, revolution, and freedom (Uranus) merge well with creative and spiritual goals (Neptune). In the late 1940s, many children were born with Uranus in Gemini trine Neptune in Libra. Uranus in Gemini indicated children born during this seven year cycle would have unique ideas about technology, communications, and travel. When this group came of age they ushered in the computer, video, space age technology in the late 1960s to the present. Many also had the trine to Neptune in Libra, creating the extreme idealism of the anti-war protesters, flower children and the Woodstock generation of the late 1960s and early 1970s. Generations with Uranus trine Neptune really want to save the world.

Uranus sextile Neptune

This generation born between 1965 and 1968, when Uranus was in Virgo and Neptune in Scorpio, entered during the sexual revolution of the 1960, when many institutions were in turmoil. Many of these children had parents with Neptune trine Uranus and they are just as idealistic and creative. They will also rebel against the established order and wish to have their say. When they came of age in the 1980s and 1990s, they brought the entrepreneur's spirit of independence. Since they see their world as global, they are likely to participate in world government in the future.

Uranus opposite Neptune

Here the technology and individualism of Uranus can be used to control the spirit of the masses. This aspect may indicate religious wars and battles over cultural ideals. This aspect occurred in 1914 and 1915 about the time of World War I. Natives born under this aspect came into a world of political unrest and nationalism.

Uranus square Neptune

Here technology and the rights of the entitled

are weakened by misplaced idealism or spiritual values. This combination occurred between 1952 and 1956. This was a conservative time when change was feared. The conservative Uranus in Cancer became fanatical with fear of Communism and the mentality of Joe McCarthy, when it squared Neptune in Libra. The Cold War replaced World War II, and conformity replaced creativity for a period.

Uranus conjunct Pluto

When Uranus (freedom) conjuncts the intense power of Pluto, people will go to extremes for individual, economic, and political freedom. When these children born between the years of 1963 to 1967 came of age, they were avid environmentalists and entrepreneurs.

When the conjunction occurred from 1963 to 1967 in Libra, astrologer, Robert Pelletier, explains its influence as follows:

Rachel Carson's book, <u>The Silent Spring</u>, was a grim reminder of how seriously we are upsetting the balance of nature. The United States Government on <u>Smoking and Health</u>, pointed to the much higher incidence of cancer and heart disease among smokers than non-smokers. Along with disturbing reports of these publications, there was increasing use of mind altering drugs such as hallucinogens, LSD, marijuana, and "hard" drugs such as heroin and cocaine. The use of thalilomide by pregnant women in Europe produced deformed children, until the side effects of this medication were understood. (Planets in Aspect, by Robert Pelletier, Para Research, Gloucester, MA p 65)

Uranus trine Pluto

Here change and freedom are welcomed by Pluto. These natives value personal expression and creativity. The last time this aspect occurred was during the Roaring Twenties from 1921 to 1926 when Pluto was in Cancer and Uranus was in Pisces. Since they were in a water sign, Spiritualism was at its peak as well. Many gifted psychics, such as Boston's Margery Cransdon, made headlines. Optimism was high, the stock market soared, and jazz and art deco were the rage.

Uranus sextile Pluto

Here freedom and change are also popular, but not as dramatic as the trine. These natives were born in 1957 to 1970 with Pluto in Virgo (health care for the masses) and Uranus in Scorpio (changing values and morals, and regeneration). These natives saw a revolution in birth control for the masses as the birth control pill gained popularity and new psychiatric drugs replaced lobotomies and strait jackets. Tranquilizers and psychotherapy became popular. Business was booming as many cities underwent urban renewal. When these people come of age in the 1990s, they will be interested in continuing health care reforms, and rebuilding not just urban areas, but the globe. Uranus recently sextiled Pluto October 1997 to November 1998, a period that brought prosperity in the form of low interest rates, low inflation, and increased consumer confidence. The global market expanded (Pluto in Sagittarius) and the technology, especially, the biotech industry, grew - the results of new inventions, (Uranus in Aquarius).

441

Uranus opposite Pluto

The masses (Pluto) were suspicious of Uranus' new fangled ideas in 1900 to 1903 when Pluto was in Gemini and Uranus was in Sagittarius. The inventions of the airplane and car were not accepted by the public at first. These natives hold strong views which are not easily swayed. Later when they came of age in the 1930s, Uranus would square Pluto. Their strong nationalism present at their births set the stage for World War II. Their lives were forever changed by new inventions of aircraft and tanks now used for war.

Uranus square Pluto

Between 1931 and 1934, Uranus in Aries (individual rights) squared Pluto in Cancer (nationalism) sowing the seeds of World War II. In the United States many lives were put on hold by the Great Depression. Innovation and change took second place to survival. During this period of depression, Hitler gained his power, promising prosperity and a new order to desperate Germans.

When those who survived the war came of age in the 1950's, they resisted change, preferring conformity and the materialism of the fifties.

Neptune conjunct Pluto

Here desire for social reform and a new social order is strong. This aptly describes the mood of 1914 to 1916 when both Pluto and Neptune were in the sign of Cancer, disrupting many families during World War I.

Neptune trine Pluto

While this has not occurred in this century, it represents a sustained period of social and creative (Neptune) advancement (trine) for the masses (Pluto). Unfortunately, it does not occur in the next century either.

Neptune sextile Pluto

This aspect occurred from 1976 to 1984 when Neptune in Sagittarius sextiled Pluto in Libra. There was a tremendous surge of freedom. New ideas about marriage, law, and psychology were explored. The equal rights amendment, affirmative action, and new ideas about social justice were on the agenda. This aspect will occur in 2,024, ushering a sustained period of peace as the masses (Pluto) work for universal peace and brotherhood. Neptune will be in Pisces, bringing in a new surge in religious faith. China may even embrace the ideas of Christianity during this cycle. Pluto then enters Aquarius in 2,025 bringing freedom and brotherhood to the masses.

Neptune opposite Pluto

Neptune square Pluto

Fortunately neither aspect has occurred in this century or in the next century.

CHAPTER THIRTY-SIX

RESEARCH ON DEGREES OF THE ZODIAC

The following research on degrees of the zodiac came out of a study with my teacher, Dorothea Lynde. She constantly encouraged her students to keep careful records. While the scope of research is limited, it is hoped it will inspire other future students of astrology to continue research on the degrees. Observations from Aldrich, Carter, Robson and of course, Dorothea Lynde are recorded in these notes.

Esoteric astrologers often find that the planets highest in degree presents the most frustration to the native. Also degree of the Zodiac which conjunct fixed stars are very important for good or ill. For example, the fixed star Regulus, which is at 27 Leo, rules royalty. Its light is a thousand times more brilliant than our Sun. It is the most courageous star both in stamina and power. One born with their Sun conjunct Regulus will rise in life and have the power to come back again and again after a failure. On the other hand, Algol which is a 25 Taurus, has a very bad reputation. It is said to cause beheading and disgrace in an afflicted chart.

Aries

Afflictions in Aries may indicate accidents. According to C.E.O. Carter 22 degrees of the cardinal signs are frequently present in accidents. Also, when Mars is near the end of the sign, it is more prone to accidents.

FIXED STARS

Calculated by Vivian Robson

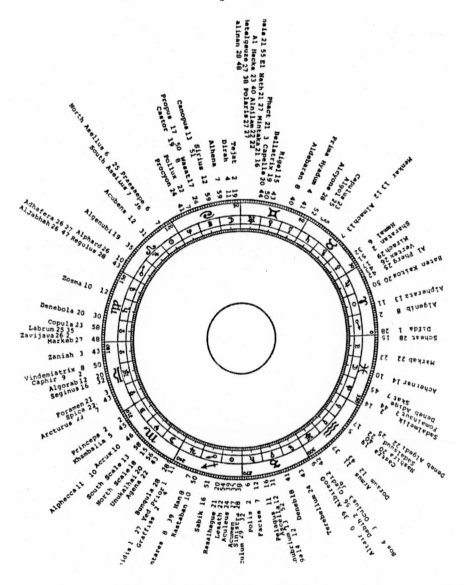

One degree, 28 minutes is associated with Difda which has the nature of Saturn.

Two degrees of Aries is considered the degree

of a surgeon.

Three degrees of Aries may be involved with abscesses or if afflicted, accidents to the eyes.

Four degrees of Aries is said to be the degree of birds and is found to be prominent in the chart of aviators.

Five degrees of Aries may indicate homicidal tendencies, when afflicted according to C.E.O. Carter.

Six degrees of Aries may indicate creativity and is usually present with architects.

Seven degrees of Aries may be associated with jaundice and is a degree of life and death.

Seven, eight and nine degrees of Aries are considered to be military degrees.

Eighth degree, two minutes of Aries conjunct Algenib, considered to be the seat of reason. The greater number of planets aspecting at birth or Algenib on the ascendant, the greater the intellect. The late Czar Nicholas had Jupiter at six Aries in his house of death, conjunct the Moon at eight Aries, a spot also associated with assassination. At the time of his death July 16, 1918, this point was brought into prominence.

Eight and nine degree Aries is often seen in the chart of generals and is associated with immortality.

Ten to twenty degrees of Aries is associated with electricity. Benjamin Franklin had his Neptune at 17 Aries.

Ten Aries indicates spiritual triumph, the ability to rise in life.

Thirteen Aries conjunct Andromeda's Head and is found in the chart of many doctors.

Fifteen Aries may figure in suicide. Stalin died when Mars was at 15 Aries. The transiting Moon was at 15 Aries when President Franklin Delano Roosevelt passed.

Seventeen Aries is considered a degree of oratorical ability. Theosophist, Annie Besant, a noted speaker, had her Uranus at 17 Aries.

Twenty Aries, fifty minutes Baten Kaitos is associated with abscesses. C.E.O. Carter says it may indicate accidents.

Twenty-two Aries is an artistic degree, associated with music.

Twenty-three Aries is also considered a musical degree.

Twenty-four degree Aries is a degree of watchfulness and curiosity. Walter Winchel, noted gossip columnist, had his Mercury here, giving him good detective ability.

Twenty-five Aries is connected with literature.

Twenty-six Aries is associated with discovery and exploration, sometimes controversy. Sir Francis Drake had his Neptune at twenty-six Aries trine Saturn and John Cabot had Uranus here.

Twenty-seven Aries is seen in the chart of generals and military leaders. Hitler had his Mercury here and Al Capone had his Moon at twenty-seven Aries.

Twenty-eight Aries may denote generosity, and power to realize a lofty ideal, and is sometimes associated with red hair. It can also denote teachers and philosophers.

Twenty-nine Aries is associated with Mirach, which give personal beauty, a love of home, a brilliant mind, and good fortune in marriage. However, when it is conjunct the Sun, it can indicate trouble with the opposite sex due to expectations, but it is otherwise favorable. With the Moon, it also brings trouble with the opposite sex due to indiscretions. Here it is also considered unfavorable for domestic affairs. With Mercury, it brings vacillation and instability. With Venus, it brings bad morals, voluptuous figure, scandal, drinking or drugs later in life. With Mars it brings ill manners, boisterous behavior, and recklessness, sometimes with evil associates. With Jupiter, Mirach brings help from women, but danger of scandal, much travel and sometimes legal difficulties. With Saturn, strong passions, debauchery, misdirected talents, and sometimes when well aspected mechanical genius. When it is conjunct Uranus, the mind is unbalanced leading to crime, insanity or occult studies. Here it is also bad for domestic affairs and may be associated with peculiar or violent death. Associated with Neptune, strong passions, ambition, eccentric or dishonest qualities may be present. Under affliction, it can also indicate a painful and lingering death.

Taurus

Zero Taurus can indicate an independent person, who needs to watch relations with the opposite sex. Adolph Hitler had his Sun at 0:46 Taurus.

One degree Taurus may indicate a reserved, diplomatic person with a strong will. It may also indicate a strong, heavy neck.

Two degree of Taurus denotes a person with original, independent ideas and strong ambition. Queen Elizabeth II has her part of fortune here.

Three degrees may show sympathy, sensitivity, and psychic ability. Two degrees, 51 minutes has a Mars-Saturn quality according to Aldrich. Frederick the Great had Neptune at one degree Taurus trine Uranus at six Virgo, Marshall Foch had Uranus at three Taurus, and General Patton Mercury three Taurus conjunct the Sun at five Taurus. (Check Petain)

Four Taurus indicates strong dominate qualities.

Five Taurus gives a friendly disposition.

Six Taurus, 32 degree is the placement of the

fixed star Hamal, which has the influence of Mars and Saturn. President Franklin Delano Roosevelt with his interest in helping others in difficult times had his Saturn here.

Seven degrees gives a love of comfort and luxury; often a successful marriage. According to Charubel: One liable to torture in one form or another. Look at planets and aspects involved with this degree to determine influence. Hamel's influence is also felt.

Eight degrees of Taurus denotes one who obtains peace through belief in higher power.

Ten Taurus may indicate mathematical or mechanical ability.

Eleven Taurus may show wealth and fame obtained through shrewdness.

Twelve Taurus shows a sympathetic and hopeful nature.

Thirteen Taurus conjunct the fixed star Menkar at thirteen degrees, twelve minutes which has a Saturn quality.

Fourteen degrees Taurus shows a peaceful person who may be rewarded for service to others. This degree also rules circulation. President Franklin Delano Roosevelt had Neptune at fourteen Taurus in the ninth house. He loved to travel by sea, and had an interest in the Navy. He was also charged with bringing on monetary confusion. The fixed star Thyge at fourteen Taurus is associated with the loss of fortune and has a Saturn influence. Conjunction of Jupiter and Saturn at fourteen Taurus (1940 and 1941) brought a time to try men's souls. This fixed star Mankar may let evil cruelty manifest. When coupled with Saturn, it is a great soul tester, with Jupiter it can give courage to overcome eventually.

Fifteen Taurus indicates a studious, self-reliant person.

Sixteen Taurus shows a prosperous marriage and one fond of food and luxury. Venus at sixteen degrees, fifty-eight minutes indicates artistry and music.

Seventeen Taurus shows a good, faithful person. May also give a powerful mind and interest in art and music.

Eighteen Taurus indicates a fiery, ambitious

person who believes he is right.

Nineteen Taurus shows a gentle genius who may need encouragement.

Twenty Taurus indicates one who will rise by his/her own efforts.

Twenty-two Taurus shows industry and thrift.

Twenty-three Taurus can be keen to detect fraud or deception.

Twenty-four Taurus is trusting and serves others.

Twenty-three, three minutes Taurus is famous for fixed star Algol. This is said to be a degree of beheading - literally and figuratively. In an afflicted chart, it often brings disgrace.

Twenty-six degrees, twenty-eight minutes is the most destructive region of the zodiac. Power and authority may be used unscrupulously - sometimes death.

Twenty-seven Taurus indicates wealth and success gained through thrift.

Twenty-eight Taurus by some accounts shows a happy, contented life. By other accounts, it is associated with heavy drinking.

Twenty-nine Taurus is associated with Alcyone which has a Moon-Mars influence. It is a famous acting degree, ruling fate, plot, and dramatics. This famous point in the Pleiades is said to be very bad for eyesight. Other degrees to watch for bad eyesight; six Leo and eight Sagittarius. When the Moon or Moon is afflicted in these degrees or planets here are afflicted by one of the malifics at birth, the person has trouble with the eyes. With severe affliction a person can become blind.

Gemini

Zero Gemini gains wealth and influence by helping others.

Two Gemini indicates a sincere, happy person, who prospers through friendship.

Zero to three degrees of Gemini may indicate draftsmanship abilities.

Four degrees, forty-one minutes is a degree of Prima hyadum which has a Saturn-Mercury influence. These positions are related to sharp intelligence and aviation ability.

Five Gemini indicates an all around person.

Six degrees, seven minutes is one of the most brilliant and intellectual degrees of the zodiac. Dante had his Mercury at six degrees, thirty minutes. This position is also good for reasoning and languages.

Seven Gemini shows a kind and generous person who is popular. It is considered to be one of the degrees of the heart. Shakespeare had his Neptune at seven Gemini.

Eight degrees, forty minutes relates to Aldebaran which is one of the four royal stars of Persia. Its influence is similar to Mercury, Mars and Jupiter conjunction. The person may have an ability for selling, trading or business.

Nine Gemini shows ability for solving other people's problems.

Ten Gemini indicates healing ability with a knowledge of human nature.

Eleven Gemini is associated with a desire for travel.

Twelve Gemini indicated original ideas.

Thirteen Gemini shows superior ability, but a roving tendency unless married to the right person.

Fifteen degrees, forty-three Gemini conjunct fixed star Rigel which Ptolemy and Lilly said has a Jupiter-Saturn influence, which can indicate lasting honor if well placed in the chart.

Sixteen Gemini indicates one who loves to help and advise others.

Seventeen Gemini shows reverence for advanced humanistic thought.

Eighteen Gemini gives ability for writing, selling or entertaining with keen mental powers.

Nineteen Gemini indicates success after many difficulties.

Twenty Gemini denotes a positive nature which wishes to aid humanity.

Twenty-one Gemini seeks knowledge and truth and is inclined to independent, progressive thought.

Twenty-two Gemini is fond of music, poetry, or art and has a strong desire for peace.

Twenty-three Gemini indicates the determination in order to succeed. The fixed star Capella here gives a Mars influence.

Twenty-four degrees denotes a sociable

person.

Twenty-five Gemini indicates mental ability to achieve great recognition.

Twenty-six Gemini shows ambition and self-esteem.

Twenty-seven Gemini shows applied artistic ability. It is also a degree of astrology. Polaris is at twenty-seven Gemini, twenty-seven minutes Betelgeuse twenty-seven degrees, thirty - eight minutes is very military with a Mars-Mercury influence.

Twenty-eight Gemini may indicate a love of friends and success in practical pursuits.

Twenty-nine Gemini shows original ideas and ability for writing. Rudolf Valentino had his Mercury at twenty-nine Gemini.

Cancer

Zero Cancer is a degree of diplomatic and political ability.

One Cancer denotes a contented person who has a happy family life.

Two Cancer often has a love of nature.

Three Cancer is said to govern sight and may give success to scientific research.

Four Cancer is a medical degree near Dirah, a fixed star at four degrees, eleven minutes that has a Mercury-Venus influence.

Five Cancer, seven degrees is a part of honor.

Seven Cancer, fifty-nine minutes (almost eight degrees) is the fixed star Alhena, which has a Mercury-Venus influence.

Ten Cancer is considered a degree of history. Calvin Coolidge, a president who had a passion for history, had his Sun here.

Eleven Cancer is sometimes associated with retentive memory; other astrologers view it as a degree associated with addiction and the disease cancer. Look to the aspects in the chart for more information.

Twelve to sixteen degrees of Cancer are known as business degrees.

Twelve degrees Cancer fifty-nine minutes is the placement of Sirius. Esoteric astrologers viewed Sirius as the great central Sun of our universe.

While its influence is that of Jupiter and Mars; it is sometimes associated with the disease cancer. Sirius also rules large animals such as horses, elephants, and camels. People with their Neptune at this degree may have magnetic powers over animals.

Fifteen Cancer is considered to be one of the degree of suicide.

Sixteen Cancer is associated with duty.

Seventeen cancer denotes honorable acquaintances.

Nineteen Cancer is associated with Castor. Many with affliction here have sine physical defect.

Twenty-two degrees, seven minutes is the fixed star Pollus. It may be connected with disease Cancer.

Twenty three Cancer is often given to forethought.

Twenty-four degrees, forty-one minutes is the fixed star Precyon, which has a Mars-Mercury influence.

Twenty-six Cancer to the end of the sign may be prominent in the disease cancer, according to Maurice Wemyss. Napoleon had his Saturn at twenty-six Cancer opposite his Moon at twenty-eight Capricorn.

Twenty-seven Cancer is a degree associated with farming.

Leo

Astrologer, C.E.O. Carter found Leo especially on the ascendant to be high in accidents and sometimes involved in infant mortality under affliction. However Sagittarius has a higher rate of accidents. In any event Leo is the sign of children, speculation including risk-taking, and romance.

Zero Leo is associated with acquisitions.

Three Leo may denote a tendency to biliousness.

Six Leo is in the Ascelli and has a Mars-Moon influence. It denotes a masterful person with a special mission in life. Sometimes it causes blindness or in a rising sign trouble to the left eye.

Six Leo twenty-five degrees is in the North Ascellus and has a Moon-Mars influence. It may denote fevers, quarrels, and slander.

Seven Leo thirty six degrees is the South Ascellus and it also denotes fevers, quarrels, and slander.

Eight Leo denotes leadership and visionary passion.

Eight Leo fifty-three degree conjunct Daybrethren.

Nine Leo is said to be associated with alcoholism as nine degrees in any fixed sign may give this influence.

Ten Leo is associated with love of brethren as Neptune north node is placed a ten degrees Leo, twenty-seven minutes according to George White.

Twelve degrees of Leo verging on thirteen is considered to be a degree that gives the most attractive personal appearance. Actress Lily Langtry had Mars at thirteen Leo. Acubens is here which has a Saturn-Mercury influence.

Thirteen Leo is considered a degree of literature.

Eighteen to twenty-two Leo may give medical ability.

Twenty Leo is a degree of faith.

Twenty-one Leo rules comedy in particular.

Twenty-three Leo is associated with the stage. If afflicted, it denotes anarchy.

Twenty-four degrees Leo, seven minutes is associated with travel by land.

Twenty-five Leo and twenty-five degrees of any fixed sign may have a tendency to alcoholism and suicide.

Twenty-five degrees, twenty-nine minutes Leo is connected with astrology. Astrologer, Alan Leo, had Saturn at this degree and astrologer Aldrich had twenty-seven Leo rising. The opposite points are also stressed as having great astrological interest.

Twenty-six degrees, ten minutes is the fixed star Aljabhah. This star has a Saturn-Mercury influence and may be associated with poisons and suicide. Alphard is also here and it has a Saturn-Venus influence.

Twenty-eight degrees, forty-three minutes is the degree of the fixed star Regulus which is one of the four royal stars of Persia. It is said to send out a thousand times more light than the sun. However we do not receive its light for 160 years after it is transmitted to us. If rising Regulus gives great honor and wealth according to the ancient astrologers. However, it can also bring violence and trouble if afflicted. Often it favors great victory over trouble. It is the most courageous star, giving stamina and the power to rise in life and come back after failure.

Virgo

Three Virgo is said to be associated with appendicitis.

Four Virgo is said to be associated with asthma.

Seven Degrees, ten minutes denotes a natural instinct for dress.

Seven Degrees, eighteen minutes Virgo is a dangerous degree

Eight Virgo is sometimes said to have homicidal tendencies.

Eleven to nineteen Virgo is said to rule beer and is prominent in the chart of brewers.

Eleven Virgo is a degree of astrology according

to Aldrich. Other degrees of astrology included twenty-seven Leo, twenty-seven Aquarius, and eleven Pisces.

Twelve to sixteen Virgo is considered a business area.

Thirteen and Fourteen are given as areas of transformation and versatility.

Sixteen Virgo is associated with Christian ministry. The Virgin Mary's birthday is celebrated on September eighth when the Sun is at sixteen Virgo.

Seventeen Virgo rules gliding and flowing and is common in the charts of yachtsmen. Franklin Roosevelt had his Uranus here. It is also a degree of abortion. The Moon placed here may deny children.

Twenty degrees Virgo, thirty-six degrees denotes the fixed star Denebola which has a Saturn-Venus influence. Well aspected, it may give riches, however, it is usually considered unfavorable.

Twenty-two Virgo is considered a military degree.

Twenty-three degrees, fifty-eight minutes Virgo is the placement of the Great Nebula Copula, which has a Moon-Venus influence. It rules poisons and the insect kingdom. It may also give strong passions, blindness, and disappointments, It is interesting in character and astrologically important.

Twenty-four to twenty-six Virgo is associated with painting.

Twenty-seven degrees, forty-eight minutes of Virgo is the star Markeb which has a Saturn-Jupiter quality. It is favorable for piety, educational work, and voyages.

Libra

Three degrees, twenty-three minutes of Libra is the location of Zaniah, a fixed star with the influence of Venus-Mercury. The degree often gives refinement, honor, and congeniality.

Six Libra is creative and is often present with architects.

Eight degrees, fifty minutes is the location of the fixed star, Vindemiatrix has a Saturn-Mercury influence. This star is often associated with dishonesty and may give loss of a partner. Many became interested in astrology when Uranus conjunct

Vindemiatrix in 1969 and 1970. Uranus here may also cause spinal trouble.

Nine degrees Libra, twenty-two minutes Libra is the placement of Caphur which has a favorable Mercury-Venus influence. Marie Antoinette had her Jupiter here and Annie Besand, born October 2, 1847 had her Sun here.

Twelve degrees and twenty minutes Libra is the fixed star Algorab. It is considered an adverse star with a Mars-Saturn influence. The Sun or Moon transiting this point is adverse. John Baird, the inventor of television had his Uranus here, Sir Oliver Lodge had Jupiter here and Eddie Rickenbacker, his Sun in this position.

Thirteen Libra which is connected with food and drink is often prominent in the chart of tea and coffee planters.

Fourteen Libra is a degree of lawyers and singers. Thomas E. Dewey, the fighting prosecutor had his Moon at fourteen Libra in the twelfth house. Interestingly enough, he was undecided on whether to choose a musical or legal career. His ascendant 27 Libra is considered to be a degree of pugnacity.

Fifteen Libra falling between Algorab and Seginus is considered to be unfavorable and may be a degree of suicide, under affliction.

Sixteen degrees, thirty-two minutes of Libra is the fixed star, Seginus, which is considered unfavorable with a Mercury-Saturn influence.

Seventeen Libra is favorable for electrical matters. According to Maurice Wimyss, sixteen, seventeen, eighteen, and nineteen degrees have been passing over the world's ascendant which we have made great progress in electricity. Benjamin Franklin had Neptune at this point. Volta, who received the Copley medal for his electrical research in 1791, had Sun opposite this point at sixteen Aries.

Twenty-one Libra is connected with stage and comedy. Under affliction it may be connected with suicide.

Twenty-one, three degrees of Libra is surrounded by the keyhole nebula and give danger to the eyes as do all nebula. With the Sun, it is said to give shipwreck.

Twenty-two Libra is artistic.

Twenty-two degrees, forty-three Libra is

the degree of Spica whose Venus-Mars influence is considered favorable. It is associated with success, renown, riches, love of art and science, and a sweet disposition. J.B. Priestly and Max Heindel had their Saturn here. William O. Douglas had his Sun here.

Twenty-four Libra is musical

Twenty-five Libra along with twenty-two and twenty-four is a degree of literature.

Twenty-six rules detectives.

Twenty-seven Libra is said to be a degree on consumption. Thomas E. Dewey had his ascendant here as did Hitler.

Twenty-eight Libra is a degree of hospitality.

Scorpio

Zero Scorpio gives a passionate and sensitive nature.

Two degrees Scorpio, two minutes is the location of the fixed star, Princeps, which has a Mercury-Saturn influence.

Five degree Scorpio, forty-five minutes is

the location of Khambalia, which has a Mercury-Mars influence. Neither Princeps or Khambalia is very well known or understood in astrological literature.

Six degrees of Scorpio is considered to be a degree of the occultist and healer when combined with Cancer and Capricorn. If afflicted, it can indicate a tendency to criminal activity, as it represents slippery people and things like serpents.

Eight Scorpio gives a strong desire especially for luxuries.

Ten degree Scorpio, forty-six minutes is the location of Acrux, which has a Jupiter influence. It bestows religious benefits, ceremonial magic, and mystery. Often it is found in the charts of occultists and astrologers. The Duke of Windsor had his Uranus conjunct Acrux trine the Moon, making him magnet to the opposite sex during the 1920s and 1930s.

Twelve degrees to sixteen Scorpio is said to be connected with business.

Thirteen Scorpio is connected with pleasure.

Thirteen degrees, fifty-eight minutes is the

location of the south scala, which has a Saturn-Mars nature. It is considered to have an adverse influence and may cause health issues if afflicted. Saturn placed here indicates karmic debts.

Sixteen Scorpio is considered a degree of growth.

Sixteen and seventeen Scorpio are degrees of painting and music.

Nineteen Scorpio in connection with Venus and Uranus is said to rule animal life.

Twenty degrees of Scorpio, fifty-six minutes is the location of Umrulhai a little known star. Its influence is most unpleasant as it is said to give accidents, immorality, violence, and danger from poisons.

Twenty-one Scorpio rules the bronchial tubes.

Twenty-two degrees, forty-three minutes is the location of Bella Centauri which has a Venus-Jupiter influence. It gives position, friendship, refinement, morality, health, and humor.

Twenty-five Scorpio is an unfortunate degree which is said to rule dumbness and alcohol. Einstein had his Pluto here.

Twenty-seven Scorpio is considered a fine degree associated with literature.

Twenty-eight degrees, twenty-eight minutes is the location of Alpha Centauri, is the nearest star to our Earth and has a Venus-Jupiter influence. The ancients called it "Toliman", which means the hereafter.

Twenty-nine Scorpio rules Antares, the most poisonous star in the constellations. Many wealthy business men and women have their Sun in the latter part of Scorpio.

Sagittarius

Zero degree, three minutes is a degree of draftsmanship; as is zero Gemini. Early degrees of Sagittarius have been prominent in the world horoscope at the time of building, great and enduring buildings of historical note.

Two Sagittarius is the location of Graffias, which has a Mars-Saturn influence. It is said to make one susceptible to contagious disease.

Four Sagittarius is a degree of aviation. Five Sagittarius, five Leo and five Aries are considered to be a degree of homicide.

Seven Sagittarius is considered the degree of the heart. It is said to be strong in the charts of children with planets here between the years of nine and ten.

Eight degrees, thirty-nine minutes is the location of Antares, which is one of the four royal stars of Persia in 3,000 BC as the "Watcher of the West". Its influence is that of Mars and Jupiter. It is marital in nature and seen in the charts commanders. It is said to give honor and preferred treatment. However, it has also been associated with eye trouble and some consider it a violent star.

Nine Sagittarius is a degree of homicide.

Twelve Sagittarius is a degree of satire. Walt Disney had his Sun here. Many of his productions are believed to be political thrusts at conditions here and abroad.

Thirteen Sagittarius is associated with accidents to wheeled vehicles.

Fourteen Sagittarius is known as a degree of acting.

Fourteen degrees, thirty minutes is considered a degree of indecision.

Seventeen Sagittarius is considered a degree of transition and a degree of curiosity. Walt Disney, developer of the animated cartoon, had his Uranus, the planet of novelty, here. Seventeen degrees of each is known as rash.

Eighteen Sagittarius is a degree of royalty, many monarchs have their Jupiter in Sagittarius.

Twenty to twenty-three Sagittarius are degrees of faith and is prominent in the charts of clergymen. Other degrees of faith and hope are twenty-three Aries and twenty-three Libra. Twenty-three Aquarius and twenty-three Leo are degrees of faith, hope, sympathy, and charity. Lewis Carroll had Venus rising in twenty-three conjunct Mars, sextile Jupiter. He had great faith in himself as did his "Alice in Wonderland".

Twenty-one Sagittarius is associated with growth. Twenty-two Sagittarius denotes one restless in nature and uncertain in temperament, one who ever seeks for the unobtainable and becomes worried because he cannot get it. In his cry, there is poetry - the poetry of a sad, hopeless nature, a kind of foreboding. It is a symbol of sighing.

Twenty-three Sagittarius is a military degree.

Twenty-four degree, forty-nine Sagittarius is the location of Asuleus, which had a Moon-Mars influence. When conjunct or opposite the Sun or Moon it may afflict the eyes.

Twenty-five Sagittarius is a degree of neuasthenia.

Twenty-seven degrees, thirty-five minutes Sagittarius is the location of Accumen, which also affects the eyes, if the Sun or Moon are conjunct or opposite.

Twenty-eight Sagittarius is a degree of consumption.

Twenty-nine degrees is considered a degree of imitation and acting.

Capricorn

One Capricorn is very ambitious. Thomas Edison had his Mars here.

Three Capricorn is a degree of sight. Charles

Dickens, who had such wonderful spiritual sight, had his Saturn at three Capricorn.

Four Capricorn is a medical degree.

Six Capricorn can be possessive.

Seven Capricorn is a degree of analogy. Facies is at seven degrees, twelve minutes of Capricorn, a cluster, one of the points which cause defective eyesight.

Ten Capricorn is a degree of history. President Wilson had his Sun close at eight Capricorn.

Eleven Capricorn is a degree of records. Manly Hall who collected and published vast amounts of ancient literature dealing with the occult and delivered hundreds of lectures on the occult and astrology had his Jupiter here. Jupiter at eleven Capricorn is common in the charts of historians. Manly Hall had his Moon at twenty-six Aquarius, a degree of communications, and his Saturn at fifteen Capricorn, a sense of duty.

Eleven degrees, sixteen minutes is the location of Pelagus, which has a Jupiter-Venus influence. For the most part it is favorable and gives religious inclinations. Often it is prominent in the charts of churchmen.

Twelve Capricorn is associated with religion.

Twelve degrees, thirty-one minutes of Capricorn is the location of Ascela, a star of favorable influence, not to be confused with the points of Asselli at six degrees, twenty-five minutes Leo and seven degrees, thirty-six minutes Leo.

Thirteen Capricorn is a degree of science.

Fourteen degrees, twelve minutes is the location of Vega, which has a Venus-Jupiter influence. Often it gives idealism, thoughtfulness, hopefulness, and refinement. While it makes natives grave and formal, it may also be very sensual, even promiscuous. When Uranus conjuncts Vega, the native may be critical and abrupt, and will suffer disappointments. Many children born in 1992 have this aspect.

Fifteen Capricorn brings out a sense of duty.

Sixteen Capricorn is also a degree of duty.

Seventeen Capricorn a degree of solid matter.

Eighteen Capricorn is a very intellectual degree and is associated with government. President Coolidge had his Saturn here.

Eighteen degrees, forty-one minutes is Deneb,

fixed star with a Mars-Jupiter influence.

Twenty-two Capricorn is a deep and scholarly degree. Charles Dickens had his Mercury here.

Twenty-four Capricorn is connected with government and authority. President Lincoln had his Moon here.

Twenty-four degrees, forty-three minutes of Capricorn in the location of Terebullum, which has a Venus-Saturn influence.

Twenty-six Capricorn is a degree of carefulness. Charubel, however, termed it "too revolting to be given". Einstein had his Mars at twenty-six Capricorn.

Twenty-seven Capricorn and adjacent degree are connected with land and farming.

Twenty-eight Capricorn denotes endurance. Al Capone's Sun was here opposite his Mars at twenty-eight Cancer, a degree of accumulating, square his Moon at twenty-seven Aries, a degree of enmity and pugnacity. His Mercury was at six Capricorn, possessions, and his Jupiter, the planet of expansion, was at eight Scorpio, a degree strong in desire, especially for luxuries.

Twenty-nine Capricorn is a degree of accumulating. When Saturn is here, the natives likes to accumulate old things.

Aquarius

Zero to five Aquarius are sometimes given as degree of homicide.

Zero degree, nine minutes is the location of Alberio, which is a fixed star with a Mercury-Venus influence. It is said to give beauty and a lovable disposition.

Zero degrees, thirty-nine minutes is the location of Attair, a fixed star with a Mars-Jupiter, which confers a bold, confident, ambitious, liberal nature. It is said to give great and sudden, but emphermeral wealth, as well as a position of command.

Two degrees, forty minutes of Aquarius is the fixed star, Geidi, with a Venus-Mars influence. It seems to bring many strange events into the world and may be a degree of beneficence and sacrifice. Neptune touched this area in May of 1998 and will be transiting February through December 1999.

Four Aquarius, a sensitive degree, in which health is greatly affected by home conditions. President Roosevelt had his Venus within two degrees in the fifth house of pleasure. Venus was also the ruler of the ninth and second houses. Money did not bring home the satisfaction it might have and his pleasure in travel was curtailed by his affliction. He would have been a most ardent sportsman, if not for his physical limitations.

Five Aquarius is a degree of strong, commanding nature with good business instincts.

Six Aquarius is said to give a gentle, chaste and retiring nature.

Seven Aquarius is docile in nature, often contented with little.

Eight Aquarius is original, daring and masterful. Often given to dangerous pursuits, not to be taken alive in battle.

Nine Aquarius has often been given as the President's or executive degree. Note: January through November, 1998, Uranus is on this degree, stirring up scandal in the White House with allegations of an affair between the President and

Monica Lewinsky. Later, Neptune will be on this degree off and on 2001 to 2002. The electoral college may be dissolved at this time.

Ten Aquarius is resourceful with good organizing ability.

Eleven Aquarius is considered to be a degree of sound judgment and is excellent for career. The person may have a tendency to incomprehensible behavior and isolation.

Eleven degree of Aquarius, thirty-seven minutes of Aquarius of fixed star, Arumes. President Roosevelt had his Sun here. Unfortunately there is not much information on its influence.

Twelve Aquarius denotes a psychic disposition, a sympathetic nature, and misfortune through inheritance.

Twelve degrees, forty-five minutes Aquarius is the location of Dorsum, which has a Saturn-Jupiter influence. It is said to give danger of bites from venomous creatures. Other than that, little is known of its influence.

Thirteen Aquarius is famous for good looks. When Mars is placed, between twelve and thirteen, assassination may result. It is also associated with literature.

Seventeen Aquarius is a degree of matter, associated with air and gases.

Eighteen Aquarius is a degree of explosiveness.

Nineteen Aquarius rules the back. Castra is here, a fixed star with a Saturn-Jupiter quality, which seems to have a bad reputation.

Twenty Aquarius is a degree of faith, associated with religion. Nashire is at twenty degrees, forty minutes of Aquarius. This fixed star is said to give danger from beasts. It may also give ultimate success. Some say it gives accidents from reptiles. More research is needed to clarify its influence.

Twenty-two Aquarius is the placement of Sadalsuud and Deneb Algirdi. The influence is mixed in nature and similar to Saturn-Jupiter.

Twenty-two to twenty-eight Aquarius is the high point of Aquarius. These degrees are associated with astrology. President Roosevelt with his Mercury here was said to be interested in astrology and the occult. Jeanne Dixon visited him in his last year in the White House.

Twenty-three Aquarius is a benevolent degree. President Lincoln, our most beloved president, had his Sun here.

Twenty-five Aquarius is a degree of alcoholism. Jack London, who was born January 12, 1876 at 2 P.M. in San Francisco, had his Saturn at this point. He was drinking heavily, when Saturn progressed to the exact degree.

Twenty-six Aquarius is a degree of communications. Manly Hall had his Moon here.

Twenty-seven Aquarius is an astrological degree, as is twenty-seven Leo and eleven of Virgo and Pisces. President Roosevelt, known for his understanding of human nature, had his Mercury here.

Pisces

Zero to five Pisces is connected with ideas of renunciation.

Two degrees, fourteen minutes is the location of Sadalmelik, a fixed star with a Saturn-Mercury influence. Its unfortunate influence causes persecution, sudden destruction, and possibly the death penalty under affliction. This does not apply to favorable aspects.

Four Pisces is a degree of asthma. The fixed star, Daneb-Adige which rules dog bites is at four degrees, fourteen minutes of Pisces. However, there is not much information to confirm its influence.

Eight Pisces is associated with knees and anemia.

Eight and nine degrees of Pisces seems to be connected with tragedy in some way. Eight degrees is said to deal with assassination.

Eleven Pisces is connected to astrology.

Twelve to sixteen Pisces is connected with business.

Thirteen Pisces is a ministerial degree, often enhancing a clergyman's oratorical or acting ability.

Thirteen and fourteen Pisces is connected with the stage.

The second decante of Pisces is said to rule beer and drunkenness. This decante covers ten to nineteen Pisces.

Seventeen Pisces is a degree of liquid matter.

Eighteen to nineteen Pisces is associated with physical handicap. Nineteen to twenty Pisces is associated with digestive ailments.

Twenty-two Pisces is called the novelist's degree. It is also a military degree and is associated with appendicitis.

Twenty-two degrees, twenty-two minutes of Pisces is the location of the fixed star, Markab, which is said to give honors, but also dangers from fire and fever.

Twenty-three Pisces. Albert Einstein, who revolutionized physics with his theory of relativity, had his Sun here. The Sun here gives a strong imagination and the ability to synthesize. He also has keen analytical ability with his Sun trine Pluto at twenty-five Scorpio. With his Mars in Capricorn, he made careful observations. His Moon at fourteen Gemini, its position is frequently found in astronomer's charts.

Twenty-four to twenty-six degrees are considered degrees of painting.

Twenty-five Pisces may sometimes indicate afflictions from Cancer.

Twenty-seven Pisces indicates the high possibilities of a mission and is considered to be a degree of spiritual enlightenment. Queen Elizabeth II has her Uranus here.

CHAPTER THIRTY-SEVEN

CASE HISTORIES

Drew Barrymore

Feb 21, 1975

Culver City, CA

11:51 A.M. P.S.T.

Source: Lois Rodden

Profiles of Women

With the Sun at the top of her chart, Drew Barrymore was born to shine! Jupiter and Venus bless her tenth of career as well. Her sensitivity is strong with Neptune in Sagittarius square her Sun at 2 Pisces. With Gemini rising, she seems friendly and carefree, hiding her sensitivity and innate shyness. The ruler of the chart is Mercury in Aquarius in the ninth house square Uranus, making her impulsive by nature. In the past, she has had a reputation as a difficult child. Drew, who won our hearts in E.T. was in a drug rehab program at thirteen. This "wild child" however, is greatly misunderstood. Her Venus is exalted in Pisces, conjunct Jupiter, she is at heart a humanitarian. With five of her ten parents in water signs, Drew is ultra sensitive, even naive and trusting. Problems with her parents, shown by the Moon conjunct Saturn, may be the root of her early difficulties. This indicates a child more "sinned against than sinning".

Fortunately Drew did not stay down for long. She has a grand trine between the Moon at three Cancer in the first house, Uranus at two Scorpio in the fifth house, and the Sun at two Pisces in the tenth house. She is slated for life-long success on the silver screen, if she can overcome a tendency toward depression (Moon conjunct Saturn) and addiction (Sun square Neptune). She has three planets in exaltation to help her. The first is Venus in Pisces which adds to her charm and artistic nature. The second is Mercury in Aquarius which gives her an excellent memory and intelligence. The third planet, Mars exalted in Capricorn, in the eighth house makes her a fighter, willing to work hard at life's battles.

Her soul cycle, the south node in the twelfth

house, indicates one who has been reclusive in a past life. In this life her destiny is to be "in the world, but not of it". The lucky north node in the sixth house indicates one who benefits from work. However the nodes both square the Sun indicating a karmic relationship with her father, John Drew Barrymore, who suffered from substance abuse himself. Such a square eclipses the father's influence and may indicate problems with men. Drew's impulsive marriage to Jeremy Thomas on March 20, 1994 lasted only 29 days! Since then her career has skyrocketed. The transit of Pluto conjunct her lucky north node brought an abundance of screen opportunities in 1997 and 1998.

Her future does include another marriage. With Gemini rising, she wants a Sagittarius style partner to "pal" around with. A nurturer at heart, Drew would make a conscientious mother. Success and romance are strong in 2,001. She may well receive an academy award nomination in 2,001. By 2,003 Neptune will conjunct her Mercury in Aquarius in the ninth house, bringing a change of residence, perhaps abroad. International success is seen in her chart at that time. Look for a compassionate side to emerge in Drew as she matures. Her early struggles will turn out to be "blessings in disguise".

Drew Barrymore

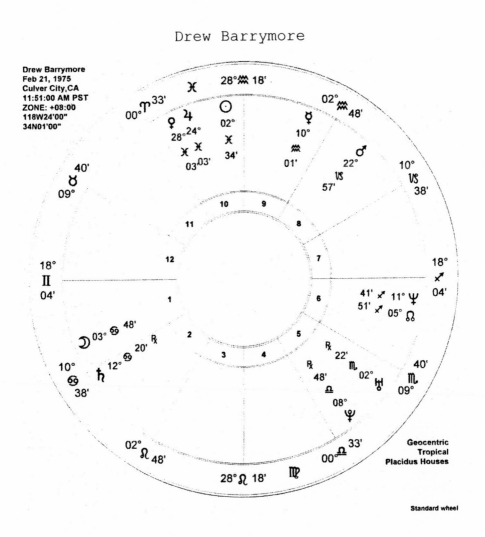

Edgar Cayce

March 17, 1877, 3m, C.S.T., Hopkinville

Kentucky

Edgar Cayce, "America's sleeping prophet", was born under the mystical sign of Pisces, with his Moon in Taurus and a Leo ascendant. With eight of the ten planets on the right hand side of the chart, much of his life would be dedicated to helping others, with little concern for his own needs. Indeed he continued giving readings even against the advice of his guides, which many believe caused his death in 1945. With five of his planets in earth signs, he could be conservative in his outlook, but with four planets in water signs, he was a "soft touch". His one fire planet, Uranus in Leo, is one ascendant, giving him a temper at times, and a strong independent streak.

His sun in the mystical sign of Pisces in the eighth house of the occult definitely indicates a psychic nature. The Sun sextiling Pluto in Taurus in the tenth house of career shows he would be recognized for this unique talent. His Moon in

Taurus gave him an easy-going nature, unless crossed - then Cayce could show a stubborn streak. His Moon conjunct Neptune in the ninth house of the higher mind and dreams gave him easy access to the world beyond through the trance state. The Moon esoterically rules the astral body and Neptune the cosmic world. The combination also added to his charisma. The Moon in Taurus trine Jupiter and Mars in the fifth house gave strong family ties and love of children. He was a Sunday school teacher for many years - always attracting large classes.

He married his wife Gladys early, Venus in Pisces sextile the Moon and Mars; and took his marriage vows seriously, Venus conjunct Saturn. His marriage was by all accounts a happy one, the lucky north node in his house of marriage. However, it was not without financial struggles. Early in his work, his guides predicted he would be very rich or very poor. With Uranus on the ascendant, he was destined to extremes in temperament at times and in finances. While his psychic abilities, Uranus ascendant, Pluto midheaven, were extraordinary, he dervied little benefit from them personally - the south node in the first house.

However weak in resources, Edgar Cayce always attracted supportive females. His wife Gladys conducted the readings, while his secretary, Gladys Davis, recorded the sessions. Both remained devoted to Cayce throughout his life. Cayce's chart is not without its flaws. His moon in Taurus makes a wide square to Uranus in the first house indicating a strong will and ego. However Edgar Cayce worked hard to maintain a spiritual perspective. Disciplined by nature, he read the Bible each year of his life and placed great faith in his teachings. He also took seriously the advice given by his guides.

For a complete analysis of Edgar Cayce's chart and past lives, read <u>Toward a New Astrology</u> by Ry Redd.

Edgar Cayce

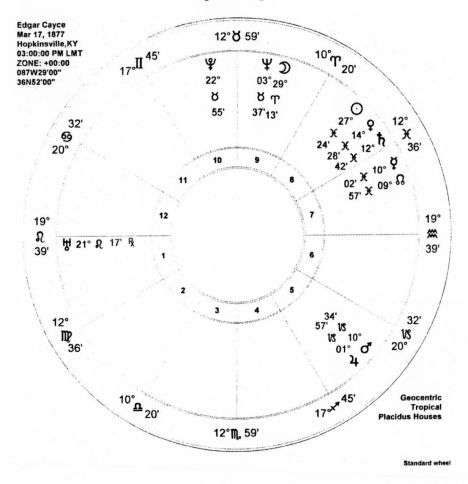

Edgar Cayce
Mar 17, 1877
Hopkinsville,KY
03:00:00 PM LMT
ZONE: +00:00
087W29'00"
36N52'00"

Geocentric
Tropical
Placidus Houses

Standard wheel

495

Bill Clinton

The most obvious feature of Bill Clinton's chart is his intelligence with five of his ten planets in air signs, joined by his ascendant and lucky north node. Next there is a generosity of spirit with four planets in fire signs. There are several sextiles between the group of fire and sir planets, creating protection and good fortune. His one earth planet the Moon in Taurus is not well placed. While the Moon is exalted in Taurus giving great charm it is poorly placed in the eighth house of sex and joint finance. Both have been issues for Clinton with scandals involving White Water and Gennifer Flowers, Paula Jones, and Monica Lewinsky. John F. Kennedy also had the Moon in the eighth house. Like Kennedy, Clinton faces more danger in July of 1999 to about July of 2,000. During this cycle his health bares watching!

In analyzing Clinton's chart, he has an abundance of free will with eight of his ten planets on the left hand side of the chart. He is definitely a self-made man. However, with his Sun at 26 Leo in the eleventh house of friends, his friends are

ever ready to aid him. With his Mercury in Leo he
is popular and likes to have fun. Since his Sun
conjunct Mercury, he has a difficult time seeing
himself as others see him. His Sun also sextiles
Jupiter in Libra giving him a strong interest in
politics and diplomacy. Since the Sun is also
sextiled by Uranus in the ninth house of law, he
is an excellent lawyer and destined to be noticed
with Uranus conjunct the lucky north node. His
north node in Gemini, in the ninth house, indicates
good luck in law, higher education, and foreign
affairs. Since the north makes an exact trine to
the midpoint of his Venus-Jupiter conjunction in
the fifth house, Clinton was destined for great
recognition and many steps up in life. His soul
cycle indicates leadership especially in foreign
affairs.

His noble nature, the Sun in Leo; however, is
undercut by the earthy Moon in Taurus. The two
planets square each other, making a deep dichotomy
in his personality. However strong his Leo nature,
his Moon earthy Taurus is equally strong. On one
hand he has great pride and a strong ego willing to

fight for his beliefs; on the other hand desire for personal gratification is strong.

With Libra rising, Clinton has a strong charm, but is easily lead. In Hillary, he found the strong mate the type one with Libra rising desires. Perhaps, she more than anyone is responsible for putting him in the White House. However, the marriage will undergo even transformations starting about the Spring of 1999. Hillary may begin to distance herself from the union. Since his Sun squares the Moon, Clinton doesn't really understand women. However, with Mars, Neptune, and Venus in Libra he has a great desire for partnership and for emotional support. He can be persuasive, charismatic, and socially adroit.

In terms of politics, Clinton is very protected with Pluto trining his Sun until October of 1998. By 1999, this aspect recedes, and he may have more legal difficulties in the spring of 1999.

Even though acquitten in 1999, his career looks stagnant until 2006.

Bill Clinton

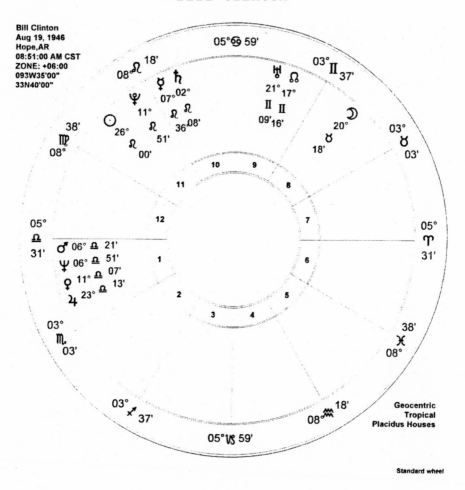

Bill Clinton
Aug 19, 1946
Hope,AR
08:51:00 AM CST
ZONE: +06:00
093W35'00"
33N40'00"

Geocentric
Tropical
Placidus Houses

Standard wheel

Hillary Clinton

At first glance, one can see the strong, ambitious image the First Lady has with the Moon at the top of her chart in the tenth house making a harsh square to Uranus in the twelfth house of hidden enemies. It is no wonder she is so controversial! However, the rest of the chart tells a very different story. Her Sun in Libra in the fifth house of creativity and children makes a hidden trine intellectual veneer. Gemini rising often has a complex Mercurial nature. With the ruler of the chart in the sixth house conjunct the unlucky south node, her image is often challenged and is not always flattering in the media. Her opposite node, the north node in Taurus in the twelfth house indicates intuitive ability. Her soul cycle: the power behind the throne.

With her Sun in the fifth house of children, she is a most devoted mother - even indulgent. She idealized Chelsea with Neptune in the fifth sextiling Mars, with Pluto and Saturn in the third house. This insures a sincere and lasting bond between mother and daughter. Interestingly enough, while she does have her daughter's interest uppermost in her mind, Mrs. Clinton is not particularly domestic, preferring her career to "hands on motherhood." This is seen by the Moon in the tenth squaring Uranus. She may lack patience at times with domestic matters. Her temper is also quick and unrelenting in nature. Her pride and loyalty are strong. However, disappointment can lead to temper tantrums.

In addition, her Venus, which is not well placed in Scorpio, is blocked by material Saturn, cruel Mars, and powerful Pluto. To avoid errors in judgment, Mrs. Clinton needs to heed her advisors in matters of state, but she is not inclined to do so as her Mercury in Scorpio is also squared by Mars, Pluto, and Saturn. On one hand she may work very hard but on the other, it is doubtful her efforts will escape criticism and controversy.

While appearing confident, even defiant at times, Mrs. Clinton often lacks faith in herself. This seen by her Mercury in Scorpio conjunct the unlucky south node. She needs the support of her husband and daughter or those close to her to function successfully. Mrs. Clinton is prone to depression and moodiness. As President Clinton's influence is weakened in 1999, she may show increased instability. Daughter Chelsea and health may be a concern for the First Lady as transiting Neptune squares her Sun in the fifth house. This also indicates a loss of popularity and emotional, if not physical, separation from her husband and/or concern for Chelsea's future.

Her nerves of steel may fray when transiting Uranus squares her fifth house of Venus between April and August in 1999. However, Hillary will emerge even stronger in 2,001 as transiting Pluto trines her Mars in her third house of writing, teaching, and travel. She may well be appointed to a prestigous and well deserved position on a senate committee. Meanwhile, she needs to realistically review her relationships, watch her health, and bide her time. May and June of 2,000 could definitely be a turning point for her when Jupiter conjuncts her South node in the sixth house of work.

Hillary Rodham Clinton

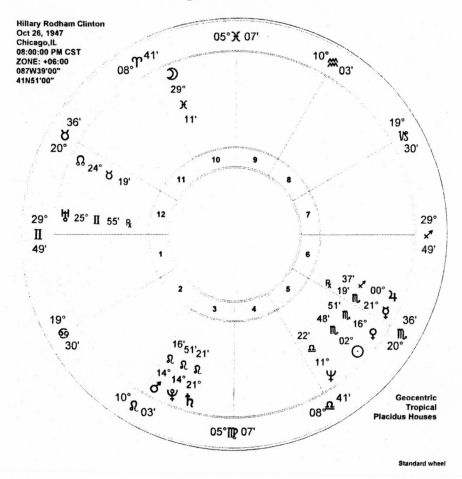

Hillary Rodham Clinton
Oct 26, 1947
Chicago,IL
08:00:00 PM CST
ZONE: +06:00
087W39'00"
41N51'00"

05° ♓ 07'

10° ♒ 03'

08° ♈ 41'

☽ 29° ♓ 11'

19° ♑ 30'

36' ♉ 20°

☊ 24° ♉ 19'

10 9

11 8

♅ 25° ♊ 55' ℞

12 7

29° ♊ 49'

29° ♐ 49'

1

2 5

☊ R 37' 19' ♐ 00' ♃
51' ♏ 21° ☿
48' ♏ 16°
22' ♏ 02° ♀

3 4

6

19° ♋ 30'

16' 51' 21'
14° ♌ ♌
14° ♌ 21°
☌ ♆ ♄

10° ♌ 03'

♏ 20°

11° ♆

08° ♎ 41'

Geocentric
Tropical
Placidus Houses

05° ♍ 07'

Standard wheel

Leonardo DiCaprio

November 11, 1974

2:27 A.M. P.S.T.

Los Angeles, CA

Source Lois Rodden's Data News #70

Leonardo DiCaprio has one lucky chart with five planets in his second house of money - three of which are part of a grand trine to Jupiter in sixth house of work and Saturn in the tenth house of career. Literally, he would make money in any career he chose! One, he loves to work and two, he's willing to work hard.

At first glance this does not seem the chart of an actor, with shy Virgo rising and Saturn, the reality planet in the tenth house of career. However, his ruling planet in Libra conjunct Uranus, giving a magnetic personality and the Moon in Libra shows public appeal. Saturn, while practical, does trine Venus, the artist's planet and Jupiter the planet of good fortune. His soul cycle is more telling of acting ability with the lucky north node conjunct Neptune, planet of illusion, in third house of communications. He truly is a reincarnated artist!

On a personal note, he is a private person. With Virgo rising and Sun and Venus is Scorpio, he prefers to keep his personal life quiet. However, he has two sides to his personality. His Moon in Libra in first house, which accents his handsome features, give great charm. The ladies do love him. Warning: women are a potential source of trouble for Leonardo. With his charming Moon square Saturn, he is attracted to older women, and also women with a past. However with Neptune sextiling Moon he can easily regroup.

With transiting Jupiter conjunct his seventh house of public, 1998 was Leonardo's year! However, look for even more dramatic success in 1999 and 2,000 as Pluto conjunct his Neptune. He may well receive another Oscar nomination! 2004 could bring relationship adjustments.

Leonardo DiCaprio

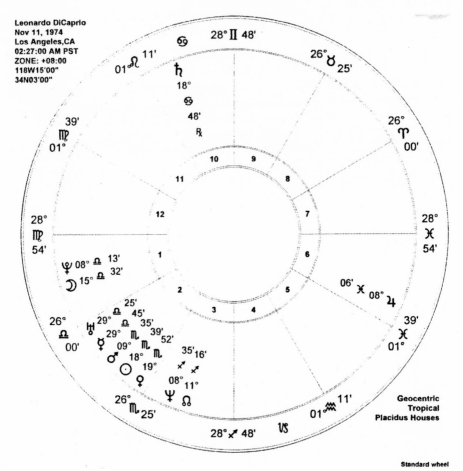

Leonardo DiCaprio
Nov 11, 1974
Los Angeles,CA
02:27:00 AM PST
ZONE: +08:00
118W15'00"
34N03'00"

Geocentric
Tropical
Placidus Houses

Standard wheel

Clint Eastwood

May 31, 1930

5:35 P.M. San Francisco, CA

Source: The American Book of Charts

Clint Eastwood's star quality was evident from birth. His midheaven is a degree of royalty, the planet of glamour, Neptune, conjunct. His power point are the Sun in Gemini in the seventh house - good for working with the public, Moon in Leo in the house, giving him a flair for drama, and a very private Scorpio ascendant. He is careful to guard his privacy, which at times can be at odds with his need to shine, Moon in Leo. While ruggedly handsome at 6'4", he keeps a tight rein on his emotions. With the Sun square Neptune, he can be shy at times. In fact his soul cycle indicated by the south node in the 12th house is one of a past spiritual seeker, destined to be in the world in this life.

With the majority, eight of his ten planets on the right hand side of the chart, contrary to his "macho" image, he is very much a "soft touch". However, he is rugged, with his ruler, Pluto in

Cancer in the eighth house of ambition, opposite Saturn - "the school of hard knocks". Pluto at eighteen Cancer makes a wide conjunction to Venus at eight Cancer. Both planets trine Uranus at fourteen Aries in the fifth house of art and drama cinching his success. Children are very important to Clint Eastwood. However, he is also a very passionate man, Venus square Uranus, and given to affairs. Unfortunately, his marriage of twenty-five years ended in divorce in 1979, producing two children. After a well-publicized split from actress Sondra Lock, he has happily remarried for a second time.

Women may be a source of concern for Eastwood, stemming back with his relationship with his mother, as the Moon square Mars and the North node in the sixth house. His early family may have lacked warmth and financial support. However with Jupiter in the eighth house, he was quite capable with hard work and endurance to make his own success. His Jupiter in Gemini sextile Mars in Aries give athletic and mechanical ability. Mars also conjunct the lucky north node in the sixth house, giving him a strong desire to be his own boss.

His Mercury at 23 Taurus shows a stubborn streak - one who will definitely not back down if he feels he is in the right. Mercury makes a hidden trine to the Moon at 1 Leo giving him excellent concentration and a long memory.

In 1999, Clint Eastwood needs to watch his health - particularly the lungs. Male family members may also be a source of concern this year as well. He is due for some deep psychological change in 1999 and needs to guard against emotional losses. On the positive side his fame continues and his pictures should do well at the box office through 2,003. He may well be drawn into national politics by the year 2,001. Even greater success is seen at that time. He may well decide to have more children which would be a definite spiritual benefit. Any illness, he may encounter will be overcome by 2,001.

Clint Eastwood

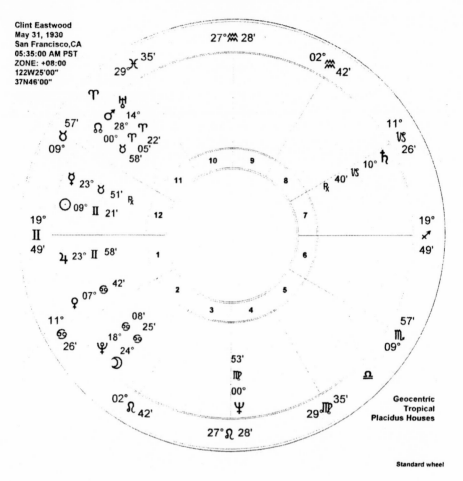

Clint Eastwood
May 31, 1930
San Francisco,CA
05:35:00 AM PST
ZONE: +08:00
122W25'00"
37N46'00"

Geocentric
Tropical
Placidus Houses

Standard wheel

Jack Kerouac

March 12, 1922

5:00 P.M.

Lowell, MA

Source: The American Book of Charts

Jack Kerouac began life in a lower-middle class family of French Canadian descent in the mill town of Lowell, MA. He went to Columbia University on an athletic scholarship. His Bohemian concepts started in what he termed the "beat generation". His chart shows he was destined to be before the public with Moon conjunct the ascendant and his Sun conjunct Venus in the seventh house. Kerouac was a complex man with two sides to his personality, the mystical, creative Sun in Pisces, opposite his Moon in the analytical, perfectionistic sign of Virgo. Born during a full Moon, he was full of life.

His career is shown by Pluto seven Cancer in the tenth house of career making a trine to Uranus in the sixth house and sextiling the Moon in Virgo. He had great determination and original ideas, coupled with good writing skills of the Moon conjunct his Virgo rising sign. Often Virgo rising makes a good analytical writer, but with Kerouac's Sun in Pisces he was also a poet. His ruler, Mercury at 24 Aquarius, falls in his sixth house of work, indicating he would make an excellent writer, salesman, or teacher. With Mercury trines Jupiter showing great intelligence, but opposite Neptune, little personal benefit. Indeed, he died with few personal possessions. With a soul of a poet, Kerouac seemed above the mundane affairs of life.

With his Mars in Sagittarius, he craved adventure - not creature comforts! Since Mars squared his Moon, he remained rootless most of his life. It also indicated a conflicted relationship with his mother who remained devoted to him throughout her life. His Mars in the fourth can indicate domestic problems, of which Kerouac had plenty. An early marriage which produced a daughter, ended in divorce after a few years. His daughter, an only child, was estranged from him at the time of his death. His last wife, Stella, a maternal figure, took care of him after his own mother died.

These relationships are foretold by his Venus at 29 Pisces - the planet highest in degree in the chart which is usually the most problematic. With Venus conjunct the Sun, Kerouac could be self absorbed and at times myopic in personal relationships. While a gentle lover, Venus is exalted in Pisces, he would not make a practical mate. Indeed with Pisces on the seventh house, he craved a "dream girl" which he never found in human form.

His soul cycle indicated by his lucky north node at eight Libra conjunct the fixed star Spica is one destined to lead. He was truly a pioneer in literature. His <u>On the Road</u>, now a classic, started a whole new genre in literature. Unfortunately the north node also squared Pluto in the tenth house and he was not destined to benefit from his fame. Indeed his time on Earth was short. He died at 47 - leaving legions of fans.

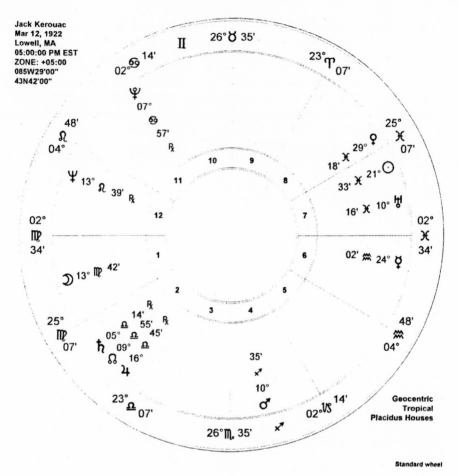

Jack Kerouac
Mar 12, 1922
Lowell, MA
05:00:00 PM EST
ZONE: +05:00
085W29'00"
43N42'00"

Geocentric
Tropical
Placidus Houses

Standard wheel

Martin Luther King, Jr.

January 15, 1929

12:00 noon

Atlanta, Georgia

Source: Circle Book of Charts

At first glance, Martin Luther King, Jr, was a born leader. With the north node in the first house trine his Sun at 25 Capricorn, his soul cycle indicates a magentic personality, destined for public life. He had the kind of charisma which inspired both men and women. Furthermore, Jupiter, the greater benefic, rising star - a clear indication of one on a mission in this life. With Neptune in his fifth house of inspiration trine Jupiter conjunct the ascendant, his personal courage inspired a whole generation to fight for civil rights. Saturn completes the grand trine to Neptune and Jupiter showing a great personal protection and guidance from Above.

With eight of his planets on the side of free will, Martin Luther King was a self-made man. He worked hard, Jupiter square his Sun, and was determined, Sun opposite Pluto, to succeed.

However fate would intervene swiftly in his life and remove him from life's arena all too soon. The Sun opposite Pluto indicates unpopular beliefs, coupled with danger from violence, (Mars opposite Saturn) demonstrates he was destined for a short life.

He seemed to know his destiny.. Indeed sometimes he seemed to be a prophet as well as a preacher! The ruler of chart, Venus, in the psychic sign of Pisces, conjunct the Moon which is also in Pisces. The two combined gave him great compassion and intuition. He knew how to read people intuitively. Since the Moon and Venus trine Pluto, he was destined for a place in history. Women would also play a significant role in his life. His wife, Coretta Scott King, has dedicated her life to his memory.

If he had lived, he surely would have written many books. His Mercury is exalted in Aquarius, in the tenth house of career, indicating writing and lecturing abilities. He was a genuine scholar, receiving his doctorate from Boston University. However, his greatest gift was his humane heart -

the spirit of which lives on in his "I Have a Dream" speech.

Martin Luther King Jr.

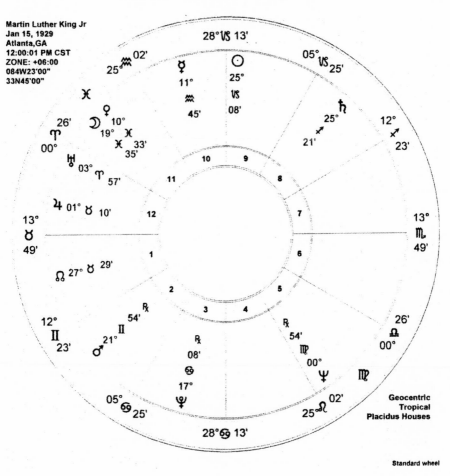

Steven Spielberg

December 18, 1946, 6:16 P.M.

Cincinnati, Ohio

At first glance, Steven Spielberg's chart indicates he was destined to make big money - serious money, with Pluto and Saturn in his second house of finance. These planets trine Mercury in the sixth house of work, indicate large sums of money would come from writing, communications, and commerce. Pluto-Saturn conjunction also benefits from a sextile to Neptune in the fourth house adding to intuition.

His closest aspect in the chart - the lucky north node making an exact trine to Neptune, shows a Divine destiny. This soul cycle, the north node in the twelfth house, gives much "behind the scenes" support. This lucky north node conjunct Uranus in the twelfth house of the unconscious mind accounts for uncanny success. Spielberg has great creativity combined with "mass appeal". His finances, which should take another step up in the spring of 1999, are greatly protected!

The key to any chart is the ruling planet. Spielberg has a Cancer ascendant which makes the Moon his ruling planet. Cancer rising adds a gentle paternal quality to this otherwise dynamic chart. With the Moon in Scorpio, he can be intense in his pursuit of fifth house pleasures - adventure, romance, children, and creativity. His Moon in Scorpio is warmed by a conjunction to Jupiter expanding his creativity. Jupiter conjunct Jupiter indicates an artistic temperament.

This would dovetail with his Sun in the fiery sign of Sagittarius. Steven Spielberg is as much a visionary as he is a film maker. In films such as Schindler's List, he inspires as much as entertains. He works hard at his craft, indicated by the Sun conjunct Mars in the sixth house. This Mars is exalted in Capricorn which gives excellent methods of organization and the ambition to attempt great works. Since Mars is the only planet in an earth sign and four in fire signs, Spielberg is interested more in creating than earning a buck.

Private by nature, nine of his ten planets are below the horizon, he prefers to live away from Hollywood, with his wife Kate Capshaw, and his children. With Neptune in the fourth house, his home is his sanctuary. While his Sun is in the outgoing sign of Sagittarius, his Moon square Saturn conjunct Pluto, he may have had difficulties with one parent. He is prone to depression, and tends to take his time before placing his trust in others. While Spielberg may have examined these early wounds in therapy, he is not likely to share them with the world.

In his future, which is good, his intuition is due for a boost in 2,001. Spielberg may even produce a film with a reincarnation theme in 2,003! Meanwhile the box office will be kind to him in the Spring and Summer of 1999. Assets need to be safeguarded as there could be a lawsuit as early as the Spring of 2,000.

Steven Spielberg

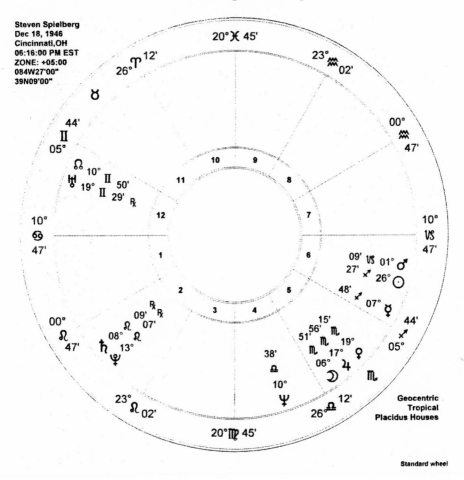

Steven Spielberg
Dec 18, 1946
Cincinnati,OH
06:16:00 PM EST
ZONE: +05:00
084W27'00"
39N09'00"

20° ♓ 45'

23° ♒ 02'

26° ♈ 12'

00° ♒ 47'

♉

44'
♊ 05°

♌ 10° ♊ 50'
⛢ 19° ♊ 29' ℞

10°
♋ 47'

10°
♑ 47'

09' ♑ 01' ♂
27' ♐ 26' ☉
48' ♐ 07° ☿

09' ℞ ℞
08° ♌ 07'
♄ ♌ 13°
♆

15'
56' ♏
51' ♏ 19°
♏ 17° ♀
06' ♃ ♏

44'
05°

00°
♌ 47'

38'
♎

10°
♆

23° ♌ 02'

26° ♎ 12'

20° ♍ 45'

10
9
11
8
12
7
1
6
2
5
3
4

Geocentric
Tropical
Placidus Houses

Standard wheel

Martha Stewart

August 3, 1941, 1:33 P.M. EST

Jersey City, N.J.

Source: Profiles of Women

by Lois Rodden

At first sight, one can see Martha Stewart was born to be an entrepreneur as the marjoity (eight) of her planets are above the horizon, with her Sun 10 Leo the highest planet in her chart close to her 18 Leo midheaven. Her ambition and hard work are indicated by Scorpio rising. She can also keep a secret well!

Her ruler, Pluto, is in the ninth house of writing and publishing, indicating talents in that direction. The two planets below the horizon are in the money house: the Moon at 25 Sagittarius in the second, giving her a penchant for collecting, and Mars at 16 Aries in the sixth house of work, giving her a zeal for hard work around the house and garden. These two planets form a grand trine to her Sun in Leo in the ninth house of publishing, promising success in career regarding publishing, writing, foreign affairs or the law. Pluto conjunct her Sun in the ninth shows her ability to influence the masses (Pluto). Her Mercury at 25 Cancer is also in the ninth house illustrating the sentimental side to her nature.

Her soul cycle, the north in Virgo conjunct Neptune, trining Saturn and Uranus in the seventh house indicates success with the public. Martha's chart shows a noble nature - one who has given generously to others in past lives. She also has an uncanny ability to be a trend setter with her intuitive Mercury in Cancer sextile her lucky north node.

Martha may be very successful, but this success has come at the expense of hard work and her marriage, which ended in divorce in 1987. She is said to be an insomniac, sleeping some four hours a night (Rodden). Astrologically she is prone to emotional upsets with her overly critical and sensitive Moon in Sagittarius square Neptune. Her refined Venus in Virgo in the tenth, may be overly ambitious as it squares Jupiter in the eighth. This could create a sweet tooth and a tendency to have crushes. While an excellent speaker and tireless writer, she may have to watch her words or eat them later with Mercury in Cancer square Mars in Aries!

Her chart shows expansion into foreign countries as Pluto trines the Sun in Leo and a romance for

Martha all by the year 2,000. However, before this Pluto squares her Venus, some deep soul searching in 1998 and 1999 and possible health problems, which she will definitely overcome, will have to be addressed. Her 2003-4 legal problems are indicated by transiting Neptune opposite her Sun she will regroup in 2005.

Martha Stewart

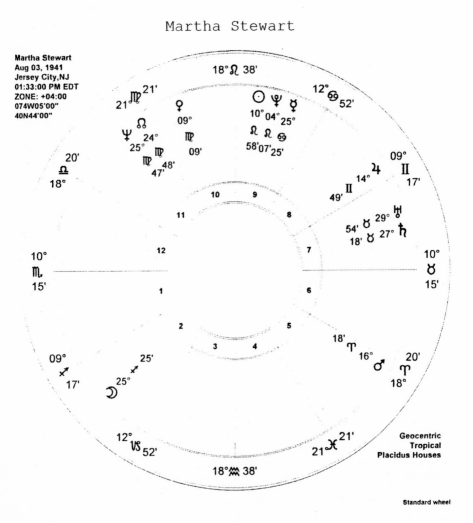

Martha Stewart
Aug 03, 1941
Jersey City, NJ
01:33:00 PM EDT
ZONE: +04:00
074W05'00"
40N44'00"

Geocentric
Tropical
Placidus Houses

Standard wheel

CHAPTER THIRTY-EIGHT
THE TIMING OF DEATH: JOHN DENVER'S CHART

Once an astrologer masters the basics of the natal chart, the next step is to check the current transiting planets for their influence. This phase of astrology is called predictive astrology. In general, when transiting planets are trine or sextile the natal planets, their influence is beneficial. When transiting planets oppose or square natal planets, their influence is detrimental. In terms of conjunctions, look to the nature of the transiting planet. The Moon may sensitize, the Sun brighten, Mercury highlight, Venus sweeten, Mars energize, Jupiter expand, Saturn limit, Uranus change, Neptune mystify, and Pluto transform.

In general, if nothing is promised by planetary aspect, little will be gained by planetary transit. The natal chart is the promise at birth; the transits are timing of these "promised" events. For example, if you have Venus in Aquarius trine Uranus in Libra, you are idealistic in love and it is likely you will have an opportunity to marry for love. When? Look at the transits. If Uranus in Libra (sign of marriage) trines your Venus at age 25 and you are available, it is probable you will meet and marry someone you love within that year. If, on the other hand, Uranus made no aspects to Venus natally, you may have a romance at 25, but it might be more an interesting interlude than a marriage.

The most important transits are the outer planets - Jupiter, Saturn, Uranus, Neptune, and Pluto. These planets stay in aspects for months and in the case of Neptune and Pluto sometimes a year or two. Naturally, they indicate the big changes of life. The Sun, Mercury, Venus, Mars are indicators of daily events, as they remain in orb only a few days. The Moon, which changes a degree approximately every two hours, may indicate the exact moment of an event.

Such was the case in John Denver's death, when the Moon made an exact square at the moment of his untimely accident. The following article - which was written for the American Federation of Astrologers is a good example of the power of transits

John Denver

Complexity in Life

Pluto, the planet of the underworld, can bring on death out of the blue. Such was the case for singer John Denver, who died at 5:33 p.m., October 12, 1997, while flying an experimental aircraft off the coast of Monterey, California. Pluto was the ruler of John Denver's eighth house of death. (John was born December 31, 1943 at 3:55 p.m. in Roswell, New Mexico, according to Astro Data II).

On the day of his death, transiting Pluto, joined by Mars and Venus, opposed his twelfth house Mars conjunct Uranus, showing the probability of an accident that day - timed to the minute by the transiting Moon at five degrees Pisces squaring his natal Mars conjunct Uranus. Literally, he never knew what hit him.

Natal Chart

With his natal Sun in the eighth house, he had the promise of longevity in his chart (barring accidents). He had an ambitious nature, with his Sun destined to rise in life. But with the Sun square Neptune, he was a soft touch, one who could be moved by "country roads" and "sunshine on my shoulder." His innate kindness (Moon in Pisces) was always there for his audience. He often gave out roses at concerts and insisted on playing through the band's break - something unheard of in the music industry.

His Moon in Pisces placed in the tenth house showed he would have a career before the public; but it was a reclusive Moon - squaring Saturn. His songs speak of the simple pleasures of family life. "Annie's Song" was written for his first wife. His Moon also squared Mars conjunct Uranus in the twelfth house of limitations, showing accidents (Mars conjunct Uranus) might take him from his fans. This was not his first accident; on August 21, 1994, he "totaled" a Porsche.

Emotionally, he was a complex man with two sides to his personality, shown by Gemini rising. His singing career is seen by the ruler of the chart (Mercury) sextile Venus in Scorpio in the sixth house of work. His Venus showed a love of the arts and his work. This turned out to be the undoing of his first marriage, which ended in 1979, largely because he was on the road so much. He had two adopted children, Anna Kate and Zachary, who are now grown. He married and divorced a second time, and had an eight year old daughter, Jesse, from that union. He seemed to be a loving parent; on the day of his death he had taken Jesse to Disney World.

His interest in flying is seen by his Mars in Gemini conjunct Uranus. He was the son of a U.S. Air Force officer. With these planets sextiling Pluto conjunct the North Node in his third house, domestic travel would play a strong role in his career. Interestingly, his first hit, which he wrote for Peter, Paul, and Mary in 1967, was "Leaving on a Jet Plane".

There was a dichotomy in John Denver's life. With Saturn rising, the shy country boy was at odds with his public life, shown by the Moon in Pisces in the tenth. His love for home was legendary, Saturn in Gemini sextiling Jupiter in the fourth house; however he wasn't home very often.

Capricorns can be prone to depression. A sadder Denver came out often in later years, with two divorces and drunk driving charges. But he never lost his appeal to his audiences, and it is quite fitting that this gentle idealist's last concert was for the environment.

Born in the "flower child" generation (Neptune in Libra trine Uranus in Gemini), John Denver truly believed he could make the world a better place.

John Denver

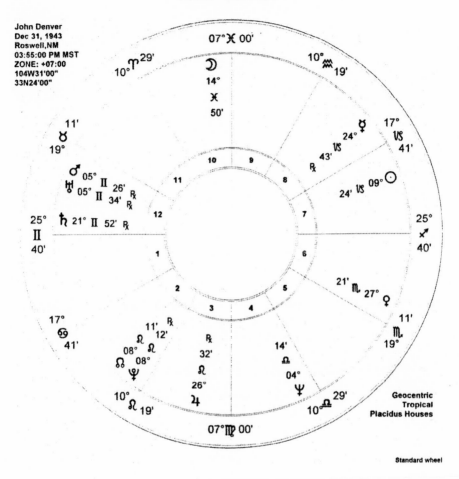

John Denver
Dec 31, 1943
Roswell,NM
03:55:00 PM MST
ZONE: +07:00
104W31'00"
33N24'00"

Geocentric
Tropical
Placidus Houses

Standard wheel

CHAPTER THIRTY-NINE

THE CHART OF THE UNITED STATES OF AMERICA

As a nation we were born in the wee hours of the morning on July 4, 1776. When the last delegate signed the Declaration of Independence in Philadelphia at approximately 2:17 a.m., The United States of America was born with the Sun in Cancer, the Moon in Aquarius, and a Gemini ascendant. While our country stands for "mother and apple pie" values, we are constantly on the go with Gemini rising. Often Europeans see us as crazy Americans. Uranus is on the ascendant giving our citizens a Uranian personality, full of enterprise and original ideas. This sign also indicates we were born from rebellion, destined to form a new order in which liberty for all would prevail. Mars in the first house adds to our independent streak, valuing the rugged individualism This is further accented with the Moon in Aquarius. We truly are "a nation of the people, by the people and for the people" with strong democratic principles.

The second house of the chart rules the nation's wealth. With the Sun in Cancer here, joined by the lesser benefic Venus and the greater benefic Jupiter in Cancer, we are a wealthy nation. The Sun square Saturn in the fifth house shows our preoccupation with the nation's youth, allocating large amounts of money to education. The stock market soared early in 1998 as transiting Jupiter trined Venus, Jupiter and the Sun. However, it may have peaked. 1999 would bring higher interest rates and inflation as transiting Jupiter squares Venus and Neptune in the Spring.

The separation of church and state is seen by Mercury at 24 Cancer on the cusp of the third house, ruling secular matters, opposite Pluto at 27 Capricorn in the ninth house ruling the church. Religious freedom is one of our hallmarks. With the lucky north node, 6 Leo in the third house, commerce is greatly favored along with communications and travel. Vast positive changes are seen in the telecommunications industry in 1998 and early 1999, when Pluto trines the north node. Our ideals and standards are noble with the north node falling in sign of Leo. Transiting Pluto will trine this node in the coming year favoring trade with United States and strengthening the U.S. currency abroad.

Leo on the cusp of the fourth house indicates vast wealth in land. Neptune on the cusp of fifth shows idealism of our youth, and trining Pluto marks a strong inspiration and vast creative energy. Speculation is favored in the chart. Saturn in the fifth shows the strong responsibility our nation feels toward its younger citizens, founding land grant colleges and a vast network of public schools. In 1998 and 1999 Neptune will square Saturn in the world chart, creating shortage and problems in world money markets. Hence, the nation's public schools will undergo transformation. Voucher systems, home schooling, and privatizing of public schools could be the way of the future in many areas. Shortages of fuel may bring some communities to cut back on busing and instead to opt televised instruction, with regional testing.

The sixth house in a mundane chart rules the military. With Scorpio on the cusp of sixth house, we believe in strong preparedness. Scorpio is organized, determined, and hard driving. Needless to say, the military-industrial complex has a strong base in our nation. With Pluto entering our seventh house in 1999, we may be sending troops out to quell problems on foreign shores.

The seventh house rules allies and open enemies. With Sagittarius on this cusp, we have a strong tendency to bind up the wounds of our enemies and aid their rebuilding effort, such as with the Marshall Plan after World War II. In 1999, we need to be especially vigilant with transcending Pluto on the cusp of seventh house. In 1998 Pluto was just touching this point. In February we did send troops to the Gulf area. However, with a trine to our luck north node in Leo, military intervention was not needed. In 1999, this protection while in force, is weaker.

Conservative Capricorn rules the eighth house of death and inheritance. Our taxation system is a stable base. The ruler falling in the fifth house shows much of our revenue goes toward education and public welfare. This spending will continue to be a controversial issue in the next two years.

The ninth house rules the legal system, including the Supreme Court. With Capricorn on the cusp of ninth house, we have a solid, but conservative, Supreme Court, which is often slow to deliberate. Issues such as States' rights have been a strong debate in recent years. In 1997 and early 1998, individual states were urged to embrace welfare reform. Great change will come in 2003 when further cuts will be made. Welfare could be phased down to a six-month program, funded partly by a marriage and/or divorce penalty tax, as the federal government withdraws its support, leaving it to the states to decide the issue of welfare.

The tenth house rules the nation's prestige. Here we have the idealistic and freedom-loving sign of Aquarius. Our democracy truly does stand as a symbol of freedom. The Moon in tenth house at 18 Aquarius shows we are a nation of people, with our president elected by an electoral college system chosen by the people. Eventually the direct election of president will be considered in 2001 as transcending Uranus trines the Moon. New leadership and progressive ideas are coming in 2000 to 2003. However, before this positive trend, there is a shadow on the presidency in the summer of 1999. Before this in the spring of 1999, President Clinton's chart is afflicted with transcending Saturn squaring Moon in Taurus in his eighth house of death. Great vigilance is needed during February through August 1999 for our president! Our prestige abroad should become stronger in 2000 to 2001 as other nations look to us for world leadership. Great spiritual leadership will enter government about 2005, when transiting Neptune begins to conjunct Uranus in the tenth house of leadership. This could signal the beginning of the Aquarian Age for our nation!

With the compassionate sign of Pisces on the cusp of our eleventh house of hopes and wishes, the United States is seen as a land where dreams do come true. The Ruler, Neptune, is in the fifth house of speculation, which fuels our stock market. 2005 may bring a complete transformation of the market as transiting Pluto, which protects by natal aspect, squares.

The twelfth house shows the karmic destiny of

nation. With earthy Taurus placed on a cusp, it is our destiny to feed the world, literally with our abundance. Our food and medical aid to others is legendary and a source of much good karma. However, materialism could also be our downfall. As we enter the Age of Aquarius in approximately 2010, the Aquarian principles of "life, liberty, and the pursuit of happiness" must be maintained - even at the expense of material comforts!

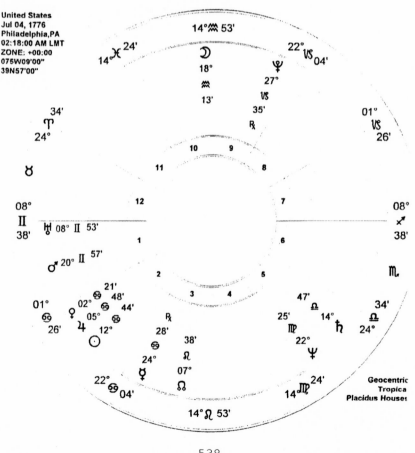

CHAPTER FORTY

A FINAL WORD: ASTROLOGY SAVED MY LIFE

Astrology has many uses. It can be a planning tool for the garden, shopping, and even the dentist! As the <u>Farmer's Almanac</u> annually advises, plant during a new Moon, harvest during a full Moon. If you wish to purchase well-made garments, shop when the Moon is in Virgo. For a car or a home, avoid signing a contract during a retrograde Mercury. As for dental appointments, choose a time when the Moon is in a fixed sign for fillings, but schedule extractions during a mutable Moon.

However fascinating such details are, never is astrology more valuable then when it saves a life! Such was the case with my own horoscope. When I first studied astrology in 1967, I learned I had Mercury conjunct Mars in the third house of communication and travel square Uranus in the sixth house of health. Mars square Uranus traditionally indicates one who is accident-prone. With the third house involved, the possibility of accidents during travel could occur during difficult transits. Such a transit, a Saturn square, was in orb intermittently from September 1971 to September 1972. Naturally, I was concerned.

I consulted my mentor, Dorothea Lynde. She was calm, but firm, "Be careful." My friend and fellow astrologer, Mary Letourney, was more practical, "Wear a seat belt and drive as little as possible!" The most disturbing warning came in a dream, early in November. Gladys Custance, my spiritual teacher, visited me. In the vivid dream, Gladys watched me digging at a splinter in my foot, and said, "Be careful." At that precise moment the splinter turned into a huge cobra which bit me in the third eye. I awoke with a sense of impending doom. A few days later, I was almost killed in a car accident! On my way to a job interview for a teaching position at Avon High School, I was hit broad side. The impact shattered my left clavicle into three pieces - one of which was just an inch from piercing the heart. Had I not been wearing a seat belt, the blow would surely have been fatal!

Since that moment, I have taken my duty as an

astrologer most solemnly. As a teacher of astrology, I remind my students to thoroughly review the horoscope. First the natal chart, to ascertain the promise at birth. Next, look at the progressed chart to see what inner changes have occurred. Finally, review the transits carefully, before discussing the client's future. I offer this advise as they prepare to read another soul's future: "Never tell the client a negative event without giving him an antidote." If you study astrological texts, there are literally hundreds of insights. It's as if God is always giving us a second chance! Basically, be more vigilant during "lazy" cycles, such as Jupiter squares. Counter erratic transits, such as Uranus square, by slowing down. For example, if you have Mars conjunct Mercury in your natal chart, you are inclined to be high-strung and opinionated. You are very likely to jump to conclusions. Try to be more flexible in your thinking and learn to pace yourself. Utilize the time dampened by a negative Uranus transit as a planning period. Slow down. While there may still be some mishap, it is better to break a dish than a leg!

Hindu astrologers go a step further. They take a pro-active stance on difficult transits, advising mantas and gems to break the cycle. For example, a client might be told to wear an emerald or jade ring to counteract a difficult Mercury period. For Saturn afflictions, Sapphire or Lapis Lazuli would be the gem of choice. Does it work? Perhaps. However, I am sure that prayer changes things. The best remedies to life's afflictions are prayer, a compassionate heart, and right action. While astrology is a valuable tool planning "right actions", the rest is up to you. As the poet, Omar Khayyam, wisely notes, the key to life lies within us:

> I sent my soul through the Invisible,
> The sector of that after-life to spell;
> And by and by my soul returned to me
> And answered, "I myself am Heaven and Hell."

In closing, I leave this thought with you, May Father-Mother God guide you in your study of astrology - for astrology is of the Soul!

Glossary

Ascendant The sign that is on the horizon at birth, the rising sign or first house.

Aspect The angle formed between two planets.

Conjunction The line up of two planets close together.

Cusp The division between two houses, which is named for the house which falls below the line.

Esoteric astrology The discipline of the metaphysics or occult knowledge of astrology.

Horoscope A map of the heavens at the exact moment of birth, calculated for when the baby takes his first breath. The horoscope is also called the natal chart.

House One of the twelve divisions of the chart. Each house presides over a different department of life.

Midheaven The highest point of the chart, also known as the tenth house cusp.

Nadir The lowest point of the chart, also known as the fourth house cusp.

Node Each of the two points at which a planet crosses the ecliptic. The nodes of the Moon are significant.

Opposition An aspect of approximately 180 degrees between planets, placing the two planets directly across from each other. This is considered to be an aspect of awareness, often a difficult aspect.

Retrograde A planet which appears to be moving backward from the Earth, often slowing down the affairs ruled by that planet.

Sextile An aspect of approximately sixty degrees, considered to mildly favorable.

Square An aspect of approximately 90 degrees placing the planets at a right angle to each other. This is considered to be a difficult aspect, creating tension in the chart.

Trine An aspect of approximately 120 degrees, placing the planets in a triangular position, which is considered to be the most efficient and favorable flow of energy, hence a highly favorable aspect.

Transit A planet moving in orbit through a house, or forms an aspect to a planet in the natal chart.

Bibliography

The Astrologer's Hand Book by Louis Acker and Frances Sakoian

The Astrology of Human Relationships by Louis Acker and Frances Sakoian

Predictive Astrology by Louis Acker and Frances Sakoian

Astrology, Karma, and Transformation by Stephen Arroyo

Your Rising Sign: your Astrological Mask by Jeanne Avery

Astrological Aspects by Jeanne Avery

How to Predict Your Future: Secrets of an Eastern and Western Astrologer by James Braha

Vedic Astrology by Ronnie Gale Dreyer

Encyclopedia of Astrology by Nicholas Devore

Planets in Transit by Robert Hand

A Time to Remember by Nancy Anne Hastings

Astrology: the Cosmic Science by Isabelle Hickey

Astrology: the Devine Science by Marcia Moore

and Mark Douglas

Astrology in Action by Marcia Moore and Mark
Douglas

Toward a New Astrology by Rex Reed

Karmic Astrology: The Moon's Nodes by Martin
Schulman

National Organizations

American Federation of Astrologers

P.O. Box 22040

Tempe, AZ 85282

Association for Research and Enlightenment

P.O. Box 595

Virginia Beach, VA 232450-64

Theosophical Society in America

Box 270

Wheaton, IL 60187

About the Author

Elaine Kuzmeskus, Director of the New England School of Metaphysics, was certified as a Professional Astrologer by the American Federation of Astrologers in 1975. She has taught astrology to college students she throughout New England and maintains an astrology practice, in Suffield, CT. In additional to her astrology expertise, Elaine Kuzmeskus hold a Masters Degree in Counseling and had taught psychology and parapsychology to thousands of college students. Soul Cycles combines keen psychological insight with the ancient science of astrology.